CROSSING THROUGH CHUECA

Crossing through Chueca

Lesbian Literary Culture
in Queer Madrid

Jill Robbins

University of Minnesota Press
Minneapolis
London

The University of Minnesota Press gratefully acknowledges financial assistance provided for the publication of this book from the Program for Cultural Cooperation between Spain's Ministry of Culture and United States Universities.

Material in this book previously appeared in "The (In)visible Lesbian: The Contradictory Representations of Female Homoeroticism in Contemporary Spain," *Journal of Lesbian Studies* 7.3 (2003). Portions of chapter 3 were first published in "Andalucía, el travestimo y la mujer fálica: *Plumas de España* de Ana Rossetti," *Lectora. Revista de dones i textualitat* 15 (2009). Parts of chapter 5 were first published in "Cybersex and the Cyberdildo: Dislocations in *Cenicienta en Chueca*," *Studies in Twentieth and Twenty-first Century Literature* (2006).

Copyright 2011 by the Regents of the University of Minnesota

All rights reserved. No part of this publication may be reproduced, stored in a retrieval system, or transmitted, in any form or by any means, electronic, mechanical, photocopying, recording, or otherwise, without the prior written permission of the publisher.

Published by the University of Minnesota Press
111 Third Avenue South, Suite 290
Minneapolis, MN 55401-2520
http://www.upress.umn.edu

Library of Congress Cataloging-in-Publication Data

Robbins, Jill.
   Crossing through Chueca : lesbian literary culture in queer Madrid / Jill Robbins.
   p. cm.
   Includes bibliographical references and index.
   ISBN 978-0-8166-6989-9 (hc : alk. paper) — ISBN 978-0-8166-6990-5 (pb : alk. paper)
   1. Spanish fiction—20th century—History and criticism. 2. Spanish fiction—21st century—History and criticism. 3. Lesbianism in literature. 4. Lesbian culture—Spain. 5. Homosexuality and literature—Spain. 6. Publishers and publishing—Spain—Madrid—History. 7. Books and reading—Spain—Madrid—History—20th century. 8. Books and reading—Spain—Madrid—History—21st century. 9. Geographical perception—Spain—Madrid. I. Title.
   PQ6140.L47R63 2011
   863'.7093526643—dc22

2010032603

Printed in the United States of America on acid-free paper

The University of Minnesota is an equal-opportunity educator and employer.

Para mi amor lindo

Contents

Preface: Marching toward Marriage	ix
1. A Brief History of Chueca and Madrid's Queer Space	1
2. Lesbian Literary Identities in the Madrid Book Business	15
3. The New Safita: Andalusia and the Phallic Woman in *Plumas de España*	33
4. Lesbian-Themed Best Sellers and the Politics of Acceptance	57
5. Dislocations: Identity and Communication in *Cenicienta en Chueca*	81
6. Popular Lesbian Fiction: Romance, Literature, and Legislation	101
Conclusion: Toward Lesbian Visibility	117
Acknowledgments	125
Notes	127
Bibliography	153
Index	167

· PREFACE ·

Marching toward Marriage

It was july 2005 and gay marriage had just been approved by the Spanish government. On the afternoon of my sixth Spanish Pride, I met my Guatemalan partner, Arturo Arias, and a group of our lesbian and bisexual friends for lunch in the pricey Madrid neighborhood of Salamanca, a conservative bastion on that year's parade route. The parade organizers wanted to celebrate the legitimacy the marriage legislation conferred on gay and lesbian unions by marching through the neighborhood most associated with the conservative politics of the Popular Party (PP). For the first and only time, the parade's concluding speeches would be held in the symbolic Plaza de Colón—Columbus Square—Madrid's biggest public square, adorned with an obelisk in tribute to the discoverer of the Americas. Our group included a rich but closeted real estate tycoon from Cáceres and her Filipina partner, originally from Los Angeles, dressed in identical fashion; a young aeronautical engineer who worked for the Spanish Ministry of Defense and spent most of her time chatting happily about the festivities on the phone with her father or waxing nostalgic about her pilot training at the Palmerola Air Force Base in the summer of 1992; a blond international banker who adhered to the politics of the PP; an Argentine woman who had just moved out of her family's chalet on the outskirts of Madrid and into an apartment with her partner, a Galician schoolteacher; and Sofía Ruiz, a U.S. academic colleague originally from Madrid whose book of short stories, *Sexutopías*, had just been accepted for publication by the gay/lesbian press Egales. In our long, animated lunch, boundless joy for this political triumph flowed as freely as the wine. After the meal, our spirits flying, Arturo, Sofía, and I headed to the Puerta de Alcalá, a commemorative arch in the middle of the city and the starting point of the demonstration. In front of Correos, the central post office building, we met up with two other formidable personalities, the Argentine poets Mario Merlino and Noni Benegas. Mario (who would soon marry his Brazilian partner, then divorce him shortly before his sudden death in 2009) was dressed in shorts to weather the wilting heat, and his bald dome twinkled in the sun like the usual picaro look in his eyes. Noni—who would soon take a turn as one of the city's drag kings—disguised her powerful appearance in more matronly garb. There were other friends as well. Most were suburban working-class women who had taken time off work for the festivities. It was blistering hot and most of our group stayed on the sidelines. Arturo, Mario, Sofía, and I could not wait to start; we joined the two-million-people-strong march,[1] shouting slogans about the separation of church and state. Behind us, a group of young women chanted, "Ahora sí podemos, pero nosotras no queremos" (Now we can marry, but we don't want to).[2] Sweat trickled down everyone's cheeks but we could not keep from smiling and laughing, waving to the cheering crowds. Young parents with small children whirled around on the sidelines, pointing out the banners to their little ones.

Anyone can join the parade in Madrid at any point along the route and step back out into the public when they get tired, bored, or meet someone interesting. As in the Andalusian Semana Santa (Holy Week) processions, the manifestation literally mixes the political with the festive, the sacred with the profane, in a carnivalesque blurring of hierarchy and order. No permit, identity card, or ticket is required to be a part of the movement. With the exception of the beginning of the parade, when the marchers separate by autonomous Spanish nationalities (Andalusian, Catalan, Basque, and so forth), spectators join in and are free to march behind any banner or *carroza* (double-decker parade vehicle). The music-blasting *carrozas* now have commercial sponsors—the Chueca hair salon Juan Por Dios, the slick gay magazine *Zero*—but they also have political ones, like the workers' union (UGT) and the social democrat party, the PSOE (Partido Socialista Obrero Español). In 2005, the presence of ads for Schweppes and Ballantine was not yet overwhelming. As we walked, celebrating the state's recognition of gays and lesbians as full citizens—Spain's president, José Luis Rodríguez Zapatero, famously proclaimed that a decent society does not humiliate its citizens[3]—I remembered my first Pride march back in 1998, seeing elderly gay and lesbian couples, survivors of thirty-five years of Francisco Franco's brutal dictatorship, holding hands and watching the demonstrators go by with tears in their eyes. Numerous studies have chronicled the repression and humiliation they suffered under the Franco regime, and even until 1981, when finally, as Gema Pérez Sánchez puts it, "the new Spanish democracy . . . eliminate[d] homosexuality as a category of social danger subject to security measures" (31). The manifestation itself had grown enormously since the early post-Franco years, when participants numbered in the hundreds and faced police repression. Even in 1996, there were only eight hundred participants; in 1997, three to four thousand; in 1998, six to ten thousand. It was not until 1999 that the numbers jumped to thirty thousand, and then, in 2000, suddenly there were fifty to seventy thousand demonstrators (Herrero Brasas, 315).

After the parade, the party continued in Chueca, the gay barrio (neighorhood)—on narrow, cobbledstoned streets, in minute bars, packed discos, and nineteenth-century plazas thronged with enormous crowds of revelers of all sexual and gender identities. The official Pride party that chartered buses and charged admission was held at the Casa de Campo, the equivalent of New York City's Central Park, and catered mostly to men.[4] We instead planned on running into friends and acquaintances in the spaces of the neighborhood, where the party would rage all that night and the next. It would be days until the locales on the plaza would reopen their *terrazas* (open-air bars), where we usually met friends and colleagues for a *caña* (draft beer) or a *tinto de verano* (a kind of sangria) at the end of a hot afternoon or after dinner, before the discos opened at 1 a.m.

The marriage celebration in 2005 signaled that the community had come a long way. Yet it seemed clear that women had not yet come quite as far. Most of my lesbian friends—rich and poor, yuppie and working class— were still closeted at work and with their families. They would not march for fear of their photo appearing in the press (the lesbian march would not take place until 2008, after the trans march in 2006 and Europride in 2007, and even then the female turnout would be small). And the much-advertised Visible 2005 festival of "LGTB" culture,[5] including photography, dance, theater, film, roundtables, and comics, left women almost entirely *in*visible, as gay male cultural figures and personalities monopolized discursive power in the programming and protagonism of those events.

This book is an exploration of the contours of this particular form of women's (in)visibility in Madrid from 1989 until the marriage march in 2005. Now marked by pride, feminism, neoliberalism, and globalization, Madrid still bore the marks of the machismo nurtured during the long years of the Franco dictatorship, when women's artistic production was suppressed and forgotten, their political activity severely limited, and their sexuality rhetorically linked to an exclusively reproductive morality that precluded the possibility of desire. I approach this issue by traversing the various literary spaces of the city associated with queer culture. I reference the gay barrio of Chueca in particular, not simply as a geographic location, but as a "product of interrelations" (Massey, 9), a site crisscrossed by a multiplicity of subjects who constitute it as a particular queer space through the negotiation of their identities. It is a political space as well—in the many senses that *political* may be understood—and it is a safe haven, a refuge from homophobia. At the same time, I recognize (with Henri Lefebvre, Edward Soja, and Pierre Bourdieu, among others) that the spatial and literary practices of Chueca have some basis in economic relations, in different forms of consumption that have determined the planning and use of space, as well as its representation, and I will address these issues as well.

The book is divided into six chapters. The first offers a history of Madrid's queer space, with a primary focus on the Chueca neighborhood. I am especially concerned in the first section with the intersections between class, morality, politics, and gender in the area's relationship with greater Madrid over the past centuries, and in the culmination, even celebration, of its marginality during the time of the *movida madrileña* in the 1980s. The second part of the chapter explains the emergence of Chueca as the emblematic queer space of Madrid, and arguably Spain (for gay tourists, at least), during the 1990s, in tandem with the broader Spanish incorporation into a globalized economy and a European community. This is a story of consumption and marketing, as well as identity politics. What, this book will ask, are the implications of this Chueca for women, for immigrants, for working-class people?

Delving into the clash of politics and economics in the LGBTQ book business, chapter 2 examines the bookstores Berkana and A Different Life, and the publishing houses Egales and Odisea. The founding of the gay/lesbian bookstore Berkana by Mili Hernández in 1992, and her co-creation of the publishing house Egales with Connie Dagas in 1995, signaled a new era of lesbian literature.[6] The predominantly gay bookstore, A Different Life, and publisher, Odisea, would appear slightly later, in 1999, but the latter would make a significant mark by establishing the only LGBTQ literary prize. The chapter looks at the complex intersections of politics, culture, and commerce in these types of enterprise, and at the ways in which they highlight some of the conflicts that linger in LGBTQ politics in Madrid.

The next four chapters offer readings of contemporary literary texts that situate women in relation to gay, lesbian, and/or queer spaces and discourses.

In chapter 3, "The New Safita: Andalusia and the Phallic Woman in *Plumas de España*," I analyze a novel published at the end of the *movida madrileña* by one of its few female protagonists. *Plumas de España* (Spanish plumes, 1989) is a transitional text, one that makes clear the ways in which Spanish culture from 1975 through the 1980s omitted women from the gay/trans figuration of the Spanish transition to democracy; at the same time, it signals the conversion of the Spanish book business to a more globalized economic model. Like Eduardo Mendicutti's classic novel *Una mala noche la tiene cualquiera* (Anyone can have a bad night, 1982), Rossetti's novel features a prominent transvestite character, although Patela is not the first-person narrator. It is Patela, though, who baptizes the narrator/protagonist as the New Safita. This lesbian denomination in reality marks the unnameability of female desire within sexual paradigms still marked by masculinism; Patela, not another woman, is the object of the protagonist's desire—both sexual and epistemological—and, at the same time, the model of femininity to which she aspires. She is not lesbian, but queer. *Plumas de España* also addresses the relationship between the cultural and gender production of the Andalusian province (honor codes, the local newspaper *Plumas de España*) and that of the metropolis (the Planeta literary prize). Rossetti's novel thus offers a unique opportunity to consider the ways in which the transition, and later the *movida*, as well as the book business itself, continue to marginalize women, female sexual desire, and Andalusia—even while performing a supposed sexual liberation costumed in their exoticized forms.

In chapter 4, "Lesbian-Themed Best Sellers and the Politics of Acceptance," I examine the representation of lesbians in three best-selling novels that have circulated outside of the queer space circumscribed by Chueca, Berkana, and Egales. In some ways, these novels were groundbreaking: the first, *Beatriz y los cuerpos celestes* (Beatriz and the heavenly bodies, Nadal Prize, 1998), owing to its largely positive representation of a lesbian character; the second, *Donde comienza tu nombre* (Where your name begins, 2004), for being the first novel published by a gay/lesbian press to cross over to a mainstream bookstore; and the third, *Una palabra tuya* (A word from you, Biblioteca Breve Prize, 2005), for depicting the sexuality of the lowest stratum of working women, garbage collectors. Still, I explain that the ways in which these authors write lesbian and bisexual women for a broad Spanish audience reveal the conditions under which mainstream heterosexual bourgeois readers are willing to accept lesbian sexuality, as well as the lingering prejudices that mark that acceptance.

Chapter 5, "Dislocations: Identity and Communication in *Cenicienta en Chueca,*" focuses on the work and representation of immigrant lesbians in this short-story collection written by María Felicitas Jaime, an Argentine exile living in Madrid, and published by Odisea. My emphasis in this chapter is on the use of the Spanish language and other communication technologies by the characters in the stories, and the implications of that technology for their economic, political, and social status. I argue that, by representing the communications and miscommunications in some transnational lesbian relationships that pass through Chueca, *Cenicienta en Chueca* (Cinderella in Chueca, 2003) lays bare the intersections between gender, economics, race, "modernity," and nationality in contemporary Spain.

Chapter 6, "Popular Lesbian Fiction: Romance, Literature, and Legislation" explores the intersection of legislative and literary politics in novels published by Egales and Odisea in the years leading up to the gay/lesbian marriage and adoption laws of 2005. Through an analysis of three emblematic novels—*Un amor bajo sospecha* (A love under suspicion, 2001), by Marosa Gómez Pereira, *Amores prohibidos* (Forbidden loves, 2002), by Marta Fagés, and *A por todas* (After them all! 2005), by Libertad Morán—I argue that the aesthetic choices of these authors represent specific textual/sexual lesbian politics, especially in relation to the question of lesbian marriage.

As a final word, I would like to emphasize that this book is not meant to be a comprehensive study of all lesbian literary production in or about Madrid, much less all of Spain. It is, rather, an exploration of the ways in which women's sexual identities have become visible in and through the Chueca phenomenon, and of some of the occasionally contradictory implications of that visibility.

· CHAPTER 1 ·

A Brief History of Chueca and Madrid's Queer Space

ALTHOUGH BARCELONA has arguably been more at the vanguard of LGBTQ culture and politics, the Spanish capital played a unique symbolic role following the death of right-wing dictator Francisco Franco in 1975, as the country sought first to distance itself from its recent past, and then to become an important actor in Western, and specifically European, neoliberalism and globalized capitalism. This social transformation went hand in hand with a growing tolerance of homosexuality that allowed the community to become increasingly visible, and eventually culminated in the recognition of civil rights, including the right to marry and adopt children. Economic factors also played a role in this change, as "pink businesses" prospered, and gay homeowners gentrified the area surrounding the Chueca Plaza. It was in this context that Chueca emerged as both the symbol of a new, tolerant Spain and the center of LGBTQ social, political, and cultural activity in Madrid.

Chueca is not an official denomination, but rather a loosely defined area within the Justicia district of Madrid. Ricardo Llamas and Francisco Javier Vidarte stake its territory as: "Behind Gran Vía to Fernando VI Street, between Fuencarral and Barquillo Streets *(grosso modo)*" (207). The name "Chueca" derives from Federico Chueca, a composer of musical zarzuelas, and it is actually the name of the plaza at the heart of the zone, which is also a metro stop. The same zone has gone by a variety of names, however, as Bernardo Veksler explains:

> Before, it bore the names of the small neighborhoods of Barquillo, Salesas, Maravillas, Refugio, and Hospicio. Later, it came to be part of the Central district institutionally known as Justicia. But its transformation in the past few years imposed the name of Chueca,

and the people of Madrid gradually began identifying the area with the name of that plaza. (n.p.)

Chueca boasts an enviable proximity to major centers of culture and learning: it is only blocks from the National Library on Recoletos and the Círculo de Bellas Artes on Alcalá, in one direction, and the Espacio Cultural Conde Duque in the opposite direction (through neighboring Malasaña). Theaters, the Ateneo, and the cinemas of the Gran Vía lie just outside its borders toward the south, and, toward the east, on Prim, we find both the headquarters of the Spanish Armed Forces and the national headquarters of the ONCE (National Organization for Blind [Disabled] Spaniards).[1] The traditional San Antón Market was in the district until it was closed in 2006 in anticipation of its transformation into a smaller, modern shopping center. The nearby Fuencarral Market had been converted in 1998 to a site dedicated primarily to the sale of secondhand and "alternative" clothing and the promotion of a culture of goth, skateboarding, piercings, and rave music. Its presence transformed Fuencarral Street from a dark, grimy street off the Gran Vía into a fashion district ("El mercado de Fuencarral"). The headquarters of the country's principal labor union, the UGT (Unión General de Trabajadores [General Workers' Union]) is also in the neighborhood, on Hortaleza. Significantly, the UGT, which participated in the Spanish civil war on the losing Republican side and was subsequently banned during the Franco regime, supported legislation in favor of domestic unions, marriage, and adoption for gay and lesbian couples. All of this means that the people crossing through the Chueca Plaza could be characterized—that is, stigmatized and/or empowered— not only by their sexual orientation, but also by their labor membership, artistic interests, fashion sensibility, social class, military status, and/or physical disability.

The history of Chueca coincides in many senses with that of the urban working class, and it intersects with questions of the church and state in Spain. According to Veksler, the Justicia division, traditionally the home of the poor working classes and those living on the wrong side of the law, began to represent marginality during the reign of Philip II, who exiled the ironworks to the Barquillo neighborhood (32). In the seventeenth century, much of the same area, dominated by Barquillo Street, and named after it, had been converted from agricultural purposes and become a zone of tile and iron works, which were soon joined by convents (Montoliú

Camps, 83). It began to embody the resistance to state authority during the reign of Carlos III in the late eighteenth century (ibid., 33, 43–44). In the nineteenth century, it was the site of cafés, whorehouses, and theaters (ibid., 60–64), to which were added a circus and movie theaters in the early twentieth century (ibid., 66–67). Some assassinations and skirmishes took place in the area toward the end of the three-year siege of Madrid during the Spanish civil war (ibid., 78–82), at which time these regions were not officially part of the city of Madrid.

The incorporation of the Justicia district into the capital responded to the Francoist policies to control and integrate the "rebellious" working class, which had supported the Second Republic, into the new state order. Montoliú Camps describes the process as a kind of quarantine:

> In a megalomaniacal desire to distance Madrid from the rest of the Spanish population, a process of annexation was begun in 1947 that would affect thirteen municipalities over the next five years. As a result, Adravaca, El Pardo, Fuencarral, Canillas, Hortaleza, Chamartín, Vicálvaro, Canillejas, Barajas, Carabanchel Alto, Carabanchel Bajo, Vallecas, and Villaverde became part of Madrid. (71)

Julius Ruiz is more blunt in his assessment of the political rationale for this process, particularly in the 1940s:

> Under the headline "A Vile Belt," a leading article in *Informaciones* on 15 April discussed the relationship between the shanty towns erected in Madrid's outer limits and the crimes of the civil war: 'In this belt which suffocates Madrid live monsters and criminals, the scum of illiterate and barbaric Spain that have been expelled from the countryside.... These infected suburbs are a consequence of the weaknesses of failed systems.' In Francoist eyes, therefore, the post-war reconstruction of Madrid necessarily had to consist of three interrelated components: physical, moral, and political. Put another way, changes to the physical landscape of the capital were to be part of the general process of "cleansing" moral and political life. (50)

Ironically, then, the creation of Chueca as a barrio of Madrid responded to the extremely conservative politics of the dictatorship, which sought to eliminate the possibility of class struggle and "moral debasement" by erasing the municipal independence of the working-class outskirts of the city that resisted a three-year siege, and by incorporating them into the center of the city that was then the capital of Franco's Spain.[2] Despite these efforts, during the Franco years the neighborhood remained a stronghold of the working class and working-class prostitutes.

The conservative ideology governing Madrid was replaced by a radical leftist and artistic one after Franco's death. The new spirit of the city, after the transition to democracy ended with the approval of the Spanish Constitution in 1978, was embodied in the Socialist mayor of Madrid from 1979 to 1986, Enrique Tierno Galván, an older, liberal professor who famously advised the city's youth to get high and have fun. As Michael Ugarte comments in "Madrid: From 'Años de Hambre' to Years of Desire":

> Tierno ... brought back carnival, financed city spectacles and street fairs, promoted rock concerts, preached tolerance of the behavior of others, delivered lectures to street sweepers on the relationship between ethics and aesthetics, discouraged ecological deterioration, and fostered an unlikely synthesis between individual social responsibility and urban pleasure. (104)

This was the carnivalesque city of the *movida madrileña*, emblematized in the early films of Pedro Almodóvar, simultaneously part of the new Europe and its seamy margin, an erotic, exotic playground, where pleasures forbidden in northern Europe were readily on hand. The *movida* nightlife was fueled by chemical energy as well: drugs were cheap, and easy to obtain and use, thanks in part to Spain's porous borders and the lax enforcement of antidrug policies. What is more, Spain in the 1980s was still inexpensive for foreign travelers, and it was relatively open in comparison to the United States or Britain, but it still had a rough, unpolished edge that was irresistible to tourists and journalists alike.[3]

The years of the *movida* could also be interpreted in the context of the reconquest of urban space. Under the Franco regime, reunions of large groups of people were forbidden by law, and the streets of Madrid were an inhospitable site of vigilance and control, decorated by signs prohibiting a variety of activities, patrolled by the Guardia Civil, documented by the secret police, with the apartment building portals controlled by night watchmen. These limitations were eased in the transition, and *madrileños* began to test the limits of the freedoms acquired with the advent of democracy. The artists and intellectuals associated with the *movida* set out to resemanticize urban spaces in a variety of ways. The movement was largely associated with the pleasures and vices of the night, and the nightlife was nomadic, proceeding from locale to locale, to private parties, to photographic and artistic sessions in the *piso* (apartment) of Las Costus, the artistic name of the duo Enrique Naya Igueravide (Cádiz, 1953–89) and Juan Carrero Galofré (Palma de Mallorca, 1955–89), and finally to the streets, where they set up makeshift *terrazas* where they could sit, drink, and talk. Encounters often happened by chance, as when the singer Nacho Canut met the now-legendary Alaska (Olvido Gara) in the Rastro (Cervera, 64). The Rastro, a marketplace associated with the poor and marginalized, became in the 1980s a kind of headquarters for the punks and comic-book junkies (ibid., 63). In this sense, the members of the *movida* were literally part of the street life, at the same time that they were the emblems of a new artistic sensibility and the city's new, liberated image.

These activities responded to a broad intellectual and artistic project regarding urban space, the scope of which is clear from the first issue of the *movida*'s main publication, *La luna de Madrid*, published in November 1983. An article by Borja Casani and José Tono Martínez titled "Madrid 1984: ¿la posmodernidad?" suggests that "we are faced with a city that has, as a whole, become avant-garde ... we are confronted with a very urban issue" (6). Another article in that issue, "El financial times de la mendicidad," by Ramón Myrata, focuses quite literally on life on the street as it explains the difference between beggars and the destitute urban poor: financial crises lead to poverty and physical need, but "the beggar does not generally have needs. He has vices" (5). As a social agent who rejects social norms in choosing the desolate life of pleasure on the streets and thus defies class-based political gestures, the beggar represents in many senses a countercultural ideal for some of these artists. Others, however, propose redesigning the city space with the view of making urban life into an aesthetic backdrop (photo shoots in bars and discos, which also housed lectures), a queer sexual and/or musical locale, or a collective experience. For example, there is discussion of an apartment designed vertically, rather than horizontally, by Enrique Fombella, with a huge window connecting interior domesticity with public living on the streets (33). Forbidden spaces come to the fore, as when an invented character, Zondra James, writes the column "Desde mi bañera" (From my bathtub), explaining that the original title was "Desde mi retrete" (From my toilet). Among the many activities listed among the "things to do instead of going to discos," we find an architecture exposition in the Colegio Oficial de Arquitectos (Official School of Architecture) on Barquillo Street, and the pages contain architectural plans, with the date, the name of the architect, and major influences, as well as a history of the various functions that the buildings of Madrid have served. Finally, on the central pages of this physically large journal appear the revolutionary drawings by the artist Rodrigo, heavily influenced by the aesthetics of comics, featuring the travels of a character as he meets, pursues, and sculpts a man, Manuel, through the spaces of the city. His movements throughout Madrid refigure places as diverse as the Metro and the pool at the Casa del Campo park, discos, his home, and the street itself as gay. His identity, not just as a gay man, but as a very masculine "bear," also re-creates the image of the male homosexual for a Spanish public.

Male homosexuality might have been reimagined in the pages of *La luna,* but female sexuality was still presented predominantly from the perspective of the nearly exclusively male contributors to the journal. This is particularly apparent in number 15 (February 1985), in which women seem to be more central than in earlier issues. An article by Carlos Sánchez, titled "Contra el placer light: Pornódromos madrileños," criticizes the "light pleasures" of those who participate in intranscendent sexual tourism out of their fear of more uncontrolled pleasures, "the most incredible and perverse libidinous madnesses" (44). For those people, Sánchez lists the *pornódromos* (pornodromes) around Madrid, with a brief discussion of the shows, which include simulations of lesbian activities. In the Chelsea:

> It's a spectacle that's put on twice each night, at midnight and 2:15 a.m., which consists of two parts: BLUE DIAMONS performs a lesbian number with a shortened dildo for their use and pleasure; and NIKI & SUSY fuck each other plain and simple. Susy gives Niké [sic] a hard-on, in a brusque and blunt fashion. (45)

Sánchez goes on to explain that another venue, El Poncho Erótico, claims that it no longer does shows for lesbian audiences. As one of the performers explains, "Once we put on a show just for women, in the afternoon, but no one came" (ibid.). No mention is made of shows put on for lesbians at night. The article describes yet another venue as follows: "The Montma[r]tre is like a cushioned vagina, decorated in red and black. There are girls to socialize with, drawings, topless shows" (44). Sánchez concludes that all of these shows, like pornography in general, become repetitive and routine. Another article in this volume, "Mujeres, mujeres, pero ¡qué mujeres!" (Women, women, but what women!) by Carlos García-Calvo, describes the women (Eva Lyberten, Paz Muro, Lola Gavarrón, Carmen Maura, Kitty Manver) who served largely as the muses for the artists of the *movida,* incarnating the visual excess of glamour and fashion, much as Evie did for Andy Warhol. The writer Ana Rossetti (Ana Bueno de la Peña, Cádiz, 1950) and the photographer Ouka Lele (Bárbara Allende, Madrid, 1957) are two of the very few women to author articles in *La luna de Madrid.*

Through the 1980s, then, Chueca was simply one of the key sites of Madrid's "queer city," which Dianne Chisholm defines as "a city of queer sites—buildings, streets, quarters, and neighborhoods that have a history of gay and/or lesbian occupation and that historians cite from city archives and sources not yet archived" (10). Llamas and Vidarte explain in *Homografías* that, in the absence of a safe barrio, or ghetto, in which homosexuals could meet, a variety of coded social intercourse, rather than geographic location, configured gay space, the *"ambiente,"* as it is known in Spain:

> There are a multitude of contexts for interaction and activities that are not explicitly marked as gay ... which, when they are performed with other gays, come to form part of those contexts in which subjects cultivate a specifically gay sociability, the *"ambiente,"* which is precisely the term used by gays to describe this form of interaction. (73)

> In order for the *"ambiente"* to exist, it is not necessary for it to be protected from the normalizing gaze. It is sufficient that verbal and nonverbal forms of communication, appropriately invisible to possible censorship, be employed. (74)

These spots would, of course, include gay bars and drag shows, private residences, galleries, and bookstores, but also any site in which coded interchanges could occur. They allowed for the construction of alternate forms of social relations—"sociabilidad entre homosexuales" (sociability among homosexuals) (Villaamil, 68)—in a geographic space not yet identified with an entire neighborhood.

Studies of gay spaces focus also on sites of male sexual encounters, and in particular, on the public places whose meaning has been transformed by the gay sexual activities that transpire there. As Dianne Chisholm explains:

> Deriving its sense from post-structuralism rather than empirical history, queer space demarcates a practice, production, and performance of space beyond just the mere habitation of built and fixed structures. Against the domination of space by abstract constructs of urban planning and the implantation of technologies of social surveillance, queer space designates an appropriation of space for bodily, especially sexual, pleasure. (10)

Some chapters of *Homografías* regarding clandestine sexual activities in bathrooms, cinemas, and metros around Madrid during the Franco years and through the 1980s exemplify this construction. Some of these spaces have been fetishized to the extent that reproductions of them exist within sex saunas in Chueca.

Significantly for my study, the focus on public sexual activity tends to leave women out altogether. The parameters of the female closet under Francoism were much more likely to coincide with the walls of the home, school, or convent, enclosed "feminine" spaces generally that could, nonetheless, be refigured by lesbian sexuality even as they kept it invisible. These spaces had been symbolically coded by heterosexist discourse in the Franco era in association with the home and hearth, spinsterhood, and chastity, respectively, significations designed to maintain female identities within the bounds of Catholic concepts of female sexuality and bourgeois notions of domesticity and maternity. These codes extended metonymically to those spaces most commonly associated with "women's work," particularly that of teachers, nurses, and domestic servants (in contrast, women who performed, or wanted to perform, physical work generally associated with working-class men were considered perversely masculine and assumed to be lesbian, as one of the slang words for lesbian—

camionera [truck driver]—suggests). Significantly, the home was figured as a sacred, spiritual space apart from the market, and the housewife and mother were thus "nonworkers," angels of the hearth, a notion that Linda McDowell thoroughly unravels by marking the contribution of domestic work to the maintenance and reproduction of the workforce (75). Several literary texts—including, for example, Esther Tusquets's *Siete miradas en un mismo paisaje*, Ana María Moix's *Julia* and *Las virtudes peligrosas*, Cristina Fernández Cubas's "Mundo," and Beatriz Gimeno's *Su cuerpo era su gozo*—have represented the homosocial and often explicitly lesbian potential of these "women's spaces."

The constitution of Chueca as a recognized queer space coincided with the end of the *movida*. Beginning in the late 1980s, a disenchantment with the ruling socialist party, the PSOE, combined with the effects of globalization, neoliberalism, and wealth accumulated from investments in Latin America, transformed Madrid in general, and Chueca in particular, from an anarchic, peripheral, bohemian utopia into more of a postutopian magnet for young, hip, well-to-do consumers. These changes turned Chueca into part of what Chisholm calls the "phantasmagoric homogenization and totalization of queer city space, its trendy circulation and abstraction in the (circuit-party's) nonplace" (17).

Although Chueca projects an image of openness that is instantly recognizable to the transnational gay community, it produces significant exclusions at the local level. Villaamil states outright that it is a predominantly male space, and that not even all males have equal access to the pleasures that attract queer tourists:

> the immense majority of the gays who frequent and sustain the "Chueca phenomenon" are young adults. At the same time, people over fifty are completely invisible except in those institutions that the two generations share: prostitution (as clients and workers) and certain locales and places that facilitate sexual encounters, generally located physically and symbolically outside of Chueca, in which the age of the public is much more diverse. (70)

Llamas and Vidarte agree, and they emphasize some of the dangers inherent in the homogeneous image of the "comunidad contenta" (contented or self-satisfied community) now identified with Chueca:

> If "Chueca" represents "homosexuality" in the eyes of society, if it is here that the community represents itself, this means (as happens at every site of representation) that there are at work in the barrio (and if there aren't, there will be soon enough) norms that define this mode of representation. When we speak (in the context of the barrio) of a gay and lesbian community, a fairly exact image comes to mind. The image of a community that we are here calling "content" or "self-satisfied." A community that has fun and spends money, that has no further ambitions, that has faltered in the struggles that were initiated a couple of decades ago (or that lobbies for new attainments politely, without stridency). A depoliticized community, assimilable to society at large in a neat, hardworking, profitable image, that of the same kind of stable couple that operates (with a few flaws) at the heart of the heterosexual community. (217)

Leopoldo Alas's critique emphasizes the vacuous self-involvement implicit in the globalized Chueca "lifestyle":

> Gay culture today consists, for example, of the veneration of the body above all else, the idolatry of the muscle; it is the tyranny of youth, a certain disdain of age and an embarrassed hiding of it; gay culture is the consumerist impulse of the Pink Pound, the purchasing power of many gays, who have become the motor of an industry dedicated to leisure, fashion, and spectacle, with all the businesses that have begun to prosper, especially since the nineties, around those universes, from the money that blooms around the new capitalist flank call Pink Business, with the promotion of businesses that have always existed—hotels, fashion, leisure, culture, services—marked, sometimes absurdly, with a specific sexual orientation. (103)

These critics argue, in other words, that the clandestine sexual sites and public meeting spaces that linked and politicized an oppressed community have given way in the globalized post-Franco age to sites of comfort, conformity, and consumption that weaken the link between oppressed groups (the poor, the ethnic minority, the immigrant, the gay) and lead to a troubling homogeneity and egocentrism. Lesbian critics like Beatriz

Gimeno also worry about the depoliticization of the lesbian community, although her body politics are the opposite of Alas's. For Gimeno, the female athletic body is not a vacuous sexual object, but the epitome of the political lesbian body: "an athletic body represents the opposite of the prescribed passivity, of feminine delicacy and sweetness" (*Historia,* 308).[4]

This depoliticizing trend coincided with an overall confidence in Spain's transformation from a politically and economically backward country on the periphery of Europe to a major world power with liberal values. Tolerance of the "gay village" of Chueca enhanced that image. Dereka Rushbrook has analyzed how such villages have come to serve as marketing devices for cities hoping to increase their financial and cultural capital and concludes: "For the entrepreneurial city, cosmopolitan places serve both as destinations for local and out-of-town tourists and as markers of tolerance and diversity that enhance the city's perceived quality of life" ("Cities," 189). At the same time, however, the state may determine the limits of that tolerance, promoting consumerist, white, middle-class images of gay life and policing queer identities and behaviors (ibid., 195). Gabriel Giorgi makes exactly this claim for Chueca: "In making gay people visible Chueca epitomize[d] the new democratic Spain" (60). That is, "In a democracy that still needs to demonstrate its strength and its resemblance to the older, so-called advanced democracies of the United States and northern Europe, gay visibility stands out as a symbol, a token of social tolerance and achieved freedom" (61). Giorgi notes, however, that this visibility does not extend to lesbian tourists, who are relegated to a footnote in most gay travel guides, where they constitute "a supplement, a formally corrective addendum to discourses and information produced by and for gay male tourists" (67).

The question of race and ethnicity is also absent from most literature about Chueca. The 1990s saw an increase in immigrant populations (economic and political exiles) in Spain from Africa, Eastern Europe, and Latin America, with the result that a country whose citizens had been exoticized as passionate, irrational Mediterraneans by their European neighbors sometimes applied the same racist stereotypes to a significant portion of the people living within its boundaries. It is notable, then, that the immigrant population has been markedly absent from Chueca, except for exiled Latin American intellectuals and young men of various nationalities making their living by prostituting themselves, selling drugs, or performing in drag or strip shows.[5] Except for that group of non-Spaniards, the vast majority of foreign-born men who socialized in the establishments of the plaza during the years of this study have been tourists.

The landscape of Chueca demonstrates yet another kind of unevenness: the majority of the upscale business establishments in Chueca—including bars, clothing stores, and gyms—cater primarily to the perceived tastes of globalized gay *male* consumers. This does not mean necessarily that they exclude women altogether, although the dark rooms and saunas—open in the days of the *movida* to men and women—now do. But even the advertisements, events, and services in free circulars like *Shangay* and *Odisea*, which are distributed in bookstores and other businesses throughout Chueca, are devoted almost exclusively to the needs and desires of gay men or metrosexuals, and, specifically, to a globalized image of male sexuality that emphasizes youth, muscles, and fashion.

The invisibility of lesbians in the image of the prosperous gay lifestyle in Chueca, is not peculiar to Spain, but has been generalized in the mediatic vision of gays. Suzanna Danuta Walters explains:

> Not only is the new campaign to get gays shopping . . . motivated by a more general trend in niche marketing, it is obviously emerging in the context of increasing gay visibility, political power, and social inclusion. . . . Given this truth—that marketing to gays is a business decision (with confusing political ramifications), it should come as no surprise that the world of the marketplace promotes a view of gays as largely male, extremely wealthy, overwhelmingly white, and ready to spend their disposable wealth with admirable brand loyalty. (237–38)

Still, the media image of lesbianism is also ubiquitous, although, as Beatriz Gimeno points out, *lesbian chic* is not directed at women so much as men: "it is the lesbian that embodies one of the most persistent (hetero)sexual male fantasies" (*Historia*, 287).

Gimeno, an important advocate of lesbian feminism, associates these media images problematically, in my view, with postmodernism, queer theory, and what she considers to be the depoliticized lesbians of the younger generation. She believes that lesbians in the 2000s allow their sexuality to be used as a marketing device for globalized capital and, even worse, buy into and emulate those images (ibid., 291). These postfeminist lesbians go so far, she claims, as to denigrate lesbian culture in relation to that of gay men: "These lesbians appear in the associations to tell us that gay men are more fun than we are, more dynamic, more open to new experiences, more liberal, more modern" (ibid., 292-93). Gimeno's remarks reflect a new transformation in Chueca, the move from a community constituted around gay and lesbian identity politics, in which the feminist consciousness of lesbians implies a (sometimes justified) mistrust of their gay male counterparts, to one in which a queer consciousness predominates, one that questions strict gender categories and identities.

Gracia Trujillo is representative of the latter group of activists. Her article "Sujetos y miradas inapropiables/adas: El discurso de las lesbianas queer" (Inappropriate/unappropiable subjects and gazes: The discourse of queer lesbians), focuses on the group LSD, Lesbianas Sin Duda (Lesbians without a Doubt), that was formed in 1993. Trujillo explains the mission of the queer group, which revolves around the AIDS crisis and homophobia, and favors street action as a means of combating invisibility (107). The group questions the notion of a permanent, stable sexual identity, but it also addresses issues that are not strictly limited to sex and gender: "LSD presents an identity discourse that is defined by sexual choice, but not only that: there are other variables that contribute to lesbian identity, such as gender, race, and social class" (ibid.). LSD's concept of politics is also radically different from that of the lesbians like Gimeno who form part of the large LGBT groups like COGAM or the Fundación Triángulo: LSD advocates "education about sexual diversity and the denouncing of homophobic aggressions; for queer lesbians, the demands are for street protests and changes in everyday reality, not for legal reforms" (ibid., 115).[6] Another primary concern of the lesbian queers of LSD is the problem of AIDS, not as a gay male disease but as a symptom of the continued neglect of lesbian sexual practices and of women's health issues in general. A concrete manifestation of this concern, and of the complex lesbian-queer political practice, can be seen in the sex shop called La Juguetería, which opened in 2004. Unlike other similar establishments in the Chueca neighborhood that cater to gay men with an array of sex toys and lubricants, the owners and staff of La Juguetería, like those of Good Vibrations in San Francisco, have pedagogical ends in mind regarding both pleasure *and safety.*

The queer lesbian movement represents a different sense of politics and identities that addresses some of the omissions in the homogenizing Chueca model, and it is therefore significant that the movement is based in a completely different neighborhood, Lavapiés:

> At the beginning of the nineties these collectives began to gather in Lavapiés, which has been called "multicultural" because of the presence of immigrants from different places, rather than in the other reference point for sexual minorities that is Chueca, where you find a commercial subculture directed above all at gays, and, to a lesser degree, at lesbians. (ibid., 110)

Lesbianas Sin Duda, then, provides a counterpoint to the hegemony of identity politics linked to Chueca.

I have sought to trace here a brief history of the relationships between a variety of identities and Madrid's urban space. The next chapter will focus entirely on the politics of literary space as it is played out in the bookstores and publishing houses of the capital.

· CHAPTER 2 ·

Lesbian Literary Identities in the Madrid Book Business

THE PRECEDING CHAPTER offered a brief history of the relationships between a variety of identities and Madrid's urban space, particularly from the end of Francoism through the consolidation of Chueca as the emblem of gay/lesbian political and economic power in the capital. It also discussed how the conception of queer sites during the 1980s in Spain focused primarily on male experiences, and, how, beginning in the 1990s, those spaces became associated with a particular form of capitalism that emphasized global consumption over national or local identities. The political gains for all LGBTQ people—not just gays and lesbians—since 2000, meanwhile, have opened a space for more intellectual diversity and dissent, and for a greater cultural heterogeneity.

Publishing and bookselling have undergone similar transformations in the past decades. Although arguably even the Spanish intellectual publishers of the 1960s through the 1980s had economic as well as political and aesthetic motives (see Santana; Herrero-Olaizola; and Robbins, "Globalization"), the globalization of the book business in the 1990s transferred control from local or national enterprises to international conglomerates in what Néstor García Canclini describes as "the passage of leadership from the cosmopolitan avant-gardes to glocalized institutions and businesspeople" (146). The books published by the editors, the merchandise stocked by the bookstores, and the layout of those stores came to be determined to a large extent by the tastes of a globalized market, with a nod toward local producers and sites ("glocalized").

This phenomenon has had mixed consequences for Spanish LGBTQ literature. On the one hand, it could be argued that globalization has allowed such literature to gain acceptance in Spain more quickly and readily than it might have otherwise, given the prominence of LGBTQ authors in the international cultural sphere. The ultra-Catholic Franco regime, after all, was crushingly heteronormative, and homosexual behavior was still illegal until 1981, which meant that few books on explicitly gay and lesbian topics circulated, and Spanish authors remained in a rigid closet. On the other hand, however, the glocalized book industry of the 1990s discouraged representations of LGBTQ experiences that were too specific to Spain, or too regional in relation to the major Spanish metropolises, in favor of hip texts that mimicked literature from Paris, New York, San Francisco, London, or Berlin. I will return to this question in chapters 4–6, where I look at lesbian-themed best sellers, as well as race and gendered sexual identities.

Gay and lesbian bookstores and publishers tend not to adhere to global norms because they have traditionally favored the local or national political mission over the economic one, providing a safe space for social, political, and cultural events and promoting texts that allow their clientele to frame their experiences and identities so as to better defend their rights. The two major LGBTQ bookstores of Madrid, Berkana and A Different Life (both located in Chueca), clearly fit this model, and it is significant that both sponsor publishing houses dedicated to LGBTQ texts, Egales and Odisea, respectively. Some problems have arisen, however, from the intersection of their pedagogical mission with their owners' economic and political goals, a phenomenon that reinforces the consumer mentality and homonormativity (Bell and Binnie, 1808) that I described in the preceding chapter in relation to the Chueca phenomenon. As a result, many lesbian texts published and sold in these venues lack literary value, reinforce stereotypes, advocate assimilation, and/or appeal to a very narrow band of queer readers. The other hindrance to the dissemination of queer literature by women has been the closetedness of queer women authors in Spain owing to the "masculinism" of the Spanish cultural sphere: as a result, the arbiters of lesbian literature have been women with little literary formation, in the case of Egales, and, in the case of Odisea, primarily men, with a preference for gay literature and knowledge of gay, including Spanish gay, literary genealogies. What is more, the publishers of Egales, particularly the Madrid branch, proved during the years of my study to be less open to bisexual and queer sexualities in texts aimed at female customers, preferring a strictly lesbian textual politics.

This chapter will explore the queer book market with these issues in mind, and with a particular attention to location, architecture, publishing decisions, and marketing. I will begin by mapping the bookstores themselves, including not just Berkana and A Different Life, but also a variety of locales in and around Chueca. I will then consider the extension of the bookstores in the publishing houses Egales and Odisea.

Bookstores

If we were to walk through Chueca, we would immediately be attracted to its bookstores. Indeed, it could be argued that Chueca has four principal spaces: clothing and shoe stores for daytime shopping; cafés and *terrazas* for afternoon and evening people watching, and clubs for nighttime frenzy. But Chueca's bookstores are open morning, noon, and night. They provide free flyers about the community; they host political and cultural events; they carry a variety of merchandise explicitly linked to questions of visibility and pride; and they are available online. They are, to some extent, the glue that binds the neighborhood. Therefore, for queer people crossing through Chueca, these bookstores are an essential stop.

The gay/lesbian bookstore has had a unique symbolic role in LGBTQ politics, arguably dating to the foundation of the Oscar Wilde Memorial Bookshop in New York in 1967. The most important such bookstore in Madrid did not appear until 1993, when Mili Hernández, a leading lesbian activist, cofounded Berkana. Although it is now an icon of Chueca, Berkana's first location was not in the neighborhood at all, but on the Calle de la Palma in the contiguous neighborhood of Malasaña. Despite the post-Franco hipness of that neighborhood, especially in the years when it was associated with the gay-friendly *movida,* the store was bracketed there among establishments that were not gay, and it was not especially visible to local, national, or international communities. It was a location that one found by chance or through word of mouth from other gay or gay-friendly people. Berkana's next location was literally in the Chueca Plaza itself. It was located on Gravina Street, at the north end of the plaza, and it was clearly visible as one exited the Metro stop or sat at one of the outdoor *terrazas* in the plaza. In 2001, Berkana moved to its current location, on a busy thoroughfare on the outer fringe of the Chueca neighborhood, nearly at the border with the Malasaña neighborhood, on Hortaleza Street, in plain sight of considerably more passersby of all orientations than either of the previous locales. (Indeed, the tattoos, piercings, clothing, and hairstyle of most pedestrians on Hortaleza and Fuencarral streets are definitively queer, even when not gay or lesbian.) The nearby shops on

Hortaleza are a mixture of globalized gay businesses—cafés with plasma screens and trance music, cabarets, clothing stores, and gyms—and traditional Spanish locales, including old-style cafés (where old working-class men still take their morning brandy), lighting fixture stores, pet shops, and, closer to the Gran Vía, the Pérez Galdós bookstore, which specializes in used books. One could say, then, that the passages of the Berkana bookstore trace a change in gay visibility from the rigid closet of the Franco days to a semicloset in Malasaña, to an openness within a larger, wholly gay *gueto* (enclave or community) in the Chueca Plaza, and finally to a borderland where queer identities mingle with a variety of others. The moves have been, in other words, not only physical but also symbolic and historical, in consonance with the broader changes in the politics and economics of post-Franco Spain.

These relocations have been accompanied by changes in the marketing strategies, merchandise, and relative prosperity of the bookstore. A few years after moving to Chueca, Berkana entered the business of selling nonprint items, which it stocked in a sister store near the Gravina location on the Chueca Plaza.[1] These items were incorporated into the bookstore proper when it moved to its current, roomier location on Hortaleza. The bookstore, in other words, is not just a bookstore, but part of a growing sector of businesses that market to the particular niche of gay people, as is apparent by its listing among pink businesses in the Shanguide, which chronicles events and sites of interest to the community.[2] Berkana has branched most profitably into pride-related items and erotica—porn videos, dildos, comics, beefcake calendars, magazines, and the like—while remaining a meeting place for cultural and political activists. And, unlike similar establishments elsewhere in Spain,[3] it is prospering—that is, it is not disappearing at all—thanks in large part to the diversification of its stock and its niche marketing to gay and lesbian consumers, in Madrid and elsewhere in Spain, as well as tourists and other non-Spaniards who buy materials in the store and on its Web site.

The other major LGBTQ bookstore in Chueca, A Different Life, is located a street away from Berkana, on Pelayo, a street running north to south parallel to the plaza and to Hortaleza. This much smaller venue caters primarily to gay men: with the exception of titles from Odisea's Safo collection, the relatively few books by or about women in this bookstore are stacked in the back, and the staff has little knowledge of them. This bias might explain why A Different Life, rather than Berkana, appeared in the 2007 film *Chuecatown* (Boystown), loosely based on the comic of the same title by Rafael Martínez Castellanos, which explores the gentrification of gay male culture in the formerly bohemian barrio. A Different Life is a considerably smaller bookstore than Berkana and hence not capable of providing a political or cultural meeting space, but it sells many of the same products as Berkana, including sex toys, which are also readily available to men in the neighborhood's sex shops.

Although Berkana, cofounded by a woman, has historically been more lesbian-friendly than A Different Life, the layout of the Hortaleza store, between its opening in 2001 until the end of this study in 2005, nonetheless suggested a preferential marketing to men. The first images one would see upon entering were those of erotic postcards and comics designed almost exclusively for gay men. Recent book releases—both gay and lesbian— were arranged on tables in the middle of the store, and the materials on the shelves were divided into "narrativa masculina" (located nearest to the door), then a large display case with gay and lesbian mugs, magnets, flags, and the like, followed by essays in Spanish, then poetry, and only then "narrativa femenina." The latter section, ironically, was located in front of the display table holding books of photography featuring male nudes. Two sections of films—commercial and porn—framed the café, where political meetings were held and through which one passed to reach the stairway to the lower level. There, after passing a section with T-shirts, one found the hard-porn books and films for men, and, at the very back, under lock and key, were dildos, condoms (for penis, dildo, and fingers), and lubricants. It seemed highly unlikely that a lesbian would buy sex toys, condoms, or lubricants at Berkana unless she knew where they were, so the setup of the store seemed to suggest that these devices and condoms were for men only. The store therefore ironically gave the impression that women did not need information or products for practicing safe sex, or that lesbian sex was never penetrative. In other words, the omission of women from this particular pedagogical and political issue reinforced the general view in Spanish society that women are not, or should not be, sexually active, or at least what form lesbian sexuality should take.

Berkana also limited the possible sales to lesbians by the "women's books" they chose not to stock. For example, by 2005, there were no books of generic interest to women, such as those dealing with maternity or menopause, and none that addressed generic social and economic inequality for women. Lesbians interested in such topics would be better served in the Librería Mujeres, a feminist bookstore near the Plaza Mayor. Librería Mujeres, however, stocked few books about lesbianism. This split between the lesbian/gay bookstore and the feminist bookstore reflected a divide typical of second-generation feminists, which still determined much of the debate about politics and sexual identity among leaders of the cultural community in Madrid.

Another omission in Berkana and A Different Life, which has more to do with the mechanisms of globalized publishing than with the politics of the bookstore per se, was the dearth of books—fiction, poetry, or essay—by Latin American and U.S. Latino women. I have discussed elsewhere the difficulty experienced by Latin American writers in penetrating the literary market in Spain (Robbins, "Globalization"). In fact, most of the Latin American writers familiar to Spanish readers have either lived in Spain for many years or have been published by firms owned by Spanish interests. Berkana and A Different Life followed this tendency: the majority of the books by Latin American authors on their shelves as of 2005 were those published by the recently founded Egales or Odisea. The stores, therefore, missed another pedagogical opportunity in relation to the queer community because their stock of books did not provide a genealogy of LGBTQ literature originally written in Spanish.

The Internet has come to play a key role in extending the borders of Chueca, as well as in integrating spaces outside the neighborhood into the dynamics of lesbian identities through Chueca itself. Berkana, for example, began to market its stock to a broader public by establishing a Web site where people outside Madrid proper could have access to the merchandise, a move that Mili Hernández has identified as political. Despite this goal of outreach, however, we should note that the Internet service does not necessarily always serve political ends, since it allows people to purchase books in privacy, without making the public gesture of entering an openly gay establishment or even strolling through the predominantly gay barrio of Chueca. In this sense, it could be said to reinforce the walls of the closet rather than bringing them down. We could also question the politics of the market: does the freedom to buy really translate into free expression or political activism?[4] On the other hand, we could say that the implications of the Web site transcend the local politics of Madrid, or even of Spain, because it makes the books stocked by Berkana accessible to readers of Spanish worldwide. In this sense, it could represent a step toward the inclusion of Spain in a transnational queer readership, or even transnational politics informed by similar texts, and it is here that the bookstore intersects with more explicitly political sites, which often include links to the bookstore on their own Web pages. Books on LGBTQ topics have not been limited exclusively to Chueca, of course, but have been distributed throughout the bookstores of Madrid. These are quite varied, from the small, traditional kind like the La Celestina or Librería Pérez Galdós that specialize in used and rare books, to those with a political history like the feminist Librería Mujeres, to those associated with publishing houses like Hiperión, to those that serve as an extension of cultural establishments like the Reina Sofía museum or the Círculo de Bellas Artes, to large commercial establishments like the bookstore of the Corte Inglés, the Casa del Libro, or the FNAC, to those somewhere in between, like Crisol. None of these is in Chueca proper, although the Pérez Galdós is just a few blocks south on Hortaleza; the Casa del Libro, a few blocks farther, on the Gran Vía; and the FNAC just a bit farther, on Preciados Street in Callao (not far from the Cine Carretas, famous as a gay cruising spot in the Franco and early post-Franco years). Although all of these bookstores now stock and advertise books with gay and lesbian themes, they do not market exclusively to the queer community but to a variety of niches, from the scholar to the student to the casual or nostalgic reader, male or female, Spanish or not, gay or straight, of any age. They therefore respond to different political and economic forces that determine how they market nonheteronormative books.

I will focus in the following paragraphs on two of the larger bookstores, one of them associated, like Berkana and A Different Life, with a publishing firm, and the other with a multimedia conglomerate that began with a clear sociopolitical mission, as did the LGBTQ bookstores.

The Casa del Libro was founded in 1932 by the famous Spanish editorial house Espasa-Calpe, but it was incorporated in 1992 into the Grupo Planeta conglomerate. The economics of glocalized publishing is laid bare in the layout and window display of the Casa del Libro: that is, the influence of the richest publishing houses often determines the visibility of literary texts in the display window and in the store itself. The less expensive *libros de bolsillo* (paperbacks) are grouped together by author, even when the book itself does not really belong to the less prestigious popular culture category of the traditional paperback. Along with this sales mentality, we may note some remnants of both the imperialist Hispanidad traditionally associated with Espasa-Calpe, along with the repressive sexual politics of Francoism: thus newly released Latin American books are grouped with texts by Spanish authors rather than with the foreign books, and the erotic books—those in the Sonrisa Vertical collection published by Tusquets, for example—are relatively hidden in a corner with other "low culture" books, like romance and detective novels.[5] Given these vestiges of traditional Spanish ideologies and the prominence of established editorial houses in the Casa del Libro, it is significant that some books published by Egales and Odisea have found their way into the store and onto the Web site, again allowing queer identities to travel beyond Chueca and the gay *gueto* in general. Admittedly, it is easier to find those books on the Web site than in the store itself, with the exception of a prominent display of Mabel Galán's *Donde comienza tu nombre* in 2004 that I will discuss in chapter 4, along with the contradictory implications of this visibility.

The literary merchandise of the FNAC is less circumscribed by Spanish national, literary, or sexual identities than that of the Casa de Libro. The FNAC (Fédération nationale d'achats pour cadres) was originally founded in 1954 in France on socialist principles and designed to make film and music products available at prices affordable to the working class. It did not begin to sell books until twenty years later, so its mission is less literary than sociopolitical. The store on Callao in Madrid opened in 1993 at the site of the defunct department store Galerías Preciados, which had been established soon after the Spanish civil war, in 1943, but then bought by its competitor, El Corte Inglés, in 1995.[6] The products sold by the FNAC are distributed over several floors of the building and are divided roughly by media: newspapers and magazines, films and TV, music, video games, books, photography, computers. The image could not be more distanced, it seems, from identity politics of any sort, yet the FNAC stocks LGBTQ books, and, in contrast to the Casa del Libro, does not confine them to any sort of literary ghetto in its displays. It is perhaps for this reason that the FNAC appears in Libertad Morán's 2003 novel, *Llévame a casa* (Take me home), as the locale where two lesbian characters first meet, their homosexuality signaled by the Patricia Highsmith book that one begins perusing (19).

The book-buying locales that queer people could frequent from 1993 until 2005, then, intersect in complex and sometimes contradictory ways with questions of LGBTQ politics. Mili Hernández has argued that those who shop for books at La Casa del Libro or the FNAC undermine the political goals of the community with their apolitical, consumerist behavior by threatening the economic viability of bookstores like Berkana and A Different Life. It is also true, however, that in the period of my study those bookstores themselves projected, through their stock, layout, and staffing, a gay/lesbian identity politics that was not always perfectly inclusive of gender and sexual difference. We see a similar tension in the editorial sector, as I will explain in the following section.

Publishing, Politics, and Literature

The publishing business in Spain has had a complex and often contradictory relationship with politics, literature, and economics over the past several decades. Despite the myth of Spanish editors like Carlos Barral and Jorge Herralde as disinterested literary intellectuals, Mario Santana has argued that the resurgence of Spanish publishing during the 1960s was largely a marketing phenomenon, the direct result of the Spanish dominance of Latin American markets, the publication of novels in all the national languages of Spain, and the success throughout the Spanish-speaking world of the Latin American Boom novels, which were published by Seix Barral.[7] This dominance was further consolidated in 1970, when Tusquets, Lumen, and Barral Editores (Carlos Barral had just broken with Seix Barral to form Barral Editores) joined five other publishing firms (Edicions 62, Laia, Cuadernos para el Diálogo, Fontanella, and Anagrama) in a distribution network that extended to Latin America as well.

Women also began to achieve prominence in the publishing business during the 1960s. Esther Tusquets, along with her brother, the architect Óscar Tusquets, inherited the Editorial Lumen from their father, Magín Tusquets, who had bought the ultraconservative religious press from his brother Joan. The leftist, antidictatorial politics at Lumen under the Tusquets siblings were similar to those of Seix Barral, but, particularly after Óscar and his then wife, Beatriz de Moura, left the firm to form Tusquets Editores in 1968, Esther Tusquets began to publish the writing of foreign and Spanish gay men and all women, including lesbians, along with children's stories and cultural theory, the kind of texts that Barral did not publish as readily. Both Tusquets and Barral, however, wanted to identify their publishing houses with products of high culture and create an international market for them (Herrero-Olaizola, 327–28). Another firm, Alianza, decided to pursue a different tactic beginning in 1966, by offering paperbacks to attract a market of commuters and beachgoers (Santana, 35). Beatriz de Moura pushed to publish this type of edition at Lumen, and it was, in part, Esther Tusquets's resistance to this ploy that led her sister-in-law to abandon Lumen.

After the dictatorship ended in 1975, Seix Barral, Lumen, and Tusquets continued to thrive and become successful international businesses, so in a way they represented the triumph of the Left after Franco. Their editors ceased to be figures combating political tyranny in the Hispanic world from the margins and began to inhabit the economic and political center of Spain. In this sense, their fortunes may be linked to the formerly banned political parties after the transition to democracy: they triumphed and prospered, but the varied goals of a Left formerly unified against the Franco dictatorship eventually split into competing factions, and economic factors began to weigh more heavily in publishing decisions.

The incorporation of Spanish publishing houses into international conglomerates in the 1990s coincided with the triumph of neoliberalism and globalization, and the disappearance of the more personal, regional establishments with strong intellectual directors and editors mirrored for many the perceived decline in the agency of individuals and individual nations in an increasingly faceless economic network. The purchase of important publishers like Lumen and Plaza y Janés by Random House also implied a loss of national identity to the capitalism of the United States, Germany, the United Kingdom, and France. At the same time, however, the internationalization of the publishing business represented Spain's incorporation into an international economy from which it had been exiled during much of the Franco dictatorship. It also symbolized the entry of Spain into a European community—Random House, after all, was at the time a subsidiary of the German firm Bertelsmann—and thus implied identification with the first-world economies, cultures, and governments of Europe. Finally, however, it meant the transfer of editorial power from artists and intellectuals to businesspeople who tended to view books as products and merchandise. It is in this economic, political, and intellectual context that we should examine the role of the LGBTQ editorial houses Egales and Odisea, associated with the bookstores Berkana and A Different Life, respectively.

In 1995, Berkana ceased to be just a seller of books and branched out into the publishing business with the cofounding of Egales with the owners of the Barcelona lesbian bookstore Cómplices, Connie Dagas and

Helle Bruun. Egales initially favored a pedagogical (and rather pedestrian) series—"Salir del armario"—for readers who were just beginning to come out of the closet. Since 2000, however, both the publishing house and the Berkana bookstore have ventured increasingly toward essays, novels by "high-culture" Spanish women writing under a pseudonym, Latin American women, and European and U.S. women publishing in translation, in response to the increased demand for such texts. In 1999, Óscar Pérez would found Odisea, whose Safo collection is directed at the lesbian community, and which, beginning in that same year, has offered a literary prize for LGBTQ literature.

The books featured on the central display tables in Berkana and A Different Life are overwhelmingly those published by either Egales or Odisea, reflecting the link between the economic and political interests of the bookseller and the publisher (in this case they are one and the same). It is striking, in particular, that although Egales was founded by women, lesbians remained through 2005 less visible than gay men in the press's publications. This invisibility extended to anthologies and histories published by Egales and Odisea as well. Sympathetic anthologists would still abide by the tacit agreement not to out authors, as Connie Dagas explained to me in July 2000. Julia Cela confirmed this pact when I asked her why she did not include Spanish women in her 1998 *Galería de retratos: Personajes homosexuales de la cultura contemporánea* (Portrait gallery: Homosexual personages in contemporary culture).[8] Likewise, Alberto Mira's exhaustive study (615 pages) *De Sodoma a Chueca: Una historia cultural de la homosexualidad en España en el siglo XX* (From Sodom to Chueca: A cultural history of homosexuality in twentieth-century Spain, 2004) does not include the literary work of a single Spanish lesbian; the only Spanish woman who merits more than a cursory mention is Carmen de Burgos, whose work Mira condemns as homophobic.

The rationale for this disparity has been explained by Mili Hernández in economic terms: as she told me in 1999, books for and about lesbians just do not sell, a view that was corroborated by Óscar Pérez in a newspaper interview in 2003 ("La editorial Odisea").[9] This reasoning, however, feeds into the gender bias of Spanish culture and seems faulty on several grounds. It does not, for example, take into account the general gender disparity in book publications and sales, an issue that Laura Freixas discusses in *Literatura y mujeres: Escritoras, público y crítica en la España actual* (Literature and women: Women writers, the reading public, and criticism in contemporary Spain, 2000), where she also notes that books by and for women sell less than those by and for men largely for the simple reason that they are *published less* (36). Current book sales, in other words, are rather unreliable indicators of future market trends, because they only reflect the status quo, which in itself may be determined by factors extraneous to the market itself, such as the assumption by publishers that women write less well than men (Freixas, 72–74) and that women's books will only be of interest to women (ibid., 70). A lesbian publisher who sees herself as an activist could reasonably be expected to address this disparity by ignoring the inaccurate and faulty reasoning used by heterosexist editors and publishing more texts by women.

The increased number of such books alone, however, would not be a reliable indicator of future sales of all books to lesbians. Lesbians do not read only about lesbians or lesbian issues. Even within LGBTQ offerings, it is logical to presume that they will also buy more general studies of homosexuality, queer theory, and novels by gay men, including classics like Eduardo Mendicutti's *Una mala noche la tiene cualquiera* (Anyone can have a bad night, 1988), Óscar Guasch's *La sociedad rosa* (Pink society, 1991), Beatriz Preciado's *Manifiesto contra-sexual* (Countersexual manifesto, 2002), and translations of Judith Butler and Eve Kosofsky Sedgwick. Egales and Odisea are not significant publishers of these texts, but both Berkana and A Different Life stock them. And, as mentioned earlier, lesbians are forced to purchase elsewhere nonlesbian books that Berkana and A Different Life do not carry and Egales and Odisea do not publish.

Even more fundamentally, however, I must point out that the claims of Hernández and Pérez regarding the buying habits of lesbians are impossible to verify because there are no data to support or disprove them. The majority of Spanish bookstores, which represent a far higher percentage of total book sales in Spain than their gay/lesbian counterparts, cannot make assumptions about the sexual identity of their clientele, and thus cannot provide data about lesbian purchases. Even Egales and Odisea cannot know the sexual identities of their customers or the ultimate destination of the books they buy, and, as far as I can determine, they do not even catalog their sales according to the buyer's gender. The market assumption regarding lesbians' consumption, then, has been made on the basis of sales, not purchasing, data. It therefore depends not on what people want or even on what they do, but on what is available to buy. Finally, the editors' assumptions do not take into account the diversity of lesbian readers, which may include mothers, older women, Latin American women living in Madrid, women scholars, and intellectuals who shop in a variety of places. All of these factors blur the distinctions drawn by Hernández and Pérez regarding the impact of lesbian consumers in overall book sales, which they use to justify an editorial policy that discriminates against women.

Another problem arises from the fact that neither Hernández nor Pérez mentioned in their interviews the relative literary quality or erotic quotient of lesbian-themed literature in comparison to similar books by and about gay men. There is a long history of "high-culture" texts by famous Spanish gay men, including Federico García Lorca, Luis Cernuda, Juan Gil-Albert, Jaime Gil de Biedma, Luis Antonio de Villena, and many others. Men have also written more explicitly about sex in Spain. Lesbian artists, on the other hand, have been almost completely invisible, meaning that there was not a tradition, or a genealogy, of Spanish lesbian writers who could serve as models for young women hoping to publish with Egales.

This might have been the context for the comments that Hernández made at the lesbian narrative roundtable of the first Visible festival of LGBTQ culture in Madrid in 2005, regarding the political immaturity of Spanish women.[10] Thus, Hernández explained that Egales primarily published coming-out stories because this was the only type of text one could expect Spanish lesbians to relate to, given that the movement was younger in Spain, and lesbian readers were therefore presumably less sophisticated than their counterparts in the United States or Europe regarding feminist and lesbian issues. This comment equated the maturity of the lesbian movement with that of individual women, and political sophistication with intellectual sophistication. It was troubling because it implied that lesbians only read for political content, that Spain was "backward" or "belated" in relation to other Western nations (a comment typically made of Western colonies), that lesbians' appreciation of cultural objects was bound to a developmentally challenged politics, that it was more important for literature to be political than pleasurable or thought-provokingly ambiguous, and even that lesbian readers might be intellectually inferior to their male counterparts. In other words, it rather uncritically reproduced colonial and even sexist notions of cultural development, politics, and sexual identity.

Hernández also asserted in her comments that lesbians did not write as much, and as evidence she explained that Egales only received one manuscript by a woman for every eight by male writers. As with her earlier assertion regarding the number of books that lesbians buy, this claim rested on erroneous assumptions and insufficient data. The fact that women sent fewer manuscripts to Egales cannot be generalized to mean that they wrote or sent fewer manuscripts overall; Egales might simply not have been their preferred venue. Perhaps they had artistic ambitions, sexual desires, or political views that were not encouraged by the editorial policies of Egales; that is, it might have been the case that Spanish lesbians and bisexual women were simply not interested in writing the kind of text that Egales was willing to publish: literature by, about, and for lesbians, as Beatriz Gimeno put it in the same panel. Hernández likewise emphasized that the author of a lesbian text must identify herself as lesbian, have a lesbian voice, and write texts full of "references to identifiable lesbian experiences." The problem of defining a "lesbian" in this context arose, and a member of the audience suggested that a lesbian was a woman who had never slept with a man, a concept that is as unverifiable as are the reading, purchasing, and writing habits of lesbians. The editors' concept of lesbian identity and sexuality, as described by Hernández and Gimeno in the roundtable, also limited the erotic potential of the press's offerings by eliminating queer, bisexual, and even penetrative pleasures altogether in favor of less "perverse" homonormative lesbian sex. Finally, it might have been the case that lesbians had more reticence than gay men about coming out of the closet by publishing an explicitly lesbian text with a gay/lesbian press. One could reasonably argue, then, that the editorial criteria of publishing books for their thematic content and adherence to a particular form of lesbian identity and sexuality, rather than their aesthetic qualities, might have served to reinforce stereotypes about women, women writers, and women's literature in the "Salir del armario" phase of Egales's trajectory.

In all fairness to Hernández and Gimeno, I should point out that they have served primarily as activists, and important ones at that, but they are not literary critics or highly regarded authors, although Gimeno had recently published a novel. The level of discourse in their roundtable therefore suffered in comparison with the critical sophistication of the roundtable of gay male literature, in which the respected writers Luis Antonio de Villena, Álvaro Pombo, and Leopoldo Alas participated.[11] The poor showing by lesbian or bisexual writers and/or critics pointed to a larger problem in the Spanish culture: the widespread denigration of women as artists and intellectuals, which leads the best among them to eschew any association between their gender, their sexuality, and their cultural production. Indeed, Hernández commented during the roundtable that several women writers had declined her invitation to participate.

The third, and final, participant in the Visible panel was Isabel Franc, whose first novel, *Entre todas las mujeres* (Among all the women, 1992), represented the mystical fervor of Bernadette Soubirous for the Virgin of Lourdes as a lesbian passion that she shares with her religious sisters. Franc's following four novels, written from and set in Barcelona—*Con pedigree* (With pedigree, 1997), *Plumas de doble filo* (Double-edged pens, 1999),[12] *La mansión de las tríbadas* (The mansion of tribadism, 2002), and *No me llames cariño* (Don't call me "baby," 2004)—were published with the Barcelona branch of Egales under the pseudonym Lola Van Guardia, becoming simultaneously lesbian best sellers and the objects of serious critical attention. This fact and Franc's open lesbianism explain her willingness to appear as the only successful novelist on the panel. Franc's Lola Van Guardia novels are characterized by humor and irony, particularly regarding lesbian politics, relationships, the detective genre, and the lesbian scene in Barcelona, so it should not be surprising that her comments were humorous and refused to categorize holistically "the lesbian novel."[13] Franc's interventions on the Visible panel and her satirical critiques of sexual identity politics served as a stark contrast to the identity politics in the cultural practices of popular lesbian publishers, as articulated by Hernández and Gimeno.

The explicit, but far from idealized, sexuality in Franc's novels, along with her ironic take on lesbian politics and her postmodern aesthetics, have had an enormous influence on the next generation of authors publishing with Egales (e.g., Sofía Ruiz), but even more so on those who publish with Odisea, four of whom I will examine in depth in subsequent chapters (María Felicitas Jaime's *Cenicienta en Chueca,* Mabel Galán's *Donde comienza tu nombre,* Libertad Morán's *A por todas,* and Marta Fagés's *Amores prohibidos*). Libertad Morán even goes so far, in *Llévame a casa,* finalist for the Odisea Prize in 2003, to have one of her five story lines dedicated to a gay man. These books imply that the Egales "Salir del armario" novels, and the strict identity politics of the editors, were not hegemonic models of lesbianism in Spain (or even in Egales) before 2005, despite the monopoly that they held on the image of lesbian culture in "Visible."

Conclusion

Pierre Bourdieu points out in *The Rules of Art* that the critical/scholarly apparatus is only one factor in the creation and maintenance of cultural authority: the mode of production, the intended consumer, the short-term versus long-term profitability, the popularity, and the accessibility of cultural products are also criteria used to determine their cultural (versus economic) value in the eyes of critics. The fusing of sales, production, and marketing in LGBTQ publishing and book sales has produced a contradictory political and cultural enterprise that seems to adopt the (inaccurate, prejudicial) criteria of what has been acknowledged as a heterosexist market. In this case, it is striking that, although the size and characteristics of lesbian—as well as bisexual and queer—readership have yet to be determined objectively, assumptions about women's sexuality, women readers, and "women's literature" inherited from the overall sexist cultural sphere of Spain have often shaped decisions regarding the marketing and sales of lesbian-themed books and erotica, even within the gay ghetto of Chueca.

Even as they struggle with economic models in an effort to remain alive, lesbian/gay books and businesses have been expected to perform political and pedagogical work within the community itself and within society as a whole, work that may, however, be at odds with the economic and artistic goals of authors, booksellers, and publishers. What is more, those political expectations often belie the actual characteristics of the lesbian/gay community itself by ignoring the changes and the fissures within it, and by trying to impose a single, normative model. Lesbians and gay men, of course, often have conflicting goals and income discrepancies, which manifest themselves in the separate literary spaces of the LGBTQ bookstores, Berkana and A Different Life, but there is also considerable disagreement within the lesbian community itself, as the political quarrel between Mili Hernández and Boti García Rodrigo, the president of COGAM (and Beatriz Gimeno's spouse), as well as the debate over "lesbian" versus "queer" activism make clear.[14] The communities also divide along class, age, ethnic, race, and national lines, or according to their level of education or specific sexual preferences. In other words, the contrast of the strict identity politics in the stated cultural practices of popular lesbian publishers, on the one hand, and the critique of sexual identity by intellectuals, lesbian writers published by Odisea, and high-culture writers, on the other hand, suggests a healthy dissent regarding the role of literature and business in LGBTQ politics.

· CHAPTER 3 ·

The New Safita

Andalusia and the Phallic Woman in *Plumas de España*

THE DEBATES surrounding the literariness of Egales's "Salir del armario" series touched on several questions about the gendered nature of cultural and sexual politics in Spain in a globalized age. The writer Luis Antonio de Villena, for example, criticized the series, and the Berkana bookstore itself, in an interview with the late Leopoldo Alas in the latter's 2002 book *Ojo de loca no se equivoca: Una irónica y lúcida reflexión sobre el ambiente* (The queer eye never lies: An ironic and lucid reflection on the *ambiente*):

> The cultured gay public is still in the closet, and they buy gay literature at any normal bookstore, not at Berkana. They don't go to bars in Chueca or to gay bookstores because they don't want to do that kind of militancy. The ones that go to the "foam parties" at Refugio or to the Shangay Tea Dance on Sundays are not cultured; they don't buy books. It's a mistake to promote to them, because you'll only sell three books, I told Mili Hernández. And she explained to me that it is for that reason that they're publishing all those novels at Egales, because they're easy to understand and they want to see if they can get those uncultured people to read, even if it's reading very elemental gay stories, told in a conventional way. I told her that, if she wanted to educate them, the first thing she should do is teach them their own history, which they don't know. (112)

Here, Villena suggests a hierarchical cultural split between gay intellectuals and sexually frenetic *locas*, a division that certain exemplary lives (Foucault comes immediately to mind) might place in doubt.[1] Villena splits literature into high and low varieties that he attaches to different modes of gay behavior: the sexual body, which has traditionally been feminized, is associated with "low" or popular culture, tea dances, and foam parties, whereas the bodies associated with high culture are more ravaged by vices associated with the life of the mind.[2] This concept has problematic implications for women, all of whom are generally linked in Spanish culture to the body and popular culture.

In the same volume, Leopoldo Alas complains that contemporary gay culture in Spain has the effect of homogenizing gay identities by presenting a single norm that is unrefined, unintellectual, incurious (112). Alas's book itself, however, creates its own homogeneous ideal of gays as cultured intellectuals who place little emphasis on the body (thus his elevation of smoking to a "cultural activity"). His study thus performs its own silencing of difference. Particularly silent in his text are women.

Some of the contradictions apparent in the current gay book business and these assessments of it by "cultured" gay male intellectuals reveal the uneasy convergence in democratic Spain between reality and the idealization of the liberal public sphere in the post-Franco era. Eric O. Clarke explains that

> the principles of translation from private to public retained by the bourgeois public sphere have historically contradicted its own universalist, democratic ideals. While claiming to establish a "context-transcending" sphere through which to adjudicate competing interests equitably, the conversion from private to public has involved quite particular, context-specific determinations of value. (4)

This is clear in the valuation of certain identity markers over others by gay male Spanish intellectuals, who seek to separate sexual and intellectual practices, and, with them, different qualities of gay males. As they attempt to distinguish themselves from the uncultured rabble, they seem to ignore the normalizing practices of the cultural public sphere into which they hope to integrate themselves—that of the Spanish intellectual elite, which continues to be sexist, sexually conservative, antipopular, and vehemently opposed to the (supposedly recent) incursion of capitalist practices in the literary market, which they associate with the propagation of popular culture at the expense of more intellectual cultural products.[3] As a consequence of their desire to assimilate into the high-culture realm, they create their own hierarchy of Spanish homosexuals that eschews the popular/sexual/feminine and omits women altogether, except as objects of their pedagogy—that is, the "lessons" they give Hernández or lesbians in general on pages 211–15—or as objects of scorn. These hierarchies, in effect, are shadows of the interestedness of the literary public sphere, as Clarke describes the concept: "the very ideals of the public sphere have historically been attached to a quite particular subject position: the white Euro-American, educated, presumptively heterosexual middle-class male who owns property" (8).

This chapter will examine a novel by Ana Rossetti, a contemporary of Villena and Alas, which lays bare the interestedness of the gay writers—and men in general—in maintaining preglobalization sexual-textual hierarchies. The novel, *Plumas de España,* appears at a moment of transition in Spanish publishing from the provincial practices that kept women and women writers on the periphery of literary culture to an industry driven by literary prizes of doubtful merit and dedicated to titillation and sales.[4] Rather than idealizing one model or the other, Rossetti's novel addresses the absence of the woman, and in particular, the Andalusian woman, from literary politics and the popular imagination, and her refiguration as the "New Safita." The protagonist's designation as a lesbian has nothing whatsoever to do with her sexual practices or political interests, but is, rather, the product of the gay imagination, as embodied in the transvestite character Patela, who so baptizes her, and of Spanish society's inability to recognize or name the "perverse" woman. It is a mechanism designed to discipline the woman, the woman author, and the provinces through sexuality, and it thus represents a vestige of the cultural practices of Francoism, as I will explain.

Politics and Drag in the Transition and the *Movida*

The performance of simulated femininity has been used insistently as a trope for the new identities of post-Franco Spain beginning with the transition. The parody of kitschy Francoist culture and the public parading of jubilant sexuality in the drag shows of the 1970s and 1980s seemed like a carnival, a celebratory funeral for the outdated repressions of national Catholicism. The seeming acceptance of these spectacles by traditional elements of Spanish society also appeared to signal a shift from the intolerance and isolation of Francoist society to a presumably softer, feminized, cosmopolitan culture that was more open and inviting to the outside gaze. Alberto Mira explains:

> Numerous examples demonstrate the instrumentalization of transvestism to integrate it into a heterosexist scheme. The principal strategy consists of falsely presenting the effeminate homosexual of the Transition as a sign of modernity, whose visibility is offered up as the definitive argument to confirm that social change has taken place. (*De Sodoma a Chueca*, 435)

Patrick Paul Garlinger likewise argues that "a rhetorical use of transsexuality indicates a celebratory escape from the past, a sign of authentic and profound cultural and political transformation" ("Sex Changes," 30).

More recent assessments of this phenomenon, however, suggest that the drag spectacle also served to confirm the hegemony of a heterosexist and patriarchal model, and, indeed, the continued hegemony of *masculinismo* surfaced in yet another rhetorical deployment of transvestism and transsexuals: at the same time that they were used to emblematize an authentic shift in Spanish mores, transvestites and transsexuals were accused of inauthenticity—of not *really* being women—and they were thus used to criticize the process of transition as a moving away from some essential Spanishness. In particular, the association between the transvestite, the transsexual, the transition, and, in the 1980s, the PSOE allowed conservatives to claim that all of these were equally inauthentic. Thus, Garlinger notes that, when Francisco Umbral called Felipe González a political transvestite, he revealed that "[t]ransvestism functions rhetorically as an artifice or masquerade, a reflection of the surface changes in the national body that are little more than a travesty" (ibid.).[5]

The accusation of inauthenticity assumes that the biological female is the authentic origin, the originary body that the transvestite and the transsexual inevitably lack, but, as Mira points out, the model for the *travestí*'s female performance is not women themselves but the simulations of them in popular culture: "The point is not to imitate an authentic model but to imitate an imitation of femininity" (*De Sodoma a Chueca*, 439). Baudrillard concurs that transvestism "is the parody of femininity *as men imagine* and stage it, as well as phantasize it. A femininity exaggerated, degraded, parodied . . . , the claim is that in this society femininity is naught but the signs with which men rig it up. To over-simulate femininity is to suggest that woman is but a masculine model of simulation" (14). The performance of camp and drag, then, references women but ultimately leaves them out. Indeed, most definitions of camp assert that, despite its connection to women and women's culture, it cannot be employed by women themselves. It is associated, as Garlinger and Song explain, primarily with *la pluma,* that is, with gay men, especially during the transition (6). It is, in this sense, a form of *masculinity,* not *femininity,* one that maintains a strict hierarchy based on biological sex even while it plays with the signs of gender.[6]

Baudrillard's theorization of drag performance focuses primarily on the way in which the separation of the sexed body from the overdetermined gender performance affects the spectator. That interpretation assumes, however, that the spectacle signifies in the same way at all times, and that the spectators share a common conception of gender identity with each other and the performer. I would argue, on the contrary, that drag performance has multiple implications, for both the performer and the audience, many of which are socially and historically determined. Spanish drag, for example, underwent significant changes in the years preceding and following Franco's death. During the dictatorship, camp forms of parody represented a somewhat acceptable device for publicly expressing a "deviant masculinity," so that "camp was intimately related to the silencing of homosexual experience" (Mira, *De Sodoma a Chueca,* 526).

In the immediate post-Franco period, in contrast, camp and drag became playful, provocative, and celebratory expressions of freedom that privileged sensual pleasure and humor over intellectual reflection (ibid.). This style reflects the ethos of the *movida* as well, as Borja Casani and José Tono Martínez explain in the first issue of *La luna de Madrid:*

> The city has interiorized and dissolved in itself all these experiences just like the pioneering cities of the West. Improvising, learning, and copying at a dizzying pace. *Provocando,* like an accelerated digestion, delirium. A false and luddic image of the world. A pleasant mythification of the modern. An ironclad superficiality and a reasonably sincere liberalism. (7)

This sensibility, likewise, marked the style of literary texts associated with drag: "Readers are urged to live in the moment, to take advantage of the frenzy of existence and to escape the well-worn paths of knowledge. The camp gaze forms a facet of this vital ideology and one of its primary functions will be to articulate the relationship between a liberated present and an oppressive past through humor" (Mira, *De Sodoma a Chueca*, 526).

The nature of drag performances changed, however, as they became marked by the ways in which heterosexist society accepted homosexuality in the 1970s and 1980s, so that they passed from a transgressive camp model that parodied Spanish popular culture and was targeted primarily at a gay audience to the striptease model that appealed to the curiosity of a mixed public. Again, Mira explains:

> With the advent of the transition, the popularity of drag started to fade; a new repertoire took over that included striptease and hormone-treated transvestites as a "modern" and democratic alternative to the outdated icons that the drag queens imitated.... The main act of each show was designed as a striptease whose climax could include a full frontal nude that revealed the performer's "truth." (ibid., 441)

The latter shows emphasized first the presence of the penis, and later its absence, as transvestism gave way to transsexuality.

The strip shows obviously drew attention finally away from the performance of gender and toward the phallus: even if the revealed penis likewise marks the simulation of femininity, and femininity itself, as artifice, it also reestablishes the phallic order and implies that the female and the feminine do not exist at all outside the male imagination. It signals, then, the end of gender play and the elimination of the female, even as it dictates the forms in which gay men can be visible in the new economic and social order, so that the apparent subversion of heterosexual masculinity can be neutralized. Fernando Villaamil explains this process in terms of Mediterranean forms of masculinity:

> The lack of an articulated antihomosexual response could be interpreted as related to ways in which masculinism operates, which is to reduce it to silence, from a position of power, which never feels truly threatened, as the silence itself implies.... The signs and behaviors associated with sanctioned masculinity constitute a symbolic arsenal that can be strategically employed: in a climate

that we could describe as tolerantly passive, as long as one maintains a public appearance of normality, a public adherence to the norm and a broad external conformity with the expectations of the masculine role, men are permitted a wide margin of operations, which include the subordinated forms of masculinity. (21)

Garlinger explains this same process in psychoanalytic terms. He focuses on the spectator of shows featuring the operated transsexual Bibi Andersen, and particularly on the heterosexual male's fetishistic desire for the mother's absent phallus in the case of transsexuality. His reading of Francisco Umbral is particularly incisive, linking machismo and misogyny to the writer's fascination with the transsexual Bibi Andersen:

> That touch of unicorn, that extra something that Umbral fetishizes, is that virtual phallus that Umbral seeks in his mythic union with Bibi. *She,* as the virtual phallus for Umbral, is the fantasy of a postmodern, technologically crafted, phallic woman—a myth transformed into reality.... The fantasy of the complete woman, the one who does not lack, is often associated with transsexualism. ("Sex Changes," 37)[7]

Alejandro Yarza, in contrast, examines the desire of the transvestite rather than the spectator. He claims that the *travestí* affirmed the penis at the end of the striptease in order to foreground a gendered hybridity produced by the transformation into the fetish of the mother's absent phallus ("Estudios cinematográficos," 194). In Yarza's and Garlinger's view, then, these types of performance omit women and draw attention to women's essential lack by fetishizing it.

Andalusia as Drag and Fetish

The *travestís* of the later *destape*[8] tended to perform pop or globalized musical numbers, often with lyrics in English, but early versions of Spanish drag, particularly *transformismo,* imitated Spanish models of femininity as represented by the divas of Spanish folkloric films—Lola Flores, Rocío Jurado, Sara Montiel—who popularized *coplas* and *cuplés.* Mira even argues that "the folkloric divas were well aware that they were objects of transvestite imitation" (*De Sodoma a Chueca,* 441). Some *transformistas,* including Ocaña and Mendicutti's protagonist, la Madelón, also fetishized Andalusia's economic and political castration by performing simulations of Semana Santa processions, which are also predecessors of the gay pride manifestations or parades. In this section, I will trace some of the transgressive and queer connotations of Andalusian culture that the Franco dictatorship attempted to suppress, but that reappear as a trace in folkloric films, and later as camp in drag performance.

Andalusian religious processions and flamenco came to emblematize Andalusia within Spain during the Franco dictatorship, particularly from the perspective of the capital, although Andalusia has had a troubled relationship with Madrid since the time of the conquest. These hostilities escalated in the nineteenth century because of the region's socialist, anarchist, and Marxist affiliations, and they found an expression in flamenco *coplas*:

> During the course of the 19th century, the inchoate antimonarchism and social discontent so widespread in Andalusia found new shape in Fourier-influenced proto-socialism, in anarchism, and, ultimately, in Marxism.... By mid-century the civic discontent once expressed in *bandolerismo* and fatalism was generating strikes, unions, leftist publications, open revolts (e.g., in 1868), and explicit social commentary in flamenco *coplas*. (Manuel, 49)

These were not, however, the same folkloric songs popularized in the *españolada* of the 1920s and 1930s, through which the Right romanticized Andalusian culture and instrumentalized it in the construction of an image of national unity. The Andalusia that they represented was not the least bit "authentic": some of these films were even filmed in Nazi Germany, featuring Imperio Argentina, who was born in Argentina to Spanish parents and affected a strong Andalusian accent in her portrayal of Gypsy heroines.

Andalusia's political history also contributed to the harsh treatment it received during the Franco dictatorship. During and after the civil war, the Falange sought not just to kill men on the Left, but "to take social and cultural life as well, to eradicate individual identity, to deny any claim to being proper men from proper 'casas'" (Corbin, 153). The subordination of women to men was a key component of Andalusian honor, and the concept of shame was of primordial importance in maintaining order.

The Falange's attack on men's honor therefore included the humiliation of their women:

> It was intended as a "castigo"..., a punishment to purify, to make chaste; it was part of a process of "cleaning." It asserted that the women, instead of being shamefully engaged in the production of proper life in the "casa," were shamelessly subhuman. They therefore should be treated like animals, shorn like sheep, herded through the streets as incontinent as any beast.
>
> The attack focused on domestic disarray, equating women living "in sin", those women living with leftist militants, and women stepping out of their proper role and participating in street demonstration. (ibid. 3)

The concepts of shame and honor continued to be ordering devices in the postwar period, and shameless women were therefore rhetorically linked to political disorder, and hence to sympathizers of the Republic.

There were many *coplas* that responded to this particular repression of Andalusia and the subsequent economic hardships that Andalusians suffered. José Colmeiro argues, however, that the political message was hidden in the text of many songs that appeared to support the values of national Catholicism:

> Voices of resistance under the dictatorship often had to resort to the use of a metaphorical language of double meanings and coded words, in a tacit subversion of official Francoist ideology. This subtle undermining strategy was also manifested through many popular songs of the period. Quite often those songs were recoded and reinterpreted by the listeners, who had developed the skill to read between the lines, sometimes even against the explicit message and professed ideology of their creators.... *Coplas* typically reinforced traditional values associated with old Spain (Catholicism, patriotism, and patriarchalism), and, as a matter of course, were anathema to Spanish anti-Franco intellectuals and resistance fighters. However, contrary to the classic Marxist approach that sees mass cultural products such as popular songs as the result of hegemonic thought, merely a reflection of the ideologies of the

ruling classes, it is possible to perceive the subversive potential of the canción española, particularly during the repressive 1940s and 1950s. Deconstructing the notion of the passive listener, this different approach restores agency to the listener, as an active decoder and recorder of collectively held views and images of the past. (32)

Again, these were not the songs performed in the "cine folklórico" of the 1950s, which used Gypsy stories as escapist fantasies for the poor throughout Spain even while Gypsies themselves were being brutally repressed.[9] This genre "combined clichéd, Andalusian, rural settings and idealized stereotypical characters . . . with fairy-tale, Cinderella plots . . . and unlikely narrative endings, in which conflicts and contradictions are resolved through a marriage union between unequals. Any resemblance to the 'real' Andalusia of gypsy persecution is purely coincidental" (Jordan and Allison, 98). At the same time, such films served as a kind of "regionalist tokenism attempting to project an image of a country united through variety" (Evans, 216).

Despite this elision of eroticism and Andalusian identities, the "sanitized" popular songs in these films, Evans argues, "inevitably recall their alternative, more ribald traditions of pre-Franco times" (ibid., 220). This ghostly return of the repressed fetishistic object has been theorized by Baudrillard, as Emily Apter explains: "Baudrillard here identifies the uncanny retroactivity of fetishism as a theory, noting its strange ability to hex the user through the haunting inevitability of a 'deconstructive turn'" (2). Mira observes that camp performance makes that ghost even more visible:

> if the *copla* became conservative, it was due to a process of appropriation by concrete ideologies. The camp vision of the *copla* runs in the opposite direction. The camp gaze on the *copla* contains an implicit mockery of national Catholic orthodoxies. For gay performers, this identification between the *copla* and Francoism constitutes one of the reasons that appropriation is necessary. (*De Sodoma a Chueca*, 535)

The *transformista*'s ribald performance of these *coplas*, then, arguably brings back and highlights the transgressive quality of repressed Andalusian cultures and undoes the political and sexual sanitation of the songs in Francoist popular culture.

The reference to Andalusia also invokes specifically the ghost of gay culture, which Francoism so brutally repressed. Fernando Olmeda claims that

> Throughout Andalusia it is known that the *mariquita* who could laugh at himself always existed, one who would lead the conversation with witty phrases designed to protect himself from mockery and who had the ability to return insults on the spot. Since he was usually from a humble background, he could afford to be uninhibited and even vulgar. (115)

Holy Week processions in Andalusia provided a sanctioned outlet for both political protest and sexual inversion during the Franco regime, as David D. Gilmore explains in his study of Carnival in the town of Fuenmayor:

> Under Franco (1936–1975) Fuenmayor carnival resembled a classic ritual of rebellion. Villagers masqueraded, the men usually as transvestites, paraded through the streets, singing gossipy or satirical songs (coplas) and acting out rehearsed skits—many scabrous and caustic. In some villages organized groups performed mini-dramas victimizing deviants or lampooning the authorities and the Church.... Spanish carnival was a politicized rite of inversion, ventilating the revolutionary hidden agenda of the poor. (37)

Timothy Mitchell also notes that the processions are homosocial in nature: "affective bonds that unite the men under the icon platform are as strong as those that unite them with their adoring public. Long hours of hard labor at close quarters develop a unique spirit of camaraderie among *costaleros* (porters of the images)" (108).

It should not be surprising, then, that gay culture of the 1970s and 1980s should invoke Catholicism, and, in particular, the imaginary of Andalusian Semana Santa rituals, bringing a certain popular image of Andalusia into the urban centers of Madrid and Barcelona. As Mira puts it:

> The Catholic imaginary is successfully recycled by authors like Nazario, Fernández, Cardín, Almodóvar, las Costus and Ocaña. The work of the preceding authors uses religion as an imaginary source for a discourse about sexual excesses.... It is a connection that is particular to homosexual art in the transition, but the

motivations are the same as those underlying the ironic gaze on Hollywood classics: on the one hand, religion is a discourse whose intrinsic vehemence invites mockery, but it was also a discourse of power and blame that permeates now the vengeful camp gaze. (*De Sodoma a Chueca*, 534)

> We must recognize, however, that, even as Carnival offered an outlet for sociopolitical tensions, its rituals served to enforce social norms, including those regarding gender and sexuality. The role of women in the processions is double—symbolically, as María, they are of supreme importance, but women of flesh and blood generally play only a secondary role, reinforcing the dominance of masculinity. What is more, the aggression implicit in Carnival is not directed solely at figures of authority, as Gilmore explains, but may also fall upon "deviants," including homosexuals:

> [T]he towns-people unleashed their aggressive energies in two ways: vertically against the authorities and horizontally against peer deviance. . . . Especially important was the scapegoating of sexual misconduct and other moral offenses such as miserliness, bachelorhood, pretentiousness, and what Andalusians refer to as "curiousness," that is, any abnormality. (37–38)

It would be an error, then, to interpret the performance of Andalusia in Spanish drag as an idealization of that region's permissiveness or as an emblem of its symbolic and imaginative power: it also marks the continued domination of the feminine in Andalusia, as well as the region's continued impotence relative to the center, just as the procession of the Virgin signals the continued power of masculinism, and women's relative powerlessness. The *travestí*'s Andalusian drag instead embodies these contradictions, as well as the audience's desire for the exotic sign of the south's absent phallus.

Plumas de España

It would be a mistake to read *Plumas de España* without keeping in mind the utilization of both Andalusia and drag by the center—Madrid—during Francoism and in the years of the transition. We must also remember that the experience of Andalusian women is not identical to that of men, even when those men do not conform to hegemonic models of masculinity, and instead simulate femininity. This kind of misreading has occasionally led critics to conclude that *Plumas* is a failed novel, a pale imitation of texts like Eduardo Mendicutti's *Una mala noche la tiene cualquiera* or Ventura Pons's *Ocaña: Retrato intermitente* (Ocaña: An intermittent portrait) whose protagonists are Andalusian transvestites who have relocated to the metropolis (Madrid and Barcelona, respectively), as an emblem of Spain's modernity and sexual emancipation following Franco's death (Epps, "The Queer Case," 149). What those other texts have in common, and what *Plumas* lacks, is an Andalusian transvestite protagonist. There is one transvestite and one possibly operated transsexual in *Plumas*—Patela, who pays to live in the narrator's house while he completes military service, and his "lady-in-waiting," Miguel, respectively—but the protagonist of Rossetti's novel is a woman, presumably straight, though Patela queers her by naming her the "New Safita" and queers the text by narrating for her the story of his and Miguel's paths from boy to woman.

To the extent that critics assume that transvestism is, or should be, the subject of *Plumas de España*, Rossetti's novel has been taken to task for its alleged inauthenticity. This accusation is not surprising, given that the definition of transvestism precludes the participation of women.[10] Valis and Moreiras Menor address this issue in relation to "Spanish culture," spectacle, and consumerism, rather than gender and sexuality. Epps takes gender and sexuality into account but seems uncomfortable with the female body beneath the façade. Still, in light of the issues regarding the *travestí*'s own authenticity and the authenticity of the "Andalusian culture" performed during Francoism and parodied by *travestís*, it seems, at best, disingenuous to demand that the representation of the *travestí* in a woman's novel be "authentic," especially when the novel does not purport to represent the *travestí*'s subjectivity, but rather that of the narrator, and from there, the various narrative representations of the "truth."

What is more, the protagonist of *Plumas* is not just any woman. On the contrary, the repeated references to the narrator's provincialism, her confusion, her prudishness, and her risible literary ambitions at the beginning of the novel define her as the furthest figure imaginable from the transgressive drag queen. She is, as Valis points out, a *señorita cursi*, a figure related to, but distinct from, the *travestí*: "Both . . . are saturated with culture. Insufficient cultural capital characterizes the one *(la señorita cursi)*, while the other (the *travesti*) glories in the excess(es) of culture itself"

(58). The *señorita cursi* lacks cultural capital because she unquestioningly accepts and enjoys kitschy cultural objects, whereas the *travestí* playfully and parodically performs that same popular culture, which has traditionally been associated with women (particularly, *señoritas cursis*) and the lower classes, and has therefore been devalued in relation to high culture. The *travestí* cleverly camps up what would otherwise be *cursi*, and it is this ironic or parodic take that adds cultural capital.

The distinction between the *cursi woman* and the camp gay *male* that Valis makes is not trivial; rather, it correctly identifies the gender hierarchy, as discussed earlier. The *señorita cursi* is found lacking in comparison to the *travestí*, much as Rossetti is found lacking relative to gay male authors like Mendicutti. Indeed, I would argue that the devaluation of this novel has much to do with gender, especially as it intersects with what is considered a provincial culture; that is, the novel and its author have been accused of a certain lack of cosmopolitan sophistication, and even of humor. The protagonist has been identified with the author herself, a confusion that is possible primarily because the author is a woman, as Barbara Johnson has argued.[11] The subject of the novel has likewise been confused: the narrator is obsessed with the gay male characters that she re-creates for her provincial readers. Likewise, her goddaughter, Lucrecia, has been desperate for Patela's attention since the two were children. Following the gaze of these two apparently straight women, some (primarily male) critics of the novel have focused almost exclusively on the gay characters, expecting from them a sort of titillation, of the kind provided by drag shows and male gay authors of the same period. But what many of these critics seem to forget is that the narrator herself is a character, a fictionalized representation of a particular image of Spanish femininity, one created to belittle women and their cultural achievements; that is, the narrator is a *simulation* of the Andalusian *señorita cursi*, one of several in the novel, just as Patela is a *simulation* of the Andalusian *travestí*; in other words, the narrator is a straight, provincial, feminine persona of the author, just as Patela is a gay transvestic persona of the same author. In fact, all of the narrators and readers in the text could be seen as fictionalized representations of specific sensibilities that marked both the performance and the interpretation of transvestism during the time of the *movida*. The tension between those readers' expectations and the multiple simulations of femininity, is at the heart of the novel, and the transvestism is performed by Rossetti herself, who has constructed a hall of mirrors in which to reflect (on) the ordering realities confronting the Spanish woman, and particularly the Andalusian one, which she must overcome to find autonomy.[12]

The *travestís* in *Plumas de España* allude to both the *transformista* (Patela) and the transsexual (Miguel/Milady), although the novel leaves until the end the question of whether the latter has undergone hormonal treatments and surgery. The latter detail has confused some readers into thinking that the climactic aspect of the novel, if not its climax, is the mystery shrouding Miguel/Milady's excess, or lack thereof, when, in reality, the denouement revolves around the *transformismo* and *transformación* of the *señorita cursi*. Her, and our, curiosity seems to govern the epistemology of the novel, because it obviously explores the *travestí*/fetish from the audience's angle: the narrator, again, is not a *travestí* herself, but a fascinated "public," a spectator who desires Patela and eagerly waits for Miguel/Milady to remove the final veil cloaking the "truth" of his/her gender identity, a revelation that might confirm her own gender/sexual identity, which was destabilized at the beginning of the text, when Patela aroused her desire and named her "New Safita." The biological resolution of the *travestí*'s gender identity might be deeply disappointing to some, and particularly the gay male reader (Epps, "The Queer Case," 161),[13] but it is an accurate rendering of the expectations that straight, bourgeois spectators held when they attended drag striptease shows. As Mira explains, "Whereas in the drag show, the spectator is looking for a good imitation or a good time, here the motivation is clearly 'el morbo,' sexual curiosity, the key concept for understanding the public's attitude toward the wave of *destape* in the seventies" (*De Sodoma a Chueca*, 441). The narrator represents precisely that type of public, as do the readers of the magazine *Plumas de España*, for which she hopes to describe the spectacle, despite her claims that she plans to write "a series of rigorous articles without a single concession to sexual curiosity" about Patela (23).[14] These spectators are intrigued by the gender disruption that the *travestí* represents, but they also recognize its danger and so insist that order be restored at the end of the show, when the penis reestablishes the binary gender divide and phallic order, when the *travestí* returns to a male identity. The narrator, who reveals Miguel's penis to her readers, is, in this sense, an agent of the heterosexist order, as Epps has noted: "Disruptive as Patela and Miguel/Milady at times may seem to be, the narrator herself is concerned with order, both domestic and narrative, and claims to employ tactics less associated with resolutely 'creative' writers than with certain historians, journalists, and the police" ("The Queer Case," 163). But, again, I must insist that the story of Miguel/Milady's possible castration is a red herring; it is a fanciful creation that plays on the curiosity of typical heterosexist bourgeois spectators, and it is humorously resolved when the narrator finds that Miguel has had his tonsils, not his penis, removed in the futile hope of improving his singing. The novel parodies and frustrates the narrator's desire to know, but it also brings her into the game of gender and narrative play, which finally empowers her. *Plumas de España*, in other words, is not meant to titillate, but to complicate titillation, and the expectation of it, an expectation that is repeatedly frustrated. This has relatively little to do with the experiences of *travestís*, and everything to do with the gaze of the audience that sits in judgment, which is explicitly related throughout the novel to the various mechanisms of vigilance that have imposed disciplinary limits on Andalusian women from the time of the civil war, and the complex negotiations that might allow those women to extricate themselves from the web of their cultural images.

To accomplish this goal, *Plumas de España* also complicates the folkloric image of Andalusian culture repeatedly instrumentalized by Madrid as a way of promoting an image of national unity while simultaneously depriving the region and its culture of their complexity and wealth. Rossetti's novel invokes, through the story of Miguel/Milady, the particular forms of Andalusian religion—especially the cult of the Virgin—and it addresses the simulation of flamenco culture through the description of the cabaret show of Pedro, el Grand Marnier, a presumably hypermasculine man who ironically falls for Patela only when he finds out s/he is not a woman, and hence his competition, but a transvestite. The tales told by Patela about Miguel's life also allude to the Spanish picaresque novel *Lazarillo de Tormes*, as well as to the Andalusian history of anarchism and freemasonry; that is, Miguel progresses from his family through a series of *amos* representing culture, the church, and high society, and his experiences with each reveal their pecuniary interests, their hypocrisy, and their criminality. The story of Patela's own life, however, evokes a different literary source, *La lozana andaluza*, the picaresque novel published in Venice by Francisco Delicado in 1528 about the irresistible and lusty *conversa* Lozana. Patela, likewise, is the lusty object of everyone's desire.

In addition to these literary sources, Patela incorporates into his recounting of Miguel/Milady's early childhood the particular kitsch culture in the imaginary of postwar Spain: *cuplé* shows of the 1920s and 1930s, glow-in-the-dark statues of the Virgin fabricated in Gibraltar, and serialized radio programs of the 1950s, the latter still marked by the political divides of the Spanish civil war.[15] Miguel's grandmother, Sagrario, invokes all of this kitsch culture in the battle she wages with her neighbor for control of his soul. Sagrario struggles to bring Miguel up in a home characterized by the Francoist ideal of austerity, but Miguel is thoroughly seduced by the worldly pleasures he finds in the *piso* of their building belonging to McKarena Stuart, the former *cupletista* whose *vida alegre* (wild life) Sagrario criticizes on every possible occasion, sometimes by raising the volume of her radio when her *novela* describes the punishment of "bad women." The debate also hinges on questions of religious images. Sagrario hints that the Virgin owned by McKarena Stuart—la McKarena (La Macarena)—cannot possibly be authentic because, in her mind, the loose woman is linked to anarchism. What is more, the Virgin in question comes from Gibraltar, which, along with the last name of "Stuart," puts la Macarena firmly in the Protestant camp.

"Have you ever seen by chance a single saint in her house? A stamp even?"
"Well . . . she has . . . a Virgin!"
"A Virgin? I'd like to see it. And how do you know it's a Virgin?
  It's probably one of those indecent singers, dressed like in the old days."
"It's not a photo . . . it's a statue about this big."
"That's pretty small. And how do you know it's a Virgin?"
"Because she has her hands together like this, holding a rosary, and she's completely white, face and all."
"She must be dead."
"No, but when she puts her in the pantry . . ."
"She puts the Virgin in the pantry? With the beans and ground pepper? What a lack of irreverence, by God!"
"No. The thing is that she puts her in the pantry because, since it's dark . . . the Virgin turns green and glows!"
"¡Ay! ¡Ay! She wants to hypnotize with you with the affliction of the Virgin!"

"No, grandma! . . . It's one of those newfangled Virgins! She
brought it back . . . from Gibraltar, I think!!"
"From Gibraltar!!! I better not ever see you enter that house
again!!—(¡Zas!)—Some Virgin! Some Virgin that is!—
(¡Zas!)—Don't even look at it! Do you understand? Don't even
look at it—(¡Zas!) (¡Zas!)—A Virgin that must even be . . .
Protestant! (30–31)[16]

The battle over the Virgin continues into the subsequent episode of Miguel's picaresque life, when he works for a restorer and dresser of religious images. Miguel falls in love with one of the Virgins, steals her, and brings her home, and his grandmother immediately begins a tug of war over who will dress the image:

The grandson came along and dressed her in blue. The grandmother came along and dressed her in red. The grandson brought her roses. The grandmother took them away and put nards in their place. The grandson, white. The grandmother, black.
The grandson, fed up, bought a lock, but the grandmother picked it and imposed her will on the altars.
He had no choice but to put a deadbolt on the door.
The grandmother tolerated the affront with dignity, but she carefully plotted her revenge and cautiously awaited her opportunity.
One night, while the innumerable vases were moved out into the hall, she overtook the fortress by surprise.
In effect, the grandson, paralyzed, with two fragile violet pots in his hands, witnessed how, swiftly, his grandmother set upon the image, and with one yank removed the handkerchief that covered its face, and with a tremendous noise, blew her nose in it.
"Ay," he exclaimed, stunned. "This reminds me of the days of the Republic!" (54–55)[17]

The same female figure symbolizes here two very different ideals, represented by the Virgin's wrappings, and she is literally destroyed by the battle over her image. These two episodes drive home Corbin's description of the parallel attacks perpetrated in Andalusia during the civil war: "Where anarchists attacked religion, Falangists attacked shameless women" (177), and Andalusia was left in ruins.

These are not the only stories about the relationship between gender and popular culture in post–civil-war Andalusia, however. The narrator herself adds tales from her own past, including the Catholic excesses of her Aunt Teresa, that mirror those of Miguel/Milady's grandmother. To cite one example, Aunt Teresa pulled the narrator from her secretarial school because she was learning English there:

> The end of my studies was occasioned by a workbook that I left open and Aunt Teresa's curiosity, which led her to read it. . . . Her anger built up to an unimaginable extreme, and, oozing holy wrath from every pore, she pounced on the telephone and bitterly scolded the secretary of the academy for offering such a program, which included languages outside the jurisdiction of Rome. And she canceled my enrollment with a "Scoundrels!!!" Then she went immediately to the kitchen, opened the hearth, threw in all the Britannic material that she laid her furious eyes on, and set it on fire. (168–69)[18]

Aunt Teresa was also obsessed with the conversion of "infidels" in Africa, to the point that she named her children after saints, and insisted that they and the narrator, her goddaughter, save used stamps so she could send them to the church in a program to raise money for missionaries to the continent. All of these peculiar Catholic beliefs become linked to commerce and soccer through the business of the narrator's cousin, Francisco de Javier: selling holy cloth in yellow and gold, the colors of the papacy, in Africa and later in the narrator's hometown, where they also represent the colors of the local soccer team. The scene in which the ultra-Catholic, ultraconservative Aunt Teresa waves this "holy cloth" at soccer matches, shouting "Pepón, Populorum Progressio, Pepón," and subsequently follows her angel, Pepón, the soccer star, into the locker room, is a hilarious send-up of Francoist conflations of national Catholicism and popular culture. The profits from Francisco de Javier's business become the object of family inheritance disputes following his death, and these, in turn, are linked to Patela's seductive relationship with Lucrecia, Aunt Teresa's granddaughter and the narrator's godchild. Patela, as it turns out, was a childhood friend of Lucrecia, who spent much of her time at the narrator's house, playing in the garden. The narrator, however, is unaware of this history for most of the novel, yet she too is erotically attached to Patela and becomes jealous of his attentions to Lucrecia.

All of these histories are related in some way to the narrator's own failed engagement, an event that traumatized her and arrested her sexual/emotional development. She comes to remember that she met Patela long before he came to live in her house while completing his military service. To wit, she had returned one day from taking Aunt Teresa to the doctor to discover Patela and Lucrecia in the attic, the former dressed in the wedding gown that she never had the opportunity to wear. Her recollection of this incident leads her to narrate the cause of the broken engagement; that is, when Aunt Teresa, after waving her *banderita* made with Francisco de Javier's papal cloth, followed her beloved soccer star into the locker room, the narrator ran after her to prevent her from entering, but she was too late and had to follow her in, where she was greeted by visions of "the soapy nudes, who were, of course, in better shape than those of Signorelli" (123).[19] Naturally, she was portrayed as a shameless woman in the ensuing gossip, and her fiancé broke off the engagement over this misunderstanding on a question of honor. At the same time that she discovers that Patela is "courting" Lucrecia, not out of any desire for her, but in order to convince her to rent him the property left to her by her uncle, to the profit of both, the narrator also recognizes the hypocrisy of the honor code that has so constrained her.

Indeed, all of these stories invoke not only the more kitschy elements associated with camp, but also the mechanisms by which Andalusian women have traditionally been controlled and devalued—indeed, castrated—as the following exchange between Patela and the narrator regarding castrati makes clear:

> "Don't worry, here comes the best part: the girl, but write this down, was a castrato."
> "Whaaaat?"
> "Don't get all excited, dear: the number of castrati in the world is infinite."
> "I'm surprised you take it so lightly."
> "And what about you? Haven't you ever felt that some appendage was missing?"
> "Me?" (43)[20]

After conducting some research on the topic, she learns that it is impossible to tell if one is castrated without a thorough physical examination and concludes, "In other words, anyone can be castrated without it being apparent" (59).[21] Judith Butler describes the import of this fear of castration for gender and sexual identities:

> In the oedipal scenario, the symbolic demand that institutes "sex" is accompanied by the threat of punishment. Castration is the figure for punishment, the fear of castration motivating the assumption of the masculine sex, the fear of not being castrated motivating the assumption of the feminine. Implicit in the figure of castration, which operates differentially to constitute the constraining force of gendered punishment, are at least two inarticulate figures of abject homosexuality, the feminized fag and the phallicized dyke; the Lacanian scheme presumes that the terror over occupying either of these positions is what compels the assumption of a sexed position within language, a sexed position that is sexed by virtue of its heterosexual positioning.... The oedipal scenario depends for its livelihood on the threatening power of its threat, on the resistance to identification with masculine feminization and feminine phallicization. But what happens if the law that deploys the spectral figure of abject homosexuality as a threat becomes itself an inadvertent site of eroticization? If the taboo become eroticized precisely for the transgressive sites that it produces, what happens to oedipus, to sexed positionality, to the fast distinction between an imaginary or fantasized identification and those social and linguistic positions of intelligible "sex" mandated by the symbolic law? (*Bodies That Matter*, 96–97)

This quote may serve to explain the curious name of "New Safita," given that the narrator only manifests desire for Patela, and not for a woman: she sees in his "masculine feminization" a mirror of her own "feminine phallicization," one that disturbs the very strict limits on women in a provincial Andalusian town.[22]

It is this very phallicization that allows the narrator to leave behind her *cursi* pretensions and the symbolic castration of her failed engagement, a move linked explicitly to writing in the novel. At the beginning of the novel, she is wholly constrained by the conventions of the provincial newspaper *Plumas de España*, and therefore aspires only to write a kind of documentary series about "deviants." Her "apology" to her readers at the beginning of the piece highlights the humility imposed on female writers; for these paragraphs repeatedly emphasize her lack of skill, intelligence, and knowledge:

> I would like to beg the readers of *Plumas de España* that they be generous with me and try to forgive my lack of expertise, but I have never before taken on a project as ambitious as the one that concerns me here.
>
> It was neither whim nor frivolity that I should decide to present in novelized form a matter no less profound for every day, and in a certain sense unfamiliar. If I were experienced and literate in the topic, I would no doubt manage to write an accurate and inspired essay that would bring you closer to the intimate essence hidden in each action, to the real reason at the heart of the most futile conduct. However, poor soul that I am, what else can I do, if I am no more than a witness to a reality that I can barely manage to transcribe.
>
> Hence, given that it is not written that I should penetrate into what the mind thinks and understands, or what the heart feels, or the will desires, I will limit myself to enunciating what I see done and to repeating what I hear, without entering into judgments or pausing to emit opinions that can cloud my intended objectivity. . . .
>
> I fervently hope that the tale I begin today will, more than entertain you, make you reflect, because I must advise you that I have not allowed the slightest fantasy to enter into it, and I have not omitted any detail, and I have not been tolerant with anything that might deform the facts.
>
> For these reasons, all of the characters that will appear here will not only be true, but also real, and I don't care what conclusions might be drawn from this affirmation. (25–26)[23]

Indeed, the absence of such talents is linked implicitly to the absent phallus, and, contingently, to her honor as a woman. Later, when the narrator decides instead to include explicit sexual details, she runs up against the closed-minded objections of the provincial, sexist editor of *Plumas de España*, who, despite his own philandering, insists that the topic she has suggested is not appropriate for proper women. Here is their exchange:

> "Why do you put in all those vulgarities if they don't have anything to do with the story? You know how to write like the angels, I don't know why you insist on doing it like a sinner."
>
> He's thinking about his own foolishness, that a woman has to spend her whole life writing sonnets to the patron saints, to the bridge, to the boulevard, and to "the child that is missing from my womb." (126)[24]

This incident, marking an epiphany in the narrator's continued enlightenment regarding the conventional constraints on femininity, leads her to move toward fiction. It is when she finally gets over her shame, and her involuntary and innocent fall into shamelessness, that she is able to dump her small-town, small-time ambitions to seek literary fame on a grander scale by submitting her tales in novelized form for the Planeta literary prize.

Plumas de España clearly marks the limits of female sexuality in the provincial literary climate, which extends from Andalusia to the Planeta, and from Francoism to the age of transnational publishing. These limits explain the invisibility of Sapphism, which can only be named, and even then named mistakenly, by the transvestite character Patela, who sees the lesbian as the cultural equivalent of the *cursi* old maid. The narrator, however, refigures the concept of *pluma* as a kind of phallus: that is, she might not have *pluma*, but she has the *pluma* in her hand as she pens her tale for the readers of the local, Andalusian paper *Plumas de España*, just as Ana Rossetti does as she pens in Madrid the story of the narrators, Patela's and Miguel/Milady's *Plumas*, for the readers of the novel *Plumas de España*. Rather than interpret Rossetti's absent phallus as a lack of *pluma* or a lack of authenticity, I see it as a problematization of women's exclusion from the *plumada* of the transition, and in particular, from the ways in which phallocentric performances constitute, to borrow Gayatri Spivak's words, a "text (of male discourse) [that] gains its coherence by coupling woman with man in a loaded equation and cutting the excess of the clitoris out" (Spivak, 191). This, not Miguel/Milady's possible castration, is the excision at the center of the text. At the same time, the critical misreading of *Plumas de España* corresponds to a globalized, rather than a particularly Spanish, frame for understanding transvestism and gender, and it is a symptom of the text's own liminal location between the *movida* and globalized, spectral culture.

· CHAPTER 4 ·

Lesbian-Themed Best Sellers and the Politics of Acceptance

IN CHAPTER 2 I addressed the impact on the Spanish publishing business of globalization and the increasingly neoliberal values of Spanish citizens, arguably results of the nation's integration into, first, the European Economic Community (1986) and then the European Union (1993). I argued that these factors shifted control of publication from local, intellectual editors to global conglomerates that placed greater emphasis on best sellers with the potential to appeal to a variety of markets. The political and economic incorporation of Spain into Europe also implied a liberalization of Spanish society, signaled in part by a greater acceptance of nonheteronormative practices.

In this chapter, I examine the representation of lesbians in three bestselling novels. The novels in question—*Beatriz y los cuerpos celestes* (Beatriz and the heavenly bodies, Nadal Prize, 1998), *Donde comienza tu nombre* (Where your name begins, Odisea, 2004), and *Una palabra tuya* (A word from you, Biblioteca Breve Prize, 2005)—were groundbreaking in some senses, the first owing to its largely positive representation of lesbian and bisexual characters, the second for being the first novel published by a gay/lesbian press to cross over to a mainstream bookstore, and the third for depicting the sexuality of the lowest strata of working women, garbage collectors. Still, I believe that the ways in which their authors write lesbian and bisexual women for a broad Spanish audience reveal the conditions under which mainstream heterosexual bourgeois readers are willing to accept lesbian sexuality, as well as the lingering prejudices that mark that acceptance.

Global Bi and Lesbian Chic in *Beatriz y los cuerpos celestes,* by Lucía Etxebarría

Lucía Etxebarría is not simply the author of best-selling novels; she is a media phenomenon, a superstar of the book business who has fashioned herself as a spokesperson of the counterculture. She is especially critical of the effects that the beauty business (cosmetics, cosmetic surgery, diet aids) have on the female body and psyche, but she also points out the hypocrisy of bourgeois culture in regard to drugs and alcohol, and she is an ardent foe of homophobia. She maintains a Web site, and she has had her own page on ClubCultura.com, followed by a blog, where she espouses her opinions on sex, drugs, fashion, feminist issues, and the cult of celebrity.

Etxebarría's own celebrity adds weight to these opinions, and that celebrity skyrocketed after the publication of *Beatriz y los cuerpos celestes*, winner of the Nadal Prize in 1998.[1] This novel, in which the young female narrator declares her love for two different women within the first two chapters, also gave Etxebarría—who has made very public her sexual preference for men—an entrance into the gay book market, to the extent that all of her works are now featured prominently in gay bookstores and on gay-related Web sites, as well as in mainstream bookstores. Indeed, the response to the novel shows that although the narrator and protagonist of the novel, Beatriz, might well believe that "el amor no tiene género" (love has no gender), as the book jacket informs us (in contrast to her love interests, Cat, a "lesbiana convencida" [committed lesbian], and Mónica, a "devorahombres compulsiva" [compulsive man-eater]), Spanish readers are not so gender-blind regarding sex. Thus, when *Beatriz* won the Nadal Prize, the headline of the article in the Spanish daily *El País* read: "Young Writer Lucía Etxebarría Receives the Nadal with a Novel about Sexual Initiation," followed immediately by the subtitle "'Beatriz and the Heavenly Bodies' Includes Lesbian Relations with Madrid as a Backdrop" (Moret). The article goes on to assure the readers, in the words of one of the jurors for the prize, that "It's not a lesbian novel, although there are lesbian elements.... The theme is more about how the family and a determined social setting can condition the love life and sex life of a person. It is also a hymn to the freedom to choose the kind of love you want." The title of the newspaper piece in *El Mundo*—"The Nadal Prize Is Awarded to the Eroticism and 'Poetic Charge' of Lucía Etxebarría"—was actually *preceded* by the declaration that "the winner assures that her work will be polemical because her protagonist maintains lesbian relations and is also a drug addict" (Maurell).[2] The lesbian content of the novel stimulated readers, and it stimulated book sales. In this sense, it emblematizes the concept of lesbian chic, as Beatriz Gimeno explains in *Historia y análisis del lesbianismo*:

La liberación de una generación (History and analysis of lesbianism: The liberation of a generation): "Lesbian chic is a category created from the outside: it is the lesbian converted into a product of capitalist consumption, it is an inoffensive, semipornographic lesbian, who serves to calm the patriarchy's anxiety over lesbian sexuality" (265).

If, as I argued in "The (In)visible Lesbian," "high-culture" Spanish women authors question the epistemological bases of gendered Spanish identities, and the pedagogical "Salir del armario" books simply ratify the traditional heteronormative practices with a lesbian twist, Extebarría performs a hybrid: she creates the illusion of transgressing societal norms without questioning their epistemological bases, thus appealing to Spanish readers who want to appear postmodern but are not ready to forfeit the traditional values of their own upbringing. The contemporary Spanish public, indeed, wants to see its country not in the bleak, isolated, moralistic terms of Francoism, but as an ultramodern cosmopolitan liberal state. In the 1990s, this globalized "hipness" implied an acceptance of women's rights and a tolerance of difference, including different sexual identities. Beyond even that tolerance, gay culture had begun to represent the epitome of trendiness, as Suzanna Danuta Walters notes in *All the Rage*, even if visibility also implies an increased vulnerability to antihomosexual violence.[3] "Cool" is certainly an adjective that could be applied to *Beatriz*, with its irreverence toward moral codes, its allusions to global media and businesses, its portrayal of bathroom drug use in the posh discos of Madrid, and its knowing descriptions of gay bars and their clientele. The rejection of the false values and bleakness of Francoism culminates in the final chapters of the novel, which detail the sordid life Beatriz led in Madrid, despite her family's wealth, before her father sent her off to Edinburgh. The descriptions of her drug-addicted friends, the family neglect, and the attempted rapes read like a naturalist novel, and they can be conveniently used by the reader to blame the protagonist's confusion regarding her identity on the hypocrisies and perversions wrought by the puritanical moral codes of Francoism.

For all its anger and faux-postmodern trendiness, however, the novel does not really disturb the premises underlying Franco-era sentimental novels directed at women, a genre to which the subtitle—"Una novela rosa"—alludes. The text often employs the very conventions of the "novela rosa" (female protagonist, love interest, melodrama, suspense, pat resolution) to undermine the lessons regarding morals and values—virginity, self-sacrifice, austerity, family submission to male authority—that the genre sought to teach young Spanish women. The use of suspense as a structuring element, especially between sections, also recalls the conventions of "women's literature" by creating the illusion that the novel was being published serially, as such literature often was in women's magazines. What is more, the structuring of time in the novel—repeated prolepses and analepses that whet the reader's appetite without really providing crucial plot details—also recall the narrative manipulations of that genre. The cleverness and irony of the text, along with the references to popular and high culture, suggest that it is meant as a postmodern parody of the "novela rosa." When the narrator fills in all of the gaps at the end of the text and explicitly states her criticisms of the contemporary Spanish family, however, the postmodern pretensions are dropped altogether. In other words, although the structure of the novel might provide the reader with the illusory sense that she or he is performing the kind of epistemological exploration characteristic of postmodern texts, the text itself impedes such an exploration by withholding information and by later providing that information, and, with it, closure. Readers thus enjoy the trappings of postmodernism without its unsettling implications.

Also disturbing for a lesbian poetics is the voyeuristic positioning of the narrator, the character who believes that love has no gender. This in itself is an entirely acceptable postmodern concept, but it is severely undercut by the narration itself, which distances the narrator from the characters she encounters. This is her description, for example, of the lesbians in the bar where she meets her female lover, Cat:

> The majority had short hair and wore pants, although there were a few disguised as femmes, with tube skirts and lioness manes. If you paid attention, you began to notice that there was a subtle division of territories. The radicals occupied the left flank, uniformed in their imitation man costumes, smoking cigarettes with the gestures of a longshoreman and ill-humored scowls, legs crossed with the ankle of one on the knee of the other, in a fashion that aspired to be masculine. On the dance floor, the carefree young things that were dancing wouldn't have raised an eyebrow at a straight disco. A fairly gaudy blonde had even allowed herself to wear a long dress, and she was flirting with a redhead who was eating her up with her eyes while attending to her friend's conversation with a succession of nervous, forced guffaws. (25)[4]

The narrator herself is not at all implicated in these performed identities of butch and femme, but rather occupies a voyeuristic position, and readers who see this world through her eyes thus garner an inside look into "alternative" lifestyles without implicating their own identities. The question of class never seems to enter into the equation, even though "butch" and "femme" roles are predominately associated with the working class (Gimeno, *Historia*, 268). Etxebarría thus satisfies the curiosity of straight middle-class readers regarding these lesbian subjects from outside their world, confirms to them that most lesbians are indeed "strange," avoids unsettling allusions to class disparities, and simultaneously "turns them on" with a moment of charged eroticism.

At times, the narration of lesbianism seems to be only a titillation aimed at male readers, as in the following description:

> An amusing fact I read in a textbook: In ancient Rome the dancers from Lesbos were preferred to enliven the banquets.... But the erotic fame of the girls from Lesbos did not come from their acrobatic skill, but from another specialty: oral sex, which, according to the Greeks, had been invented on the isle. A skill that the lesbians taught one another. (38–39)[5]

This voyeuristic technique allows readers to demystify some of the "how" of lesbian sexuality, but it obviously does not challenge them to confront their own prejudices, transform themselves, or feel any responsibility for the violence that often befalls real gay people when they become too visible.

Indeed, although there is considerable violence against women in the novel, none of it targets lesbian characters for their sexual preference. The lesbians, in fact, seem to enjoy a freedom from male aggression, even when they display their affections publicly: "We walked along holding hands and all the pedestrians gave us sideways glances. In part, because they were shocked by the image of two girls walking hand in hand. In part, because we were young and good-looking and it was a pleasure to look at us. I knew it and felt proud" (23).[6] Again, readers are allowed a voyeuristic glance, without the slightest insinuation that this scene could provoke any violent outbursts of lesbophobia or heterosexual desire. It is exclusively in straight bars and contexts that men become sexually aggressive in this novel, which allows all women readers to empathize with the characters' victimization without having to problematize the clear distinction between living as a heterosexual middle-class woman or "out" as a lesbian.

This representation clearly conflicts with reality. Beatriz Gimeno offers a chilling example of how between 1999 and 2002 the lesbophobic media used the sexual identity of Dolores Vásquez to convict her without evidence of murdering her ex-partner's daughter, who she herself had raised in the course of their relationship. Vásquez was granted a new trial, and she was freed after the real assassin was found, but only after he had murdered another adolescent girl (*Historia*, 319–39). Ten years after Etxebarría published her novel, in the midst of the 2008 Pride festival that specifically focused on lesbian visibility, three lesbians were verbally assaulted by the owner of a bar, who shouted: "Out of here! Sluts! Garbage! This is no place for you!" (Carranco).[7] Witnesses supported the women's version of the events, including their assertion that the owner of the bar, Nicolás Parrondo, refused to provide them with a complaint form as required by law before throwing them out of the establishment. In his defense, Parrondo brandished stereotypes of gay people in general, and lesbians in particular, claiming that the women had exposed their breasts and consumed drugs on the premises, but his version was not corroborated by any of the witnesses. In 1998, when *Beatriz* appeared, lesbians could not have counted on their fellow citizens to recognize their equal rights before the law, and thus would have been unlikely to demonstrate affection publicly without fear.[8]

Despite these contradictions, Etxebarría is a popular figure in gay culture. She is accorded respect and admiration, in part because she publicly condemns homophobia, taking on a role that many lesbian authors have been unwilling or unable to perform. She does not threaten straight men and women in the general public, and she is not herself threatened by any negative publicity regarding her sexuality, which might adversely affect her marketability. Finally, it is beyond doubt that she broke new ground by publishing a novel that featured lesbian and bisexual characters who were no more pathological than any other woman raised in the late Franco years.

Crossing Over: *Donde comienza tu nombre*

In summer 2004, the Casa del Libro prominently displayed on the "new book" table and in the front window another lesbian novel, Mabel Galán's *Donde comienza tu nombre*, published in the Safo collection of the gay/

lesbian press Odisea. *Donde comienza tu nombre* became a crossover hit, giving sudden visibility to lesbian relationships. I would like to suggest some reasons for its success among mainstream readers and some of the red flags such acceptance could raise in this case.

Eric O. Clarke has mentioned some of the ways in which mainstream culture deforms queer culture by mediating its values:

> In the first mode, queer interests are bestowed value only insofar as they conform to the heteronormative standards retained within publicity's supposedly universal moral-political principles. In mode two, this bestowal becomes the alibi for, and thus is overlapped by, the mediation of homoeroticism through the extraction of commercial value. (10)

The decision to put *Donde comienza tu nombre* prominently on display in the Casa del Libro was based primarily on economic motives, not moral or aesthetic ones. The bookstore marketed this book aggressively because promoters understand the desire of contemporary Spaniards to see themselves and be seen by others as modern and sophisticated, an image that implies an acceptance of "alternate lifestyles" and even the emulation of a certain globalized, metrosexual cool. As Susanna Danuta Walters puts it, "homoerotic imagery . . . speaks to the more legitimized public engagement of *straights* with gays, as if the new visibility of gays makes them more available for the displays of public desire that permeate advertising imagery. Connecting with homosexuals through gay-themed imagery allows heterosexuals access to the (media-constructed) hipness factor" (245–47). The cover of *Donde comienza tu nombre,* adorned with Roy Lichtenstein's *Girl with Hair Ribbon,* provides a visual shorthand for this association by adopting a postmodern "high-art" American image of a female that itself references the pop comic-book culture, and refigures it as a lesbian: it is a wink within a wink that seems to suggest a queer subtext. This image, and the public display of a Sapphic text in the window of the Casa del Libro, would confirm to passersby on the Gran Vía that Spain had indeed become a modern European nation, that it was in on the globalized postmodern game, and that it had definitively left behind the radical moral conservatism of the Franco years.

The trendy metaliterary narrative of the novel itself also allows Spaniards who actually buy and read it to feel that they are painlessly participating in the postmodern experience. *Donde comienza tu nombre* features several plotlines, all linked to a single figure, Isabel, who is simultaneously the author of the story about Rosalía and Irene, the subject of the plot about writing that story, and a tangential love interest in the story about Silvia and Ana. The styles of these different narrative lines recall a variety of literary genres and styles: the romantic melodrama, the cyberchat, the trashy tale of modern chicks in search of sex, the romance of maternal love, and, of course, the postmodern novel. The coexistence of these various styles and the interweaving of multiple plotlines suggest complexity and thereby allow readers who might otherwise have to explain their choice of a novel about the love lives of lesbians to justify their interest on purely literary grounds. Here, however, the multiple diegetic narrative levels are easily identified and neatly resolved at the end. It is pomo light that gives readers the illusion of sophistication without the philosophical premises, the difficulty and challenges, of works by Juan Benet, Juan and Luis Goytisolo, Esther Tusquets, or Ana María Moix.

The characteristics of those lesbians and their relationships, and the narrative styles in which they are recounted, appeal simultaneously to the need to heteronormatize homosexuality and the desire to participate in a kinky sexuality associated more with a Pat Califia handbook than with straight Spanish sexual mores. The following paragraphs will give a brief summary of the plots, all of which involve older women in relationships with much younger ones.

Isabel's story is told chronologically, with several analepses, in which she describes her past relationships and other brief encounters with women. She spends most of the novel in a gay bar eyeing a woman named Mar, reminiscing about her lost love, Marta, fending off hetero couples looking for a threesome, and finishing her novel about Rosalía and Irene, whose romantic tale echoes, except in its ending, her own relationship with Marta. The happy ending comes, however, when Isabel successfully begins a new relationship with Mar, whose name is a shortened version of Marta and who promises to incarnate the ideal love that Isabel lost with Marta. This resolution—the reincorporation of Isabel into happy coupledom—coincides temporally with the moment when Isabel finishes penning the ending of her novel, in which Rosalía and Irene reunite in the very same bar where Isabel is writing their story.

The novel that Isabel is writing falls into two genres: the tale of maternal love and the romance, replete with mystery, surprise plot twists, and, of course, a happy ending. In this narrative, Rosalía, a young Spanish lesbian, spots a beautiful, sophisticated older woman—Irene—while on vacation in Lisbon. Irene's manner of dress and sophistication leads Rosalía to believe she is straight, but she nonetheless follows her, meets her and finally begins a relationship with her. There is, however, a third mystery woman involved, one who Irene herself is desperately seeking and with whom she must resolve certain issues that eventually force her to abandon Rosalía in Lisbon without further explanation. As it turns out, the third woman is Irene's straight daughter, Sandra, who was traumatized because her father forbade Irene from having any contact with her once she came out as a lesbian. After searching the entire city, Irene miraculously finds her daughter in a drug den that represents the decadence of the 1960s ideals: it is *"okupada"* commune-style by strung-out addicts covered with tattoos.[9] As befits the romantic novel, Irene arrives just in time to save her daughter, and she returns to find Rosalía in Madrid, where everyone lives happily ever after.

The third narrative line is a breezy story about Silvia and Ana, who are looking for girlfriends online. When they click on the Web site chueca.com, they find that the gay and lesbian center (COGAM) is hosting a literary reading by a famous lesbian novelist (Isabel) and decide they might have more success there because at least they could be reasonably assured that they were actually chatting with women, a certainty that chat rooms cannot give them. They do meet Isabel, who briefly dates Ana, and Silvia finds a younger girlfriend who forces her to explore her assumptions about relationships.

The stories are linked together by different threads—literary, geographic, coincidence—and they all end in contented monogamy: that is, in a form of sexual relationship that is not threatening to the heteronormative order based on bourgeois family values. Even obvious signs of queer sexuality are normalized, so that they are provocative but still contained within recognizable parameters of behavior. For example, both Rosalía (Irene's lover) and her daughter Sandra are covered with tattoos and piercings, which in the novel signify a rebellion born of the childhood abuse by homophobic parents. In Rosalía's case, however, they also seem to represent the affirmation of a queer sexuality, one with markedly different attributes than typical heterosexual coitus, particularly the combination of pain and pleasure:

> When she got up to put her joint out in the ashtray on the night table, her short top exposed the round black tribal tattoo that Rosalía had on her lumbar region. Irene couldn't resist caressing

it and she traced it slowly with her fingertips while Rosalía stayed still. Leaning over her, she traced it over and over with her finger, pausing voluptuously on every point of the design as if she were herself tattooing it at that moment.

"It's very attractive," she said, reaffirming how much she liked the design that had her bewitched. "Why did you get this tattoo?" she inquired. "There's always a good reason for these impulses that last a lifetime." ...

"Well, let me tell you," Rosalía said. "I had it done precisely so that someone would caress it exactly as you are now." ...

"People usually get tattoos for love," Rosalía continued, whispering in her ear as she kissed her over and over on the mouth. "For love or spite." (82–83)[10]

That night Irene learned that the cold metallic touch of the piercings revitalized many erogenous zones on her body, that they impact you when they touch your skin and they surprise you with their coldness when the metal accidentally touches you; that every hair on your body rebels voluptuously, and becomes eroticized, standing up like a soldier on guard against an imminent attack. (84)[11]

Despite the transgressive nature of Rosalía's body art and the erotic description of her piercings, the lack of specificity regarding lesbian sexual practices in these passages allows heterosexual readers to imagine themselves in the place of the lesbian lovers, since anyone can get a tattoo or a piercing. What is more, the containment of these signs within a traditional monogamous romance normalizes queer sexuality into a morality more acceptable to the heterosexual reader. This appeal to heteronormativity also explains why other queer sexual practices, such as hard-drug use, multiple partners, and loveless sex, are treated exclusively as problems and limited to straight characters, particularly the *okupas,* with whom Irene's daughter is nearly tragically involved. This kind of evisceration of queer sexuality in the name of bourgeois decency comprises, as Clarke claims, "the conformist impulses of visibility politics" (21). What is more, the absolute separation between *okupas* and queer lesbians belies the actual strategic alliance between these groups that Gracia Trujillo discusses (109).

In addition to its cover, its narrative structure, and its allusions to queer sexuality, the novel contains other signs of globalization and postmodernism, including references to Internet chat rooms and DVD technology, but it does not engage with the political or philosophical implications of these media either. The novelist Isabel ends her first conversation with Ana, for example, with the "promise that I would get together with her some other day to tell her more details from my novel and to watch with her the movie *Frida*, which had just come out. I didn't tell Ana that I had already seen it a couple of times" (126).[12] The film *Frida* has become a lesbian favorite because it presents very clearly the famous bisexuality of the Mexican painter, splendidly embodied by Salma Hayek in several nude scenes, such as the one in which she lies on a bed entwined with the equally nude body of Karine Plantadit-Bageot, the dancer/actress portraying Josephine Baker. This vision is titillating, of course, but problematically so because the Latina and African American actresses' racialized naked bodies, locked in lesbian embrace, are exposed for the benefit of the general public in a manner that corresponds to the Orientalist eroticization of racial others and the heterosexual appropriation of female homoeroticism in pornography, which is played for the pleasure of the male voyeur. The female characters in *Donde comienza tu nombre* place themselves unquestioningly in the position of the straight white male viewer, thereby buttressing rather than questioning a sexual-economic order in which the female body serves as a ground.

In the specific sites described by Isabel in her novel-within-this-novel, we also find, despite nods to a globalized queer aesthetic and dating practices, a rhetorical normalization of the "white" heteronormalized Spanish lesbian by contrast to an exotic, erotic other, evident in the descriptions of Lisbon, and of Middle Eastern women working in restaurants in Lisbon and Madrid. The sexualized Arab, Portuguese, and Latin American women embody in *Donde comienza tu nombre,* respectively, the latent homosexual Middle Eastern origins of contemporary Iberia and the "pagan" sexuality of the colonial tropics, a move that alludes to what Ana Paula Ferreira has called the phantasms of empire (Ribeiro and Ferreira), the ghosts of Iberia's medieval and imperial past in its centuries-long occupation by Arabs and the reconquest of its territory, which culminated in the separation of Portugal from the rest of Iberia, the unification of the remaining territories into the Spanish, the expulsion of Arabs and Jews, the conquest of Latin America, and the enslavement of Africans and indigenous people.

The latter dehumanization was justified by the "hedonistic paganism" of those people, which allegedly required the intervention of the Catholicizing Spaniards. By alluding primarily to that distant imperial past, the romantic exoticizing of those cultures in this novel ignores the economic impetus for recent Arab, African, and Latin American immigration into Europe, preferring to turn those cultures into providers of recreational space and implicit sexual difference. The representation of Portugal is also problematic: whereas the novel highlights the thoroughly modern gay sites of Madrid—from the gay bar to the Internet to the COGAM headquarters—Lisbon appears still as a city of medieval, labyrinthine streets, with hidden pockets of forbidden pleasure and anachronistic hippie hangouts, the latter of which conveniently ignores Madrid's own history of "okupations" in the Lavapiés neighborhood in the 1980s and 1990s before it became an enclave for immigrants, particularly Muslims.

These phantasms are brought together in a crucial scene in which Rosalía, who has returned to Madrid without Irene, tries to recapture a particularly poignant moment in their relationship by eating in a Syrian restaurant in the Spanish capital. The image she recalls is that of a belly dancer who performed for the couple in a restaurant in Lisbon on the last night they spent together:

> In the half-basement occupied by a small Syrian restaurant located on a busy street in Lavapiés, an Arab woman with henna-tinted hair performs a belly dance for a small group of people. Rosalía, bewitched by her movements and the music, lets herself be taken away by the sensual rhythm of the dance that sways the Egyptian woman's hips in a singular way....
> The Egyptian woman sways her hips rhythmically, and Rosalía can't get out of her head a scene from that last night, when Irene, in a gesture hidden to the rest, stroked the base of her neck with her fingernails while a lovely Lebanese girl of no more than seventeen danced to the sensual rhythm of North African music. Her eyes were so green, against a skin so dark, that they leapt from her face like the multicolor handkerchiefs that covered her hips like a skirt and that would later be removed one by one by the customers in the room.... It wasn't a gay place like the ones they had visited earlier that night; it was full of foreigners, most of them Arabs, but the woman danced especially for them, dedicating the dance to them,

staying before their table, as if she wanted her dance to sensually baptize the relationship that had just begun. (143–45)[13]

Rosalía and Irene take the dancer's sensuality as a sign of her "natural" lesbian desire, one that justifies their own, given the partially Arabic origins of Spanish culture. By eroticizing the Arab districts and making them part of the lesbian story, then, the novel inverts the more unpleasant Franco-era connotations of "the Arab within," that is, the impure heretic that Spain had excised centuries earlier but that represented a constant threat to the morals of the Catholic nation ideated by the dictatorship.

Donde comienza tu nombre ends with the description of a monthly drag show that queers the disciplinary structures of heteronormativity and reminds spectators of the political struggle that made possible the safe haven they now enjoy:

> In a few scant moments there appears in the depths of the café a charming set and in the middle of the bar a dance floor opens for the night. The lights change, the bar becomes dark, the music switches to the beat of a vampy drag queen, with large silicone breasts and a flashy costume of silver chiffon and sparkling sequins, who crosses through the bar with long strides, balancing precariously on impregnable orange patent-leather boots, until she reaches the charming set that has appeared in the depths of the café as if by magic. Next to her there is an attractive, muscled, and correctly uniformed cop, with an exceptional bulge, in terms of its proportions, and a nightstick that is so exaggeratedly large that it emphasizes even more the phallic content of the scene, and he tries to frisk the drag queen while she shouts and protests outrageously, letting him feel her up, staging a false resistance for the attentive spectators. The cop insists that she show her identification, and when she refuses to hand it over, he begins to frisk her, feeling her up all over until he ends up recovering the fine in her pounds of flesh. The scene ends with an energetic simulated fuck between the cop and the drag queen, which they enjoy like mad to the tune of a police siren that ridicules the scene even more and emphasizes the hypocrisy and abuse of authority that this group of people has always been subjected to.
>
> The brief act is repeated the last Saturday of every month, at

around midnight, not only to commemorate with pride the clandestine nature of gay bars back then—nothing unites people quite as much as clandestinity—but also as an excuse to change the tone of the place over to one in which music and dancing reign. (177–79)[14]

The scene links eroticism to a resistance to power, and it carnivalizes and fetishizes the oppressive forces of authority. At the same time, however, the description of the scene seems to imply that the state oppression of gays and lesbians is a closed chapter. Given that this is the same bar in which Isabel has been writing and in which the women find their soul mates, it also seems to argue that *Donde comienza tu nombre* is a product of the current, liberated, space. It also makes a claim for a collective gay identity, a move that is paralleled throughout the novel by the intertwining stories of a variety of lesbians.

The novel celebrates those gains, and thereby makes an essential political point. Still, it is important to note some fissures. Questions of gender, race, nationality, and class are elided, and the last scene implies that gay men and lesbians share a common experience—an endless party and a particular ritual—by virtue of their homosexuality, and without the further complications of other forms of discrimination. What is more, these signs of gay life, and others of Latin America *(Frida)* and of Arab culture in Madrid and Lisbon titillate rather than discomfort the mainstream Spanish reader, and this could be one reason why the novel was able to attract a large mainstream readership; that is, it seems to be a postmodern novel about people who are seen as radical others, but it forges an implicit alliance with mainstream readers that allows them to see queer aesthetics and postmodern sensibilities as exciting, exotic, and perhaps even "normal." It does help them to see lesbians as Spaniards like themselves, but also, perhaps, as a nonthreatening source of pleasure. As an added benefit, by accepting the legitimacy of sexual others, they can see themselves as open-minded, modern, and tolerant global citizens.

Out with the Trash: Abjection and Sexual Identities on the Streets of Madrid

In Elvira Lindo's novel *Una palabra tuya,* winner of the 2005 Biblioteca Breve Prize, queer space is not one associated with middle-class sexual activity, exotic vacations, or political solidarity, but, literally, with refuse. The protagonists are garbage collectors, workers who, because of their working hours and the nature of their work, remain largely invisible in the everyday bustle of urban life, and particularly in its literary representations. What is more, the arduous physical work and unaesthetic conditions of this occupation lead to the assumption that women trash collectors are not very feminine, and from there, to the stereotypical assumption that they are lesbians.[15] Indeed, Rosario, the protagonist of Lindo's novel, spends much of her narration trying to prove to herself and to everyone around her, including the readers of the novel, that she is not a lesbian. Her abject negation of her own identity, however, leads to the novel's problematic conclusion, which suggests that "normalization" or death are the only solutions available to "chicas raras."

Two key concepts ground my analysis of this novel, Julia Kristeva's definition of the abject in her landmark essay *The Powers of Horror* and Judith Butler's analysis of Freud's concept of female gender/sexual identity in *The Psychic Life of Power*. Kristeva places ambiguous sexual and gender identity in the realm of the abject, claiming that it is "not lack of cleanliness or health that causes abjection but what disturbs identity, system, order. What does not respect borders, positions, rules. The in-between, the ambiguous, the composite" (4). The abject is also linked to death, to waste, to refuse, to excrement. The self, Kristeva explains, recoils from the abject, which is associated with "a threat that seems to emanate from an exorbitant outside or inside, ejected beyond the scope of the possible, the tolerable, the thinkable. It lies there, quite close, but it cannot be assimilated. It beseeches, worries, and fascinates desire, which, nevertheless, does not let itself be seduced. Apprehensive, desire turns aside; sickened, it rejects" (1).

This is an apt description of Rosario's attitude to everyone and everything that surrounds her, and, most particularly, to her own gender/sexual identity and her body. "I don't like my face or my name" (11),[16] she says at the beginning, and much of the novel explores her inability to admit love or desire. Thus, although Rosario seems to be most intimate with her best friend, Milagros, most of her narrative consists of a guilty disavowal of their relationship through the conversion of Milagros into the abject other: the monster, the lesbian, the intersexed, the child who never grew up, the person forced to live in intimate contact with dead mothers and children, the garbage handler, and, finally, literally, the dead. Rosario also wants to distance herself from her mother, who, when the action of the novel begins, has descended into senility and the loss of bodily control. "This was during my mother's last days, imagine, her predilection for the closet, having to tie her up, what she did, or that afternoon when she painted the walls with her own excrement" (33).[17] As the novel progresses, however, Rosario reveals repeatedly that her mother and Milagros are not absolute others but mirrors of herself, that she herself is also *rara*, monstrous, ambiguous, closeted, and even perhaps intersexed, but will become a mother herself after having overcome her desire to eliminate the waste of her own person.

The bond and identification between Rosario and Milagros arose from their marginalization during grade school, when both were identified as "chicas raras," a phrase often used to refer to lesbians. This quality is seen as a kind of Mongolian spot that differentiates them from "normal girls":

> I am marked, marked. Rosario, that's my mark. The mark of the queer child. And Milagros recognized my mark from the beginning. Since that grade, fifth or sixth, in the school patio. The queer—she—the queer recently arrived from the small town, recognized the queer—me. We queers recognize each other. The difference is that I have struggled all my life to be normal and distance myself from my tribe. But they haven't let me. Maximum aspiration of my life: to be normal. (15)[18]

Rosario claims that her queerness had gone relatively unnoticed before Milagros appeared, and it is a constant of her character that she tries to avoid abuse by blending in however she can. Milagros is quite the opposite in this sense:

> Milagros liked to call attention to herself, even if it was by playing the monster. The She-Monster, they called her. The She-Monster sat next to me in class, or they seated her next to me, I don't remember, and she infected me with her condition. They called us both she-monsters. (15)[19]

The monstrosity, as it turns out, has to do in part with Milagros's ambiguous biological sex, which becomes apparent during adolescence, when she literally has to fake menstruation:

These things were already part of my experience when Milagros peeked to watch me manipulate the sanitary napkin, folding it, rolling it as small as possible and wrapping it in toilet paper, two years in which she didn't ask anyone and no one asked her, she only listened to the other girls' conversations, spied on them, found out what constituted this monthly ritual and decided to join it even though she never bled, never became a woman, as we girls used to say. (77–78)[20]

Rosario is not so marked physically, and it is her ambivalence about her own monstrosity that drives the novel, as she repeatedly tries to "pass" as a "normal woman," to excise the abject from her self-identification. Hence, in the passage just cited she places herself grammatically with the normal girls: "as we girls used to say."[21]

The fear of recognition explains to a large extent Rosario's insistent attempts to disavow her emotional and sexual ties to Milagros in the eyes of her coworkers, who gossip incessantly about their possible lesbianism. Her male coworker, Morsa, asks her directly, and Rosario responds later, not only to him, but also to the reader: "Milagros a dyke? I don't know. I know that I am not. That's exactly what I said to Morsa" (53).[22] She sleeps with Morsa to prove that she is different, from the "monstrua," that she is a woman: "the beer helps me, along with the intense desire that everyone know that no, I am not a lesbian, and my legs spread and it seems I am all wet, that I am also wet like any other woman" (61).[23]

Another of Rosario's strategies of disavowal is to downplay the sexual aspect of Milagros's lesbianism. For example, although Rosario does admit that "Milagros slept with chicks,"[24] she claims that she did so because she herself was in need of mothering: "What I believe is that Milagros needed affection, that's all, and she grabbed onto whatever she could get, because it was not just sex that she was looking for" (84).[25] Her desire for women can thus be logically explained as an attempt to replace the mother rather than sexual desire or "perversion": Milagros "would have needed someone, that guardian angel that unfortunate children never seem to have, to help her untangle the great mental confusion generated by that inevitable loss" (247).[26] The explanation for this maternal drive comes at the end of the novel. Milagros's mother, the town heroin addict, died, perhaps committed suicide, when Milagros was eight years old, and the child lived for days with the cadaver before her Uncle Cosmo took her to live with him in Madrid (her father had already died, perhaps from an overdose). Rosario also attributes Milagros's lesbianism to an interrupted process of maturation occasioned by her absent mother, following a Freudian concept of maturation and development. Rosario imagines Milagros "making her voice become all the voices a child needs, playing many nights by a mother who was asleep or lost in a daze, acting with a maturity that she afterwards lost, stuck as she remained in a queer infancy" (235).[27] This interpretation links Milagros's hermaphroditism and her biological immaturity—the fact that she has never menstruated—with a psychological definition of lesbianism as a failure to reach emotional maturity.

We can find a theoretical explanation for this construction in Judith Butler's *The Psychic Life of Power*. Butler points out that Freud's concept of gender identity presumes heterosexuality, but that the logic of maturation actually proposes same-sex identification, which, in the case of women, would mean an ambivalent identification with the lack, with the absent phallus, which, as Teresa de Lauretis has suggested, is the mother herself, in Butler's reading. Butler argues: "Consider that gender is acquired at least in part through the repudiation of homosexual attachments; the girl becomes a girl through being subject to a prohibition which bars the mother as an object of desire and installs that barred object as a part of the ego, indeed, as a melancholic identification" (136), or as uneasy site of identification (137). Female gender, then, involves an overcoming and an internalization of a double lack: the loss of the desire for the mother and the identification with the absent phallus. Butler says that "Here Freud articulates a cultural logic whereby gender is achieved and stabilized through heterosexual positioning, and where threats to heterosexuality thus become threats to gender itself" (135).

Rosario's attempts to explain Milagros's difference through psychoanalysis mask a fundamental identification between the two women; that is, we find in Rosario's discourse strong evidence that her abjection of the other is intimately tied to her abjection of self. Rosario signals and then disavows her own ambiguity, her lesbian desire, her need for and rejection of the mother, and her tragic experience of loss.

Rosario has never conformed to a model of feminity, as her own mother points out: "She always said that she could see for me or for any other feminine woman (my mother always added the feminine part, which always hurt me) that it was better to work in a travel agency than as the head trash collector" (41).[28] Her masculinity was apparent even in childhood, when she was always assigned the male roles in school plays:

> I didn't play Pocahontas, that's for sure, they cast me in the male role in every school play, I imagine because of my serious, even grave, demeanor. On the one hand, this made it possible for me to perform in all the plays, because it seems there was no other girl who had such a boy's face as mine, but on the other hand, it gave me a complex. (79)[29]

She is frustrated at this apparent typecasting, which she sees as "one of those small typecastings that adults impose on you from the time you are born and that shape your life" (80).[30] Still, much later in the narration, Rosario admits that, as a child, she had worried that she might even be hermaphroditic:

> I have always had dark thoughts, since I was a little girl, since when I started to think, for example, that on any given day I would get up, go to the bathroom to pee, and when I wiped myself with toilet paper, I would realize that I was growing a penis. (173)[31]

What is more, several of her confessions indicate that she is not entirely straight, not "sexually normal." For example, she explains Milagros's lesbianism as follows:

> I don't know if her lesbianism was pure lesbianism, I mean that Milagros slept with chicks, I heard something about that, but she did it like I did when I was eight years old and I would go to bed with the neighbor's daughter and we would get on top of each other and the neighbor's daughter said, you have to kiss the *chichi*, like married couples do, and she would kiss mine for a while and then say, it's your turn, but I never managed to do it because my neighbor's smelled too much and repulsed me, and then she would get angry and throw me out of her house. (84)[32]

Even as an adult, Rosario's sexual preference is clearly not for men, as her descriptions of heterosexual activity make clear:

> I feel disconnected while it's happening, in mid-act. Disconnected, disconnected from the body of that man next to me and who pants on top of me. Suddenly I see him as a slobbering animal, and I move around, and I pant and I move around, so that it will all be over with as quickly as possible. (58)[33]

Finally, despite Rosario's protests that she is different from Milagros and did not love her—and she does protest far too much—we find that their relationship did, indeed, include sexual contact:

> I was not a dyke, I was not her girlfriend, or even her intimate friend, as she wanted me to admit at the very least ("No, I'm not, Milagros, and I never will be"), and that what had happened that night when she stayed over to take care of my mother and me had only been an almost pathological need for affection.
> But you let me, she would say, you let me.
> Milagros, you know what kind of physical and emotional state I was in, I was a wreck, Milagros, and it happened while I was half asleep, I said, and in the morning I thought it must have been a dream brought on by the fever.
> That's what all the fags and all the dykes in the world who are ashamed of being gay do, they pretend to be asleep so that the next day they can pretend that nothing happened. Oh, but it did happen, Rosario, although you deny it now, it happened and it happened, and I haven't forgotten a detail. It doesn't count for me what you think now, the only thing that counts is what you did that night.
> What did you say, I would tell her, what are you talking about?
> That if you come, if you come and you say, ay, Milagros, Milagros, it's because you like it. (85–86)[34]

Even beyond this manifestation of sexual desire, the lesbianism of the two women becomes clear when they nearly establish an alternate family structure. This is Milagros's goal, one that Rosario recognizes. As they are cleaning a park one day, Milagros finds an abandoned baby in the trash and persuades Rosario to allow her to bring him home and raise him as her own. Rosario figures as the father in this improvised family:

> I came slowly to her side, still recovering the balance that her words had made me lose, and she must have understood that she had convinced me, that I wouldn't tell anybody, and she stopped pressing the box against her chest and held it out to me, as if she wanted to share the infant with me. (181)[35]

Rosario, however, refuses any responsibility, much as she refuses to acknowledge the nature of her relationship with Milagros. The baby soon dies, and Milagros, Rosario, and Morsa drive to the town where Milagros was born, and where her own mother died, to bury him. Milagros, having lost any possibility of taking her mother's place, and of forming a family, remains in the town and subsequently kills herself. It is only at her funeral that Rosario accepts a kinship relationship with Milagros: "I think that Milagros would have been happy to see me there among all the women who had a physical likeness to her, to see me as one of the family" (249).[36]

Milagros's death is the event that gives rise to the entire narration, which is both a kind of confession and a form of self-therapy for Rosario, who feels burdened by guilt. Ultimately, then, the novel narrates the way in which Rosario deals with loss, and we eventually discover, in a tale she tells to Morsa and Milagros as they drive to Milagros's hometown, that the defining loss was her father's abandonment of her mother, her sister, and herself. The event was even more tragic because it involved a betrayal of Rosario in particular, because her father took her on a "secret shopping trip" for her birthday present, which was in reality an excuse for him to meet his lover, who would eventually become his second wife. Until that moment, Rosario had rather unproblematically identified with the father, and she had served happily as his accomplice because that role seemed to confirm her difference from, and her superiority to, her mother and her sister. Her father's betrayal, however, provokes a rupture and causes an irrevocable loss that coincides with Kristeva's explanation of the abjection of the self:

> The abjection of self would be the culminating form of that experience of the subject to which it is revealed that all its objects are based merely on the inaugural *loss* that laid the foundations of its own being. There is nothing like the abjection of self to show that all abjection is in fact recognition of the *want* on which any being, meaning, language, or desire is founded. (5)

This betrayal also causes a breach with the mother and a rejection of the maternal role. As she puts it: "I notice the scent of mother, the scent of the mother who has lost her mind, the scent of all I do not want to be" (61).[37] The refusal to identify with the mother and to desire the father provides a neat explanation of Rosario's gender dilemma and possible lesbianism: she, like Milagros, fails to reach maturity.

This theory is corroborated by one of Rosario's colleagues, who links lesbianism with a lack of sexual maturity and from there to a perpetual virginity: Morsa tells her that "Sanchís says you're a virgin because all lesbians are virgins and he says you're a lesbian" (59).[38] To the extent that, as Gayatri Spivak notes, the continuing centrality of the concept of virginity is one factor that maintains patriarchy, Sanchís's argument has a kind of logic:

> The indefinitely displaced undecidability of the effect of the text (as hymen) is not the transcendent or totalizable ideal of the patronymic chain. Yet, is there not an agenda unwittingly concealed in formulating *virginity* as the property of the sexually undisclosed challenger of the phallus as master of the dialectics of desire? The hymen is of course at once both itself and not-itself, always operated by a calculated dissymmetry rather than a mere contradiction or reconciliation. Yet if the one term of the dissymmetry is virginity, the other term is marriage, legal certification for appropriation in the interest of the passage of property. (Spivak, 174)

The lesbian does not enter into that system of patriarchy. It is significant, then, that at the very end of the novel, Rosario forces herself to "become straight," to become "a woman": "my legs spread and it seems that I am all wet, that I am wet like any other woman" (61).[39]

Although the entire novel could be read as a confession of love, regret, and repentance, Rosario's love for Milagros, her gender confusion and lesbianism itself, are reduced to a problem of maturation, and the only possible ends are death, in the case of Milagros, or compulsory heterosexuality and reproduction, in the case of Rosario. The novel ends with the following affirmation:

> And it was clear to me that that night and the next and the next, [Morsa] would stay at my house, each and every one of the next

steps was clear. At that moment I almost felt his body on top of me, the abandon, the come that would leave me pregnant, that would give me a child. You can't change the past, we can't avoid who we are, so let's make another life begin, I thought, a new life that will grow out of this Rosario from whom I cannot free myself, that Rosario who doesn't like her face or her name, let's make an innocent and beautiful creature that will come out of this me that I have always hated. Perhaps it is my only opportunity to erase from my soul that blemish with which I was born, I thought, to seek redemption, to make me forgive the original sin. (251)[40]

This conclusion seems highly problematic in terms of lesbian identity, which could be read as "la tara con la que nací" (the blemish with which I was born), in psychological terms, or "el pecado original" (the original sin), in Catholic terms.[41] Redemption, to the degree that it is possible, is only for future generations. Still, this might be an accurate representation of a sector of Spanish lesbian discourse at this moment in time, when it is still gay men, and not women, who occupy the center stage in discussions of everything from marriage to adoption to pink business to gay meccas, villages, and constellations.

Indeed, it seems to reflect the findings of Olga Viñuales in *Identidades lésbicas*. Viñuales interviewed members of Catalan lesbian collectives in Barcelona, women who one would expect to be out and to have positive views of lesbianism, but instead she found characteristics reminiscent of the women in this novel, such as the tendency to downplay sexual desire, given the taboo surrounding female desire in Spanish culture (79), or the tendency on the part of most Spanish gay women to dissociate themselves from the cultural image of the lesbian, and from lesbians "con pluma," because contact with such women "'can expose them by indicating, by their appearance, that they are homosexual" (84). The gender norms of Spanish society lead Spanish lesbians to construct their sexual identity around "feminine" norms of affectivity, rather than desire, and to reproduce traditional family structures. The problem, then, is the continuing disparagement of women and the negation of their autonomy and their desire, or indeed, the association between their desire and abjection, which still keeps Spanish lesbians, and indeed all challenges to heteronormative binarisms, out with the trash.

Conclusion

My readings of these best-selling novels reveal the limitations that the global book market can impose on the representation of lesbian characters, in particular the continued tendency to stereotype "deviant" females as exotic, trendy, un-Spanish and/or pathological. In the case of Etxebarría's and Lindo's novels, heterosexual readers may confirm their prejudices even while they congratulate themselves for their tolerant gaze, which the novels' famous, and famously straight, authors do not problematize but rather channel directly; that is, such readers can comfortably identify with the authors, if not always with the protagonists, and the lesbians can thereby be integrated epistemologically into a normalized heterosexist and capitalist order. Galán's novel attempts to overcome these limitations, to push beyond the closet by representing a variety of lesbians and lesbian relationships, and beyond the Chueca ghetto by appealing to a reading public beyond the target audience of the "Salir del armario" series. *Donde comienza tu nombre*, in other words, builds on the commercial success of *Beatriz y los cuerpos celestes*, but focalizes a variety of lesbian identities through a lesbian writer, Isabel, even while it maintains, in part by exoticizing Latin American, Portuguese, and Arabic others, an image of national homogeneity. To the extent that best-selling literature represents the limits of acceptability dictated by the broad national reading public, then, these texts represent the parameters of the lesbian literary closet in globalized, neoliberal Spain.

· CHAPTER 5 ·

Dislocations

Identity and Communication in *Cenicienta en Chueca*

THIS CHAPTER examines the literary representation of the forces of globalization and the neocolonial relations between Latin America, Spain, and the European Union via communication technologies. *Cenicienta en Chueca* (Cinderella in Chueca), a collection of short stories by Argentine exile María Felicitas Jaime published by Odisea in 2003, especially lends itself to a consideration of these issues. The book traces a variety of contemporary relationships between women of various nationalities and social classes, whose encounters are mediated by spatial arrangements of all kinds. In all of the stories, the purported identity of the characters is called into question by the different spaces they inhabit and the texts they write, which emphasize the constructedness of space and·identity. In the first story, "Ejecutivas" (Executives), for example, a powerful, globe-trotting Spanish businesswoman, who lets her hair down only when her work takes her to Buenos Aires, meets a woman who dominates her sexually, much as Spain economically dominates Latin America. Traveling bodies figure prominently in other stories as well, even when these are set in Madrid: in "Soledades" (Solitudes), a German and an Argentine confuse sex with love in an enduring, conflictive relationship; in "Cenicienta en Chueca," the title character is a poor Peruvian immigrant working as a maid who has had to leave her lover behind in South America; and in "Otras cartas" (Other letters) an Argentine professor living in Madrid writes to her former lover, a French businesswoman who has moved back to Paris with her daughter. However, the distances and approximations between characters are not only physical, but also psychological and linguistic, and these communications and miscommunications are occasionally represented by the texts they write to one another. For example, in "Cartas" (Letters) the main characters arouse each other by describing the sexual encounters they have outside their relationship, and the texts in "Otras cartas" are letters that the protagonist will never send to her ex-lover, Sylvie. I will focus primarily on "Chateo" (Chat), a story about cybersex between a woman in Spain and another in Uruguay who meet for an encounter in a lesbian chat room. The implications of this masturbatory relationship in cyberspace provide a conceptual frame within which to consider the implications of globalization and communication technologies for lesbians from a variety of different classes, cultures, and countries throughout the Spanish-speaking world.

The chat is an apt venue for exploring these issues in narrative because it is itself an elaborate fiction, complete with setting, plot, characters, and dialogue. William J. Mitchell points out that even the chat room space is an illusion created by communication technology, "just some computer software that brings the participants in the conversation together and thus—in some abstract fashion—performs the basic function of a room" (114). The physical location of the actual participants has little to do with the site of their interaction, although it might, in subtle ways, color their individual interventions and their interaction with others. Chatters, however, have no way of knowing for certain the physical location from which their correspondents are writing. Indeed, they cannot know anything concrete about their interlocutors, because the fictional elements of the chat room extend to the identities of the participants, who adopt nicknames and offer descriptions of themselves that do not necessarily correspond with reality.[1] As noted by two characters in the previously analyzed novel *Donde comienza tu nombre,* in the lesbian chat room of Chueca.com, "half of the chatters were unprincipled men who were passing for lesbians and the rest, neurotic, insecure, or sex-crazed women, who lied even more than they covered up" (40).[2]

The main goal of chatters also corresponds with that of fiction authors: they hope their language will have specific effects on their readers. In the sexual chat, that effect is sexual response. Sexual stimulation in the chat room, of course, is purely linguistic, with a considerable number of fictional elements, including not only the participants' description of their physical characteristics, nationality, desires, and actions, but also certain conventions of the genre. In gay chats, the key linguistic fiction resides in the description of the penis, as Leopoldo Alas points out in *Ojo de loca no se equivoca* (The queer eye never lies):

> Cybersex is very stimulating if you have imagination and know how to use language to excite that other about whom you only

know the measurements and information that he wants to dole out, which, naturally, could be false: age, height, weight, body hair, hair color—if it's long or short—and, of course, the length of his penis, which is the fundamental information to which one generally responds, especially if it's greater than nineteen centimeters, by typing an *mmmmm* . . . that tends to raise the erotic temperature of the chat. The speakers, or cyberchatters, can be frivolous, festive, and gregarious with a tendency to share secrets and draw out each other's intimacies. There are even those who send poems, as happened to me once with an Argentine from Buenos Aires . . . who had lived in Madrid and remembered it with nostalgia and in detail. (263)

Alas goes on to link cybersex with masturbation, a practice that, like writing itself, is solitary:

cybergays, solitary navigators of a space without a physical existence, seem to find pleasure in merely connecting virtually, without caring too much if the interchange of messages leads to real encounters between them. The Internet is, in this sense, a masturbatory invention, perfect for an age like ours, in which chastity and abstention are disguised as lust and hedonism. But at the moment of truth, nothing at all: just words, words, words. (264)

Alas represents virtual sexuality as a substitute for "real sex," and, in this sense, a reinforcement of the closet. It is, however, possible to frame it as a supplement, in the Derridean sense of the word, one that is associated with masturbation. We should also remember that the desires and parameters of "real sex" are equally determined by discourse, as Foucault has explained.[3]

Even the cyber-phallus that Alas describes is not a physical organ, a penis, but a discursive creation on the screen, "words, words, words." Its virtual location, its disconnection from material reality, and its circulation apart from a living body make it more akin to the dildo, in the sense that the device is theorized by Beatriz Preciado in her *Manifiesto contrasexual: Prácticas subversivas de identidad sexual* (Countersexual manifesto: Subversive practices of sexual identity). As Preciado explains, the dildo is one of many technologies elaborated to control female bodies and their social relations, orienting them exclusively toward heterosexuality and reproduction, but it has been reappropriated as a tool of pleasure for ex-centric sexualities. In the chapter titled "Breve genealogía de los juguetes sexuales o de cómo Butler descubrió el vibrador" (Brief genealogy of sex toys, or how Butler discovered the vibrator), she explains that the strap-on dildo derives from the vibrator and the chastity belt, technologies that are intimately tied to the modern regulation of female masturbation, orgasm, and hysteria:

> What we know by the name of "female orgasm," from at least the beginning of the seventeenth century, is nothing more than the paradoxical result of the work of opposing technologies for repressing masturbation and producing the "hysterical crisis." Female pleasure has always been problematic, since it doesn't seem to have a precise function either in biological theories or religious doctrines, according to which the objective of sexuality is the reproduction of the species.... Female pleasure was described as the crisis that follows from a hysterical crisis, a kind of "hysterical paroxysm" that should be produced in clinical conditions and frequently with the help of diverse mechanical and electric instruments. The orgasm, described thus, is recognized as the symptomatic crisis of an exclusively female illness, and at the same time as the therapeutic climax of a process brought on by technical efforts: massage with the hands or a vibrator, pressure showers. (92)

In particular, the therapeutic climax had as its goal the orientation of the woman toward heterosexual coitus as the sole form of sexual experience, and specifically away from masturbation and lesbianism. It was in this sense a technology that sought to regulate not only sexual practice and sexual identities, but also gender:

> The diagnosis of hysteria and the reaching of orgasm as a result of a "hysterical crisis" were associated with a certain indifference or frigid reaction to heterosexual coitus that could be related to diverse forms of sexual deviance and above all with a tendency toward "lesbianism." For example, in 1650 Nicolaus Fontanus pointed out that some women who suffered from hysteria could have an equal tendency to "ejaculate," a symptom that, according to Fontanus, could put in danger not only the health of the hysteric

but also her moral worth as a woman, given that, "it moved the female body close to certain functions of the virile organ." Just as a possible lesbianism could underlie every form of hysteria, each treatment of hysteria seems to include the risk of giving the hysteric a form of pleasure that could lead her to lesbianism. (90)

According to Preciado, the subversive, masturbatory use of those instruments elaborated specifically to prevent female masturbation and lesbianism serves to destabilize sexual and gender identities because orgasm and ejaculation were considered to be natural experiences for men only (ibid.).

Preciado marks the colonial, nationalistic, and racist implications of sexual control technologies in her argument for masturbation by linking the limits of the body with the borders of the nation:

> It is important to point out that these technologies of sex and gender do not exist in isolation or in only one specific matter, without forming part of a broader biopolitics that joins colonial technologies of producing the white heterosexual European body. In this sense, the new masturbatory body, threatened with an internal contamination of its own limits, operates as well as a physiological metaphor of the modern states in the midst of colonial expansion. The skin, subjected, in the same way as the border, to an immunological process of self-protection and self-demarcation, is transformed into the surface that registers the European sovereign states' new strategies of formation. The same economy of energetic regulation protects the body and the nation-state from "deplorable solitary maneuvers" that could become a danger to its security and reproduction. (83)

This part of her argument is clearly a homage to Donna Haraway's theory of the cyborg in her classic book *Simians, Cyborgs, and Women: The Reinvention of Nature*. Haraway focuses on communication rather than sexual technologies, but notes that they have a similar goal to control through *"the translation of the world into a problem of coding,* a search for a common language in which all resistance to instrumental control disappears and all heterogeneity can be submitted to disassembly, reassembly, investment, and exchange" (164).

Haraway claims that communication technologies, developed in the interests of particular nations, governments, and industries, can also be reappropriated by subversive, liminal practices that interrupt the control supposedly embedded in the code itself and blur the borders (150).[4] The Internet is one of those communication technologies, as Erkki Huhtamo explains:

> Automation emerged in the context of military and industrial applications, and also became prominent in the vast field of administrative applications that came to be known as ADP (automatic data processing). In his overview in 1967, John Rose listed four categories of applications: control (from various industries to traffic and air defense), scientific (from engineering design and space travel to economic research and military logistics), information (from accounting and tax records to medical diagnosis and retrieval of information), and others (including pattern recognition and problem-solving). (100)

To the extent that sexual chats fall outside these applications, they serve to interrupt the logic of the codes that underlie communication technologies.

It is not too far a stretch to extend the definition of communication technologies to include the code of language, particularly in the case of a language like Spanish, which was an important instrument in the colonization of the Americas, and, indeed, of the Iberian Peninsula itself, as Catalans, Basques, and Galicians have pointed out. The Spanish language (that is, Castilian) is still purportedly controlled by a Royal Academy housed in Madrid, the former imperial center of the Spanish-speaking world, and it has attempted to control everything from Gabriel García Márquez's writing to increasing incidences of Spanglish. The luddic distortions and disruptions of Spanish in a variety of cultural texts from within and outside the recognized boundaries of Spain for at least a century have challenged both the borders of the nation and the cultural hegemony of Castile in Spain and in what Castilianists like to denominate "Spanish America," a name that simultaneously denies inhabitants throughout North, Central, and South America the right to name themselves and erases the indigenous populations, thereby illustrating the imperialist implications of the Spanish language itself. Disruptive texts like *Los ríos profundos* by José María Arguedas, *Tirano Banderas* by Ramón del Valle-Inclán, *Balún Canán* by Rosario Castellanos, or *Mulata de tal* by Miguel Ángel Asturias, for example, sought to reinscribe cultural and linguistic heterogeneity into the literary canon. The recent hegemony of Spanish editorial houses in publishing Spanish-language texts—a power owing primarily to globalized market forces—however, has foregrounded the extent to which the former empire can still control not only publication, but, even more importantly perhaps, distribution and marketing, that is, what gets read and where.[5] What is more, the language of literary texts, and occasionally the content as well, are subject to correction by an editor (often a Spanish one) prior to publication—that is, a text's conformation to linguistic norms can be a condition of its circulation. If we consider that the newspapers that review literary texts are owned by the same multimedia conglomerates that control the major publishing houses, it becomes clear that the possibilities for linguistic/cultural subversion in the traditional media have been curtailed in the global age. This linguistic hegemony, in turn, both underlies and propagates Spain's current economic imperialism in the former colonies.[6]

The chat room, and especially the sex chat, however, can largely evade these linguistic controls. It puts different variations of Spanish into dialogue with one another in a space where none of them can dominate the others, where none is more "correct" than the other, because the value of the linguistic performance lies elsewhere, in its ability to arouse the reader, and because there is no moderator akin to the editor or the Royal Academy to police grammar, vocabulary, or the incorporation of foreign words. Linguistic performance in the sex chat rooms is akin to the masturbatory reappropriation of dildos in this sense: it uses the very communication technology developed to control bodies within and between nations—Spanish—for the sole purpose of disseminating nonreproductive sexual pleasures in clear defiance of the rules and conventions, the grammars and dictionaries, associated with the language.

All of these elements—communication technology, post- and neo-imperialism, language, fiction, chats, and masturbation—come together in the story "Chateo." The protagonist of this story is an attorney who recounts an experience she had one night while researching legal information from her home computer. Bored by the slow Internet connection, or so she says, she succumbs to curiosity and clicks on the "chat" button on the screen, but not before asking herself, as any conventional husband might, "how could it be unfaithful to chat with some chicks?" (132),[7] and, indeed, one of the primary themes of the story is the critique of conventional, monogamous sexuality. The pop-up includes chats of all varieties, so that the medium itself highlights the multiplicity of identities and possible relationships, in contrast to the single possibility of heterosexual, procreative marriage that predominated before Spain left Franco behind and entered modernity in the mid-1970s. The protagonist takes the nickname of "fulanita," an ironic move given the fact that the term typically denotes a public woman, one who does not conform to the sexual mores of a heterosexist society; under Franco, women who pursued careers over marriage were also seen as "public women." She is initially bored by the inanity of most of the young, uncultured chatters, so she invites someone to debate "serious" themes, such as "the role of lesbians in alternative families."[8] This sign of her intelligence quickly attracts a similarly articulate interlocutor, "Tania," who invites her into a private chat, not to debate, but to *follar* (fuck). The protagonist wants to meet in person, but "Tania" points out that "fulanita" may be in Spain, but she is in Uruguay, a distance which makes it impossible for them to meet, but not for them to *follar* by chat, which they proceed to do after the protagonist sheds her last traces of heterosexist guilt over "cheating" on her sleeping girlfriend, Alejandra. Given that, under the law, even women who did not exercise lesbian sexuality but merely behaved in a masculine fashion were condemned as sodomites (Sullivan, 3), the masculinist upholding of heterosexist moral values by this lawyer becomes even more ironic. We should remember as well that even the education of women in Western society was a controversial subject until quite recently because it was thought to produce mannish women.

The story ends with the protagonist, not *"follando"* again, but "haciendo el amor" (making love) with her partner; after signing off, she goes to bed and wakes her girlfriend, heating her up with language similar to that she used in her cybersexual encounter with Tania. She comments in the concluding paragraph:

> Perhaps the best part about virtual sex is that it gets you hot for the real thing, that if your partner has you a bit bored because of the routine, first you fuck one on the Internet and then you go to bed to make love, which, as the Uruguayan said, is not the same thing but still delicious. Tomorrow at the same time ... with a different

one, and my partner will have to make love every day, a custom that routine had stolen from us. Until tomorrow, my love. (140)[9]

But where is the "real" sex in this fiction? Isn't it all, as Alas said, "words, words, words"? And where, for that matter, is the "real" cybersex in this printed (not virtual) short story? The conventions of traditional fiction, placed in contrast to the interactive fiction of the chat room, highlight that all sex—"real," virtual, fictive—is a function of discourse: "sexuality is not natural, but rather, is discursively constructed. Moreover, sexuality . . . is constructed, experienced, and understood in culturally and historically specific ways" (Sullivan, 1). That is, the fact that all of the sexual acts described in the story are linguistic performances allows us to examine the fictionality of sexual stimuli in general and place into dispute certain binary oppositions such as fictive/real, public/private, homosexual/heterosexual, perverse/natural. The interactions between "fulanita" and "Tania" and between "fulanita" and "Alejandra" are framed by a first-person narrative in which the protagonist addresses the reader directly through a series of meditations and exclamations regarding the postmodern condition. In the first paragraph, she calls herself, "Una romántica del siglo XX" (a twentieth-century romantic) and, indeed, the tone in those lines reflects a romantic temperament, a nostalgia for "a written letter, with a stamp, from faraway places, a letter that we anticipate before slowly opening it, using the sense of smell to perceive the aroma of ink, of paper" (131).[10] Opening a letter, in other words, is like reading the exposition of a story: it creates the mood and sets up the reader's expectations.[11] The exposition of this story does not end with the letter, however. The second paragraph reveals that a false expectation was created in the reader's mind by the opening lines: we are no longer romantics limited to handwritten snail-mail exchanges. We have moved on to both the endless possibilities of the Internet and its endless miscommunications now that we are "modernas, muy modernas" (132) (modern, very modern), a modernity that extends to the protagonist's legal profession, which would have been denied her in the romantic age. The narrator's meditations on the pros and cons of electronic communications lead to the complication of the plot when the communication technology slips from its function of facilitating professional information that helps to maintain social structures (legal research) to its uses for pleasure (sex chats) that put the boundaries and moral underpinnings of those structures into question.

The story to this point has been recounted in a first-person narrative, but once the protagonist and "Tania" meet online, it is largely developed through dialogue meant to mimic "real" internet exchanges. The content, of course, is not the same as in the chats that Alas describes; this is, after all, a lesbian chat, not a gay one. Like the latter, it does not go straight for the genitals, but rather begins with considerable tongued foreplay, and it does not end after the first orgasm. Part of the game, of course, is the description of the effects the prose is having: as in porn videos, the participants need to provide a "come shot," in which they "prove" to their audience (their reader, in this case) that they have had an orgasm: "I'm coming, Uruguayita . . . Ahhh . . . I can't hold back anymore" (138).[12] All they have really proved, however, is their ability to describe climax and orgasm in a convincing fashion. As a supplement to these dialogues, then, the author provides occasional first-person interludes, in which the narrator describes what happens before she learns the rules of the game, as well as what she is thinking and what is going on in her apartment while she is chatting with "Tania." She describes the "reality" that "Tania" cannot see, including the details of her masturbation and orgasm, and what happens after she signs off:

> I was reading what the Uruguayan was writing and masturbating like crazy . . . with my girlfriend just a step away. . . . I stuck two or three fingers in my pussy, pulled them out, stuck them back in with force, I wet my tits with what I drew from down there, passed my wet fingers over my lips, flattened one breast while my other hand rubbed against the silk of my pajamas at the level of my lips. (ibid.)[13]

Leopoldo Alas argued that Internet chats function as closet substitution for real acts and that they keep homosexuality in narrow private spaces; however, passages like the one above actually make lesbian sexuality (a mystery to those who still believe in female sexual passivity) visible. And, of course, this story is not a private chat itself, but part of a book that is bought and sold in public places and occasionally discussed in conference papers or books like this one, so it actually performs the opposite function of the one imagined by Alas—it brings homosexuality, and, in particular, lesbian sexuality and sexual practices, into the public sphere.

The sexual acts described in the first-person narration, however, are no more real than those presented in the dialogue that mimics Internet interactivity. They, too, are no more than "words, words, words" designed to stimulate the reader, perhaps to induce her to masturbate as well, and to convince her that the orgasm was real. The extension of the stimulating discourse to the reader through this first-person narrative highlights again the notion that what we call the "real"—in this case, not only the experiences of "fulanita" in the story but also the erotic reactions of readers of this book—is conditioned by discourse. This connection between reality and fiction extends to the reader's gender just as it does to the gender of "Tania" and chat-room participants in general: in neither case does the writer have any way of knowing exactly who the reader will be. The production of erotic discourse in all cases is independent of the "real bodies" to which they ostensibly refer, but rather conforms to culturally determined codes of sexuality.

It is significant that not all of the "words, words, words" of this story are in Spanish: as the title of this story makes clear, one by-product of globalization is the proliferation of English, which is the primary language of informatics. The Spanish Royal Academy has insisted on finding Spanish equivalents for any *extranjerismo* in an attempt to maintain "linguistic purity"—an absurd concept for a language with so many words derived from Arabic and indigenous languages. It could be said, however, that this reaction to the "invasion" of the Spanish language by foreign words is part of a larger response to the country's status from the 1950s on as a kind of colony in relation to the economic empires of the most powerful NATO states. The Academy, however, has been unsuccessful in policing the daily usage of foreign and hybrid words, particularly during the post-Franco era, in the sciences and computer technology. This situation is reflected throughout the story by the numerous Anglicisms, although their foreignness is still highlighted by the use of italics: *"e-mail," "footing," "mobbing," "emilios," "chat,"* and *"nick."* I should note that the use of *footing* for *jogging* predates the computer age and comes not from U.S. English but from Great Britain. Likewise, the concept of becoming hooked, *enganchada*, is not necessarily American: "it's that once one begins this, she seems to have an addictive personality: every day she is more hooked" (ibid.).[14] In fact, drug use in post-Franco Spanish popular culture is associated primarily with the aesthetics of the *movida madrileña*, whose roots were more in

British punk than in any music originating from the United States. The idea of having an addictive personality, however, is clearly more American than European.

As I noted, the attempted regulation of American Spanish also reflects the country's anxiety regarding its own lost power, its lost imperial status. In "Chateo," the power relations between the former imperial center and the former colonies is reversed, as the Uruguayan woman educates her Spanish counterpart on how to arouse a woman with words; that is, the American demonstrates greater linguistic skill and control. The Spaniard is inexperienced, in part because she maintains a Franco-era connection between sex and love and is, in this sense, not "modern":

> "You've never done it?"
> "No, the truth is that I'm new to this . . . and it doesn't seem to me that you can make love by chat."
> "I'm proposing we fuck, not make love." (133)[15]

This supposedly higher moral ground—monogamy, the linking of sex and love—is ironic, given that lesbian relationships are considered perverse in the mainstream imagination. It soon becomes clear, however, that the protagonist's reticence to engage in loveless sex and her scorn for those who practice it come more from fear than a sense of ethics:

> "This seems crazy to me, virtual sex has no charm."
> "And how do you know if you've never done it? Try."
> "Are you really desperate?"
> "I'm horny and alone and I wish there were someone next to me to take away my horniness."
> "Well, I have my girlfriend just meters away, very absorbed by her book."
> "Well, then? . . ."
> "And . . . it's just that I'm very shy and I don't know how to do it." (134)[16]

From here, the lessons begin, with the Uruguayan leading the way as she would with a woman having sex for the first time: very slowly, but insistently, she instigates the narrator to perform as well and not just receive her partner's verbal caresses. The Spaniard does so, imitating "Tania's" style, and becoming increasingly excited, even as she worries that she is somehow being unfaithful, although "there was an ocean between us" (135).[17] The Uruguayan remains in control: "'Are you there, Spanish girl? Are you touching yourself?' And my hand went down between my legs without my authorization, the silk of my pajamas was wet, and the contact of my fingers was spectacular" (135).[18] The narrator really starts to heat up, however, when "Tania" speaks to her in "American":

"What are your hairs like?"
"Red, abundant, curly, and they get as wet as my little thing....
    What do you call the little thing in Spain?" (136)[19]

And later, she says, "I'm rocking in my chair, with my conch in the air, and I'm rubbing it against the upholstery" (137).[20] The narrator, in contrast, speaks of her *"coño"* (cunt), and at a crucial moment yells out, "¡Joder, joder, joder!" (139) (Fuck, fuck, fuck!) before "Tania" signs off: "Ciao, Spanish girl.... As we say, may you screw well and deep" (ibid.).[21] This interchange of regional sexual vocabulary takes on a different charge, however, when, after signing off, the narrator applies the lessons she has learned from the Uruguayan on her girlfriend. She wakes her and asks, "Do you know what they call this in South America? The little thing" (140).[22] The Uruguayan's words become resignified as "exotic" and "erotic" signs that add spice to the stale domestic arrangement as the narrator begins to exercise the linguistic control that the American taught her; they are, in this sense, a form of "Orientalism," as Edward Said figured it. We are left, then, with an important question: does this mimicry signify the submission of Spain, Spaniards, and Spanish to the superior creativity of Latin Americans, or does it represent the ways in which the imperial power adopts skills from the colonies in order to perpetuate control?

Part of the answer may be found in the story "Ejecutivas," which deals more explicitly with the neo-imperial relations between Spain and Latin America. In this story, Paula, an ultrapowerful international banking executive from Spain, seems to surrender sexual control to her colonized subjects in Argentina, but this masochism is in fact a further exercise in control, as Gilles Deleuze has explained (20). Critics of gay male culture have examined at length this masochistic desire for the colonized subject (particularly those of the British Empire), but their observations have rarely been applied to lesbian relations, particularly in the Hispanic world.[23] The protagonist of this story is most certainly a prototype of the powerful imperial subject, albeit one who uses a simulacrum of femininity to overpower her male peers in the Spanish banking world:

> Paula is attractive, seductive, active, intelligent, elegant, and good-looking besides. She is the director of major accounts of the most important bank in this country. She lives hanging on the phone, climbing onto planes, with an agenda that leaves her no time even to see her mother, who she has put up in the most expensive locale in Madrid and for whom she pays a round-the-clock assistant to take her place. Anything to avoid more complications. She doesn't have time, and the time she has she wants to keep for herself.
>
> She answers only to the owner and the general director of the bank; she's chummy with him and they decide the institutional policy in Latin America, the drop in the stock market, even how much they can afford to lose.... She knows that part of her success is her person, her way of dressing, her way of moving, her skirts just long enough, which distract the men and provoke the envy of women, her pastel-colored suits, her authentic silk hankies, glasses that are unnecessary for seeing but indispensable for her ultrasympathetic sincerity. (9–10)[24]

She relishes the power of her position and her power over men, but her work and her image are revealed to be elaborate closets; she can only come out in Argentina and among a very different circle of friends—different from her colleagues and different from her because, although they are also powerful women, they do not live in the closet. Paula loves Buenos Aires: "In spite of its crises, in spite of its decadence, in spite of its nighttime bookstores that are no longer open, Buenos Aires was a second home for her: there she was comfortable and let her hair down, twelve thousand kilometers managed to relax her, make her forget she was an executive" (11).[25] The irony, of course, is that the crisis resulted in part from the business practices of Spanish firms in Argentina, including banks like the one where Paula herself works. What she loves about Argentina is its exoticism: "speak to me in Argentine, your language fascinates me" (16).[26] This fascination, however, does not preclude her from seeing the country as a colony, a provider of natural resources (including lovers) and business opportunities, which she will leave devastated when she returns to the "madre patria" (motherland).

The banker Paula's relationship with Argentina, and with Argentine women, parallels the relationship between Spanish banks and their Latin American counterparts. This economic imperialism was the subject of a special issue of the journal *Quórum* dedicated to the "Internacionalización de la Economía y la Empresa Española: El Caso Latinamericano" (Internationalization of the economy and Spanish business: The Latin American case). In an article titled "La expansión de Santander Central Hispano en Iberoamérica" (The expansion of Santander Central Hispano in Spanish America), Juan Manuel Cendoya writes:

> In Spanish America we find, definitively, a zone with a great potential for growth in the banking sector and where the cultural affinity with Spain, together with the knowledge we have of the principal markets where we were already present in specialized businesses, gave us a competitive advantage over European and North American competitors. (78)

Cendoya goes on to point out the advantages of this investment for Latin Americans, who benefit from the technology and modern business practices that Spanish enterprises brought with them. As Pablo Toral makes clear in the same issue, however, Spain's investment in Latin America was an act not of beneficence but of economic necessity, one that took advantage of the economic crises throughout the former colonies:

> Banks were the leading Spanish investors in Latin America, driven by the fall in returns from the Spanish market resulting from the saturation of the market and the fall in the differential between loans and deposits.... Banking's solution was to diversify its investments, geographically (investing in new markets) as well as in its areas of activity (the energy sector and telecommunications). Its expansion in Latin America was favored by the openness and liberalization of the Latin American banking market, which following the banking crisis of the 1980s. What is more, Spanish banks found little local competition, and they had important comparative advantages. On the one hand, many local banks found themselves faced with closure during the crisis, and others ended up seriously weakened. On the other hand, the liberalization of banking in Latin America increased the competition among all financial institutions (not only banks) for the provision of every type of financial and

banking service, breaking the monopoly that banks traditionally held as savings institutions. (136)

The "openness and liberalization" are represented in "Ejecutivas" as sexual freedom and open lesbianism, which irresistibly attract Paula. As a closeted lesbian, she can exploit but cannot fully participate in this freedom and openness. We see this acquisitive side of the love story between Spain and Latin America even in the description of Paula's "transformation" into lesbian as she changes her clothes after her business meetings are over:

> every time she took off her executive clothing she lost little by little her feminine manners, and began to feel like a seducer: she liked the game of seduction between women because she felt that she occupied a dominant position, that her attractiveness inhibited them; and to counteract the effect, she acted a bit masculine, earthy. (14)[27]

If we recall the fate of Don Juan's women, we know that this does not bode well for the women who sleep with Paula, and our suspicions are soon confirmed. Sexually, Paula wants to lose control, to play the game of submission, and she meets a young woman in Buenos Aires who dominates her sexually and linguistically. Clara tells Paula to bite her:

> "You like to bite.... Bite me [*Mordé*, in Argentine Spanish]...,
>   I like to be bitten.
> "Mordé... Mordé..., I like that dialect so much... I like your
>   entire city, your country. You Argentines don't know what you
>   have here."
> "Mordé yourself, and I'll tell you what we have. A shitty government that steals everything and a shitty populace who lets them." (18–19)[28]

Paula, the Spaniard, presumes to see more and better the riches of the country, including the "exotic" dialect of Castilian Spanish, but Clara points out that Paula's attitude simply exoticizes the American other, performing a kind of Orientalism. The sense of superiority is clear, but it does not last. When Clara orders her to kiss her, Paula obeys: "And she obeyed docilely, kissing her with an open mouth, her tongue reaching down to her throat" (19).[29] This submissiveness, however, will only last as long as Paula remains in Buenos Aires with her lesbian friends. When she leaves for Spain, she goes in her executive guise and forbids Clara to come to the airport. When they see each other again in Spain, Paula is too busy to dedicate much time to Clara, and it is obvious that she prefers to keep her lesbian identity distant, and, preferably, in exotic America: "They agreed to meet a few months later in Rio de Janeiro, without the agenda and without the executive pose" (26).[30]

In "Ejecutivas" the forms of Spanish neo-imperialism are reflected linguistically in the battle between two forms of Spanish. The Spanish woman sees Argentine Spanish as a dialect of Spanish in general, by which she means Castilian Spanish, which would then be the mother tongue. The dialects are her children, and they may very well be charming, but they are still subject to her pedagogy, her control. Or they could be her lovers, her other tongues, that service her and reassert her centrality. American dialects, however, are mestizos, bastard children, like Donna Haraway's cyborgs, and their superior musicality—a quality that thoroughly seduces the Spaniard—is akin to the superior insight that Americans might have into the workings of their own societies, as Clara points out, despite the apparent omnipotence of Spanish business.

Other stories in *Cenicienta en Chueca* sound similar linguistic chords. In "Soledades," for example, the fissures of the European Union appear in the imperfect control that foreigners exercise over the language. In "Cenicienta en Chueca," the exotic Latin American is not always prized in Spain; social class, ethnicity, and education enter into Spanish reception of Latin Americans. A "white" Argentine executive or Uruguayan chat mate who is interested in politics is clearly more prized than a woman like the protagonist, a poor, mestiza Peruvian immigrant who had been a nurse but is forced to work as a maid when she goes to seek her fortune in Madrid. The first part of the story describes how the protagonist discovered her lesbianism with her friend, then lover, Susana, how the two struggled to pursue careers and live together, how they felt isolated, with no gay/lesbian community to support them. The protagonist is forced to leave her country, and Susana, behind because the devastating effects of globalization on the economy have made it impossible to find work and live without the protection of a man: "But the crisis worsened: they fired them from the shop, they couldn't support themselves, there was no work, the violence was daily, every day. Lima was a hell, Peru and all of Latin America, a tinderbox that pushed everyone into exile" (182).[31] She hopes to work as a nurse in Madrid, but prejudice makes it impossible, especially for a woman with indigenous physical traits: "Spain, the motherland, felt a certain phobia toward Peruvians! They didn't have the good fortune to be European and white, even if they were Western and Catholic, they were from the Third World!" (ibid.).[32] She ends up as a maid working for an elderly Spanish woman typical of the Franco era, and her attitudes toward Latin Americans—"they just want money, but they don't want to work at all" (183)[33]—reveal the prejudices of that regime. The woman's granddaughter, Charo, however, is able to see the queen beneath the protagonist's current image. She falls in love with her and rescues her from her miserable life:

> She put her arm around her waist and brought her to the dance floor. They had barely put their arms around one another when she kissed her. . . . They left, got into Charo's car and went to her house. Finally, she was no longer fucking, but making love. She felt that . . . anything was possible, even to make it in this city. Charo made her leave her grandmother's house, she rented a little apartment two streets away from Charo's, got a semilegal job in a clinic, waiting patiently to be awarded her title, and she lived happily ever after. (190)[34]

This story, which closes the collection, has a happy ending, but the very language used to describe it suggests that it is no more than a fairy tale.

By representing the communications and miscommunications in some transnational lesbian relationships that pass through Chueca, *Cenicienta en Chueca* lays bare the intersections between gender, economics, race, "modernity," and nationality in contemporary Spain. The text, with its allusions to communication technologies and globalized capital and its imaginative re-creation of women's worlds, sexualities, and relationships, seems to fit nicely Haraway's definition of the cyborg:

> A cyborg is a cybernetic organism, a hybrid of machine and organism, a creature of social reality as well as a creature of fiction. Social reality is lived social relations, our most important political construction, a world-changing fiction. The international women's

movements have constructed "women's experience," as well as uncovered or discovered this crucial collective object. This experience is a fiction and fact of the most crucial, political kind. Liberation rests on the construction of the consciousness, the imaginative apprehension, of oppression, and so of possibility. The cyborg is a matter of fiction and lived experience that changes what counts as women's experience in the late twentieth century. This is a struggle over life and death, but the boundary between science fiction and social reality is an optical illusion. (149)

Cenicienta en Chueca reminds us that language itself is a communication technology and that, even if print texts do not circulate in exactly the same way as words in cyberspace, literary fiction can still mark and disrupt the free—and sometimes, the costly—flows of resources, people, identities, and words across the new boundaries of the globalized world.

· CHAPTER 6 ·

Popular Lesbian Fiction

Romance, Literature, and Legislation

IN THE EARLY 2000s, Spain's LGBTQ community activists—including those involved in the gay/lesbian book industry—campaigned for what they described as equality before the law, in the form of gay/lesbian marriage and adoption legislation. Several autonomous communities (Catalunya, Valencia, Navarre, and Aragon) had already approved measures recognizing civil unions between same-sex partners at the end of the preceding decade, but in 2001, the Popular Party, which still controlled the majority in the Parliament, rejected calls for national recognition of common-law gay/lesbian marriages *(parejas de hecho)*, and stated categorically that such unions could never be called marriages. Although the PP's argument rested on a religious foundation, the explanations the party put forth in the debate were couched in terms of science (sociology) and law.[1] In 1997, the party had rejected a similar measure, claiming that legally recognizing unmarried life partners would occasion an unacceptable increase in government expenditures for social security and the like. The leftist opposition, meanwhile, maintained that this was a question of human rights and of the separation of church and state, linked, then, to the liberalization of Spanish society and government, and representing another step away from Francoism. This strategy had been elaborated by the LGBTQ organizations themselves since the early 1990s (Villaamil, 36).

Obviously, constitutionally guaranteed equality for all citizens, regardless of gender or sexual identity, is an important and laudable goal; it could be argued, however, that lesbian and gay marriage does not completely accomplish this end. In order to attain congressional approval of gay and lesbian marriage, activists would need to convince the state and society as a whole to recognize gay men and lesbians as acceptable life partners and parents according to this model, which meant making lesbians visible, to begin with, and replacing the hypersexualized and/or feminized image of gay men with one of accomplishment, maturity, stability, and monogamy.[2] The campaign implied, as well, a contradictory relationship with the state: at the same time that gay and lesbian activists demanded privacy regarding sexual acts that were, until 1981, illegal in Spain, they would invite the state into the private realm as a legitimizing force by making their relationships subject to laws regarding the contracts of marriage, divorce, custody, and adoption. Bisexuals, queers, and transgendered people were excluded from this project, which suggests that the battle was, indeed, more about legitimacy and normalization than about equality, and that it would require gay men and lesbians to conform to the ideal of the bourgeois Western family, headed by monogamous parents with the goal of raising children.[3] As Judith Butler puts it: "Gay marriage obviously draws on profound and abiding investments not only in the heterosexual couple per se, but in the question of what forms of relationship ought to be legitimated by the state," with the result that the "sphere of legitimate intimate alliance is established through the producing and intensifying regions of illegitimacy" ("Is Kinship Always Already Heterosexual?" 232). Gay and lesbian marriage, then, could be seen either as a first step toward equality for the LGBTQ community or as a reinforcement of gendered sexual identities (male/female, gay/lesbian), and a consolidation of a disciplinary, heternormative institution, expanded to include those lesbians and gay men who conform to its norms.

This chapter will examine the ways in which these contradictions manifest themselves in lesbian novels published by Egales and Odisea in the years leading up to the marriage and adoption legislation. I will begin with a novel that could be considered the prototype of the Egales "Salir del armario" lesbian romance, *Un amor bajo sospecha* (A love under suspicion, 2001), by Marosa Gómez Pereira. Although this text addresses the oppression of lesbians during the Franco dictatorship, it upholds that government's model of the family (with the obvious exception of the parents' gender) to such an extent that it even invisibilizes lesbian sexuality, which is subordinated to motherhood and romance. The second novel I examine was a finalist for the fourth Odisea literary prize, *Amores prohibidos* (Forbidden loves, 2002), by Marta Fagés. This suspenseful novel departs from a specific premise regarding feminist politics in relation to the state to argue that the homophobic rhetoric deployed by patriarchal institutions (families, schools, churches, neighborhood gossip) is a form of aggression with potentially fatal consequences. It is a text that urges political action—and words—to protect gays and lesbians from discriminatory and violent acts. The third novel, *A por todas* (After them all!, Odisea 2005), by Libertad Morán, seems entirely apolitical in its representation of the dating habits of a modern young lesbian in the Spanish capital, and, in fact, it provides an explicit critique of identity politics in contemporary lesbian literature and sexual practices. In this sense, the text represents a queer utopia, in which the gender divide falls away and monogamy becomes one option for relationality that does not delegitimize the others. The characters, nonetheless, participate in the LGBTQ collectives, even as they eventually reveal their corruption, thereby moving the sphere of political action from a consecrated institution—an NGO, no less—to an alliance of freethinking individuals. Taken together, these novels outline some of the parameters of the debates about gay and lesbian marriage in the context of a changing Spanish society.

Un amor bajo sospecha represents lesbian identity and lesbian relationships in ways that echo the identity politics of the first generation of lesbian activists of post-Franco Spain. In fact, it could be the prototype of the ideal lesbian novel, as described by Mili Hernández and Beatriz Gimeno at the 2005 "Visible" festival discussed in chapter 2. In that same roundtable discussion, Hernández and Gimeno prescribed the literary style and form that lesbian novels should take—the sentimental romance with a happy ending—and Gimeno went so far as to recount for the audience that she was required to change the ending of her own novel, *Su cuerpo era su gozo* (Her body was her pleasure, 2005), because the editors felt that the unhappy ending would be too discouraging to lesbian readers.[4] That happy ending is intended to remove the stigma of homosexuality, to put conflicts with society in the past, and to give hope and inspiration to readers struggling to assert their right to sexual freedom. Unfortunately, it has the further effect of reinforcing heteronormative morality, particularly through its insistence on an idealized eternal love expressed in an absolutely monogamous relationship. As a consequence, the lesbian romance novel, in essence, reproduces the gender roles outlined in the genre of romance itself, even if both the masculine and feminine roles are being filled by women; this is the same critique that some theorists have made regarding gay and lesbian marriage (Lehr, 25).

Un amor bajo sospecha recounts the life story of Lucía, who begins her first-person narration in the present, and recalls her past in a series of analepses as she prepares to meet her son's fiancée, Marta, for lunch.

Lucía had married a merchant marine in Galicia during the waning years of the Franco dictatorship and had three children with him before falling in love with Matilde, a local waitress. When Lucía's husband, Sebastián, returns on one of his rare visits home (he traveled nine months of every year), he immediately notices that his wife and Matilde are in love, and he takes that opportunity to confess to her that he is himself gay. He explained that, although he initially hoped to fall in love with her and be "saved" from his nature, he never felt passion for her. Finally, he suggests that they remain married to avert suspicion, but draw up appropriate legal documents to protect all involved (especially the children, whom he naturally adores) in case some accident should befall him on the high seas, and then, except for brief cameo appearances, he conveniently disappears from the narration.

The descriptions of Lucía's relationships with Matilde, Sebastián, and the children conform to most sentimental clichés regarding romantic love and maternity, which allow the author to represent Lucía as a "normal woman," despite her lesbianism, which in turn is presented as an unchangeable natural condition. Thus, while attempting to "legitimize" lesbian relationships as "natural" as opposed to "perverse," the text unwittingly endorses the concept of biological determinism that has so often been used to justify gender roles in heterosexual unions. Not surprisingly, then, the text draws a distinction between male homosexuality (and male sexuality in general) and lesbianism: men are shown to be more aware of their sexual orientation and more responsible for their behavior in relation to it than are the women. The result is often contradictory (though never problematic to any of the characters), especially given that this is a narrative about a working mother who becomes the head of a household run by women. For example, Lucía admits that, before marrying Sebastián, she had only fallen in love with women and in fact never felt any passion for her husband (8–9), yet she feels used and betrayed when Sebastián admits to similar emotions: "He had used me, and he had also used the children; the four of us had been his great cover" (36).[5] But then she will use this same *tapadera* when she sets off to live in Madrid with her children and "Aunt Matilde," with whom she maintains a seventeen-year relationship. By the same token, she suspects that Sebastián's family and her own guessed that he was gay but hid this knowledge from her, hoping that it was just a phase and that she would "cure" him with her love (35). She recriminates them for not recognizing his true identity: "Didn't they ever imagine that that could be what it was, his true identity, and that living by my side was a farce, and, therefore, we could never be happy?" (ibid.),[6] but she does not blame her family for not recognizing her own sexual identity, nor does she blame herself for attempting to hide her relationship with Matilde from her husband (and later, from her children). Sebastián, of course, was not deceived because, as a gay man, he was immediately able to perceive the truth about Matilde's sexuality when he met her. Why, then, could Lucía not perceive that Sebastián was gay? She even admits that he was the one "who attracted me the most, and whom I also attracted" (8),[7] implying that there was a kind of unconscious recognition when they were courting. These confused identities and misrecognitions suggest, on the one hand, that lesbians were still invisible in the 1970s when Lucía began her relationship with Matilde, but, on the other, they reveal a continued belief in stable, "natural" sexual identity, a "true identity."

The presumed sexual ignorance of middle-class girls and the general invisibility of lesbianism during the Franco years might explain some of the misrecognitions in the novel. For example, "everyone" suspected that Sebastián was gay, but nobody recognized that Lucía was a lesbian, even though she had an affair with another girl when she was a teenager (9). What is more, the same lesbian identity that was imperceptible to "straight" people was clearly visible to a gay man. No one else can see that the women's relationship was sexual because it was assumed that women, being passive, could only engage in sexual activities with an "active," male partner. Companionship between women was expected, but sexuality was not even contemplated.

Indeed, although sexuality between the women is implied in the novel, it is never described. Rather, the author employs imagery of the sea and the Galician landscape to portray nearly all of the emotions and sensations that the characters experience. Lucía and Matilde's first sexual experience is described thus:

> In her arms I felt like a ship stranded in a solitary inlet, with fine sand and gentle waves that rocked me rhythmically, licking my sun-bleached wood, penetrating all my fissures, refreshing them, wetting them with small salty drops, entering all my pores, all my knots, and dilating all that wood shaped as a boat. (18–19)[8]

Given that these images form part of a system of maritime imagery that pervades the entire narrative, they imply that sexual activity is only one aspect of lesbianism. The extreme conventionality of these metaphoric evasions also serves to normalize lesbian sex for a heterosexual readership, or for women who are just coming out and do not want to be considered or consider themselves *raras* (queer). The description, however, covers up the actual sexual practices of the women, as do similar passages in "straight" romance novels, and it thus maintains the sexist norm of keeping women in the dark regarding the workings of sexual activities that they might not yet have experienced. At the same time, the conventionality of the passage inscribes lesbian sexual activities within the bounds of heteronormativity, excluding any possible "deviant" activities (sadomasochism, bondage, use of sex toys, anal penetration, etc.). Eric O. Clarke's assessment of this phenomenon is helpful:

> With regard to eroticism, only those private vices that conform to a heteronormative moral code are translated into legitimate public virtues. Thus elements of queer life that do not conform to this code are expunged with little, if any, regard for the imaginative diversity of queer life.... Because the ideals of bourgeois publicity use unduly universalized moral codes to govern the distribution of equity, conformity to a historically particular, class-inflected, and often racially homogenized heteronormativity determines what precisely will and will not become valorized representations of queer life. (9)

Indeed, the relationship that the women subsequently form is also entirely conventional. Matilde, who works as a waitress before meeting Lucía, takes the role of the mother to the children because Lucía has a serious career as a designer and cannot spend enough time with them. Lest we imagine that Lucía thereby becomes "masculine," she assures us that "I didn't stop using makeup, plucking my eyebrows, putting on eye shadow, and painting my lips, things that I still do and will no doubt continue to do until I can no longer hold the tweezers or the lipstick in my hands" (25).[9] And she is, nonetheless, a perfectly loving and responsible parent at all times. Even when she falls in love with her son Sebas's fiancée, she resists the temptation to date her until her children reveal to her that Marta is not, in fact, in love with Sebas at all, but the whole engagement has been a ploy on the part of Matilde's children to arrange a meeting between their loving mother and the woman they think would be perfect for her. The novel ends with all parties happy, well adjusted, and successful, the message clearly being that lesbianism is normal and should have no negative consequences within the family or in society. These institutions are, in fact, upheld in this "novela rosa," albeit in a format that accepts, accommodates, and celebrates the productive, nurturing lesbian.

The second novel I will discuss is *Amores prohibidos,* a finalist for the Odisea Prize in 2002. Although the book was published in Madrid, a city that appears as a mecca for the lesbian protagonists, the story is set in Andalusia, in the urban setting of Seville. It is one of the few novels published by a gay/lesbian press that depict violence toward lesbians, opening with a newspaper report of the act of arson that has destroyed the home of Lucía and Julia, and nearly killed the two women. Most of the other families living in the apartment building with the lovers maintain some level of discomfort with the couple's lesbianism and are therefore suspects, but the prime suspect is presented as an anomaly—nearly un-Spanish in the sense that he converted to Evangelical Christianity while in jail for a heroin-related murder he committed in Madrid. Only Marquina, the president of the building, and his wife Amelia, view Lucía and Julia as a family and tenants like any other, and they thus serve as a model of tolerance that contrasts sharply with their neighbors' hypocritical condemnation of the couple's "immorality."

The style of the novel's third-person narration could best be described as realist, and, although the narrator is omniscient, recounting the unspoken thoughts of the characters, the structure takes the form of a whodunit, presenting motives and clues, but hiding the identity of the perpetrator until the very last chapter. This technique obliges the reader to engage critically with a variety of characters and the causes of their homophobia, and to see both the dangers that these various rationales represent to lesbians and gays and the ways in which the homophobic characters themselves are victims of an unjust heterosexist society.

This last theme is presented explicitly in the second chapter, which recounts the beginning of the protagonists' relationship, nine years before the crime, when Lucía was a university student and a companion of Julia's then boyfriend, Jaime. The argument regarding the subjection of women in patriarchy is, ironically, advanced by Jaime himself, who will become violent when Julia leaves him for Lucía:[10]

> Lucía was convinced that activism was the only possible route for women, lesbian or not, while Julia firmly believed that equality had already been achieved and there was no need to keep worrying about it.
> The topic that provoked [their first] disagreement had been brought up by Jaime.... He wanted Julia to realize that her point of view was completely erroneous, the product of a tendentious discourse elaborated by Power to control the progress of women. He argued that what women had achieved could be erased with the stroke of a pen. Everyday life demonstrated that the most fervent defense of patriarchal values could be found precisely among women; and that these women, continual volunteers in the practice of discrimination, would be the first vehicles to transmit *machista* and sexist ideology. Lucía agreed. (60–61)[11]

Indeed, one of the primary mechanisms in the novel for enforcing patriarchal logic is the gossip of the three older women in the building, Carmen, Irene, and Amelia (though she is portrayed as a reluctant participant), who represent the generation of women who married and/or raised their children during Franco's dictatorship. The interconnected stories of these women, who live on different floors of the same apartment building, are in part an allusion to Antonio Buero Vallejo's *Historia de una escalera* (Story of a stairway), which serves a kind of shorthand reference to relations among members of the working class in Francoist Spain. Here the economic stultification of the working poor and the premodern technology that hangs over from Francoism is also represented by the staircase and by the building itself, which still does not have an elevator.

At the same time, the women's gossip brings to mind Federico García Lorca's *La casa de Bernarda Alba* (The house of Bernarda Alba), an allusion that reinforces Jaime's argument. The main object of the older women's gossip is the lesbian couple in their midst, but, as it turns out, these women themselves, like Bernarda Alba, have secrets they want to hide behind a supposedly unstained image. Carmen, for example, was unhappily married and always coveted Amelia's husband. Irene's son, Carmelo, became a heroin addict in Madrid and ended up in the Carabanchel prison, but she covers up this disgrace by telling her friends that he received a scholarship to study in Colombia. In an act of dispassion, disguised as salvation for her own son, she also travels to the slum where Carmelo's pregnant companion lives to break off the relationship, against her son's wishes, an act she soon regrets when the television news reports the woman's death of an overdose. To add to her sense of shame, we later discover that Carmelo is the offspring of Irene's incestuous relationship with her own brother, Jacinto, the same person who emphasized to her the supreme importance of maintaining appearances. Amelia, for her part, is a basically decent person, but she nonetheless sets part of the book's tragedy in motion with her lack of discretion and her need to be accepted by her neighbors. The gossip of these women, then, serves the purpose of distracting others from their own sins and shortcomings by converting the lives of a marginalized group (homosexuals) into the sole focus of moral approbation. The omniscient narration, however, reveals not only their hypocrisy, but also the extent to which they themselves are products and victims of patriarchy.

Irene's son Carmelo returns to Seville from Carabanchel as a Pentecostal preacher, but he wields the pulpit not to preach love, but as a form of self-empowerment. The Argentine spiritual adviser who trained him in jail (a woman) expresses considerable reservations about his ministry owing to Carmelo's overweening pride and his misogyny. From his church, the Iglesia Evangélica de Estudios Bíblicos y Defensa de la Familia "Nuevo Pentecostés" ("New Pentecostal" Evangelical Church of Bible Study and Defense of the Family), he preaches about an idealized family threatened by moral degeneration, particularly as represented by homosexual unions. His sermons in this sense replicate the function of the women's gossip, singling out a marginal group to incarnate sin and reinforcing a conservative concept of family, but they are even more dangerous because his hateful discourse is cloaked as the word of God. When his church is featured on a local television series about the different religious practices in Seville, and the star of the series is replaced with a lesbian subordinate for his segment, he avenges the affront by changing the topic of his sermon from brotherly love to the evils of homosexuality. The program allows his homophobic fury to reach an even broader audience, prompting Lucía to respond in her column in the local newspaper about the violent potential of words, especially when wielded by people in power. Her column has the effect of provoking Felipe, who had allowed Carmelo to house the church in his building for free, to evict his tenant. Felipe, as it turns out, had recently left his wife for a man, and was one of the targets of Carmelo's televised diatribe. Despite this indictment—and punishment—of Carmelo's pride and his abuse of power, the omniscient narrator reserves a measure of compassion for him by revealing his devastation upon learning, in jail, of the death of his companion Rosa and the loss of his child, and the utter hopelessness of his life. Finally, he is also a victim of the normalizing function of gossip because he loses most of his congregation when they discover he did time in jail.

The dangerous potential of homophobic speech is finally realized in an act of arson that threatens the entire building. The perpetrator, as it turns out, is not any of the suspected adults, but an adolescent girl, Paulina, the eldest granddaughter of Carmen, the most intolerant and self-righteous woman in the building. The conversations between Paulina and her friends suggest a degree of ignorance about lesbianism, but the majority of them have no issue with the couple, whose mere presence infuriates Paulina. The text hints that her extreme homophobia stems from her fear of "contagion," that is, from a fear that she herself might be or become lesbian. Even in this case, the narrator evinces some degree of compassion and empathy for someone who could be seen to some extent as an unwitting tool of patriarchy.

What would have been a happy ending for Lucía and Julia—finding perfect jobs after Julia finally passed her comps, and moving to Madrid—turns into an unending nightmare for both. Lucía is not allowed to visit Julia in the hospital, where she is in critical condition, because they are not married. Julia faces years of rehabilitation and a lifetime of chronic pain. Paulina, as a minor, receives a relatively light sentence, despite the grave nature of her crime, and the victims are not compensated for their financial losses. Finally, then, the novel argues that the state, supported at times by religion, or at least religious discourse, still protects individuals according to a particular definition of family; that is, it looks out for minors, who are considered children until they reach legal maturity, but it does not equally protect people in relationships not recognized as familial by the state. Without idealizing Julia (who has taken seven years to pass her comps) or Lucía (whose own character has caused some conflicts with the neighbors), or their relationship, the novel nonetheless asserts that they are at least comparable to their neighbors and should be accorded the same consideration, civil rights, and protection. It also implicitly argues for a shift in pedagogical practices; that is, for the use of discourse (in the home, in the school, in the church, in the legal system) in a way that is loving and compassionate, and not hateful and judgmental, a philosophy that the author herself puts into practice in her representations of the novel's homophobic characters. It does not, however, question the economic underpinnings of social institutions, presenting a middle-class existence, in which both members of the couple are successful professionals, as the norm to which the characters aspire.

Libertad Morán's *A por todas* (2005) presents an entirely different view of both lesbian politics and the function of literature in furthering LGBTQ political objectives. The novel appears initially to have no political agenda at all, beyond the mainstreaming of gay and, especially, lesbian culture. The protagonist and narrator, Ruth, participates only minimally and out of a sense of solidarity in functions organized by the gay/lesbian collectives. Ruth is a typical chick lit protagonist: superficial and self-involved, given to prolonged cell-phone conversations, a party animal. Her activity in the *ambiente* revolves primarily around sex; her cultural interests are limited to pop culture (films and literature); and her sentimental relationships have lasted only a few weeks or months during the five years since she broke up with her first partner, Olga. She does not even believe in identity politics, as she herself explains: "Since I was a teenager I've advocated for a diversity of genders and orientations and where I feel most comfortable is in a place where there are men and women, straights, gays and bisexuals, whites, blacks, and any other ethnicity" (218).[12]

For most of the novel, therefore, it is not as much through her actions as through her metadiegetic comments to the readers of the novel and her conversations with her friends—especially the lesbian Pilar, the gay couple Juan and Diego, and the straight man, Pedro—that she hashes out her beliefs regarding what she believes to be the important issues in the lives of contemporary lesbians. These include the literary style of lesbian literature, the continued marginalization of gay/lesbian culture vis-à-vis Spanish society as a whole, and the relative invisibility of women in the *ambiente*. She also addresses straight people's misperceptions of lesbians, which suggests that the implied author's intended readers extend beyond the gay ghetto to the mainstream hetero world.

The narrator's crossover ambitions are explicitly stated at the beginning of the text, where she complains about the ghettoization of lesbian culture even within the quintessentially feminine genre of chick lit and film. Why, she asks, are heterosexual experiences presented as universal, and lesbian ones considered of interest only to lesbians and *progres* (the Spanish equivalent of "liberals")? The problem, she concludes, is at least partly a consequence of the state of lesbian literature itself:

Then we have the subject of so-called lesbian literature. If there's anything that bugs the shit of me about those stories of lesbians, it's their deadly seriousness. I mean that you pick up any of those little books by Sapphic imitators of Corín Tellado and what do you find? Stories of loves that are suffered, returned or not, with a happy ending or without one, with a protagonist who is one of those drop-dead gorgeous girls who has a great job and a bank account that allows her to take constant trips to bucolic spots with her girlfriend of the moment, another drop-dead gorgeous girl with a liberal profession, where they make love for hours and hours, languid hours, tender hours, pleasant hours filled with sublime orgasms, cosmic ones, that raise their spiritual consciousness and bind them until infinity and beyond ... Because that's another thing: lesbians don't fuck. No, ma'am, you're wrong about that. Lesbians make love. Always. Gays fuck. Heteros practice coitus. Animals copulate. And lesbians? Lesbians make love. Suuuure. (22–23)[13]

The novel goes on to prove that this view of lesbian literature and sexuality is entirely erroneous. Much like Lola Van Guardia's *Con pedigree* in Barcelona, Morán leads us through the *lugares de ligue* (pickup spots) and *ambiente* (queer space) of Chueca (the bars Escape, Truco, Nike; the café Colby; the restaurant Momo's; Gay/Lesbian Collectives) and Lavapiés (La Lupe, Medea) with humor and irony as her protagonist, Ruth, looks for sex, not love.

The real literary icon for Ruth, however, is not a novel of the *ambiente*, but Helen Fielding's *Bridget Jones's Diary* (1996), the topic of several pages of the "Preámbulo." Like the British novel, *A por todas* takes place over the course of a year, following Ruth's romantic adventures in the big city with her loyal friends. She seems to have an eye toward a franchise and movie options, given the style of the exposition, which often seems like an overwritten film script, or, better yet, a minute description of a movie scene: "I drop my purse on the sofa and enter the kitchen looking for a Coke. I take a sip and put it on the coffee table while I start undressing and enter my bedroom. I end up wearing only an old T-shirt and I come out into the living room where I light a cigarette and continue drinking from the can of Coke" (54).[14]

Despite these normalizing pretensions, the novel, like Ruth herself, ends up dealing rather explicitly with lesbian and gay political issues. The characters in this novel participate in the gay/lesbian (no mention of transsexuals, bisexuals, or queers) collectives GYLA (Gays and Lesbians in Action) and GYLIS (Gays and Lesbians for Social Equality), as volunteers or employees, although they often disagree with the organizations' philosophy and objectives. We come to learn that Ruth had been quite politically active when she first came out, but became disillusioned by the collectives' poor organization and the increasing marginalization of women. When the novel begins, GYLA and GYLIS have become so oriented toward gay men that they have curtailed lesbian activities with the claim that such events lose money and exclude men, and, instead they have organized "inclusive" tours of the gay saunas and dark rooms (which, by definition, exclude women). They have also just received a large grant from the government for a visibility campaign, a detail that disappears from view during the many chapters detailing Ruth's sexual and romantic adventures. It is crucial information, however: when Ruth finally remembers it months later, she asks her friend Diego, who works for GYLA, what has happened to that campaign. This, along with irregularities that Diego has noticed in the organization's payment of its employees, leads the group of friends to investigate the mystery Nancy Drew–style. They find that the all-male leaders of GYLA and GYLIS, who have made much in the press of their ideological differences and personal enmity, are actually colluding in a fraud scheme, designed to finance an all-male gay resort in Panama. Our heroes denounce them just before the Pride celebration of lesbian and gay marriage, and, although GYLA and GYLIS still appear as the event's sponsors, they are officially represented in the manifestation by a woman, a transsexual, and a gay man, none of whom was involved in the fraud scheme. The indictment in the text is not directed at gay men per se, but at the continued sexism of society, as well as at organizations that have inordinate power and symbolic capital in the community, and in which overlapping political, cultural, and economic interests have led to corruption.[15]

The action culminates in the Pride celebration of gay marriage, the notice that Ruth's ex, Olga, has given birth to a daughter (with her lesbian partner) named after Ruth, the formation of a separate lesbian political organization, and the possibility that Ruth has found true love. There are hints of the heteronormative family in the search for monogamy, and in the case of Ruth's ex, parenthood, but they are balanced by the more colloquial connotation of "family" in LGBTQ parlance as a broad web of queer support. What is more, the actions and language of the characters defy traditional gender identities, even if their sexual practices could not be defined as queer. Clearly, unlike the other two novels analyzed in this chapter, *A por todas* is a romp, more concerned with the love and sex lives of relatively frivolous twenty- to thirty-somethings in the Madrid scene than with the threat of violent abuse from society or the state, in the past or the present. The novel resists the marriage/adoption agenda of the major lesbian/gay collectives without disparaging it, as it aspires to a postpolitical queer existence, a reality in which queer people are not marginalized in culture or society. The author's aesthetic choices, therefore, are not entirely apolitical, nor is the accented individualism of the characters, who, nonetheless, manage to work together to combat corruption and change the order of things.

In their 2007 article "The Psychological World of the Gay Teenager: Social Change, Narrative, and 'Normality,'" Bertram J. Cohler and Phillip L. Hammack provide a psychological account of the narratives of homosexuality that aptly describe the disparity between the paradigms of politics and lesbian literature I have described in this chapter. As they explain, technological changes (Internet, e-mail, chats) and a greater social acceptance of diverse sexualities have produced a concomitant modification of narratives about sexual identity:

> The first narrative, which we term the *narrative of struggle and success,* depicts gay youth as the victims of harassment and internalized homophobia, accompanied by serious mental health problems such as anxiety, depression, and suicidal ideation. But this narrative also suggests success in spite of struggle, revealing the process of gay identity development, realized through social practice in the larger gay and lesbian culture (e.g., Herdt and Boxer, 1996), as a triumphant model of resilience in a heterosexist world. The second narrative, the *narrative of emancipation,* reveals the increasing fluidity in self-labeling among youth with same-sex desire, depathologizes the experience of sexual identity development among these youth, emphasizes the manner in which sexual minority youth cope with issues of minority stress . . . , and extends the concept of normality . . . to the study of sexual minority youth. We suggest that these two narratives reflect particular historical moments

in the cultural construction of homosexuality over the post-war period and into the present time. (49)

In the 2005 "Visible" panel, Hernández and Gimeno emphasized the first model, exemplified by the "Salir del armario" series, in which the protagonists, who conform to images of the good woman and mother, would prefer to legitimize their union. The result is that these lesbian romance novels often incarnate the same kinds of contradictory messages about lesbians and women in general generated by the marriage debate: they normalize homosexuality by presenting it as virtually identical to heterosexuality—the only difference being the biological sex of the people in relationships—but they do not perform a critique of heteronormativity itself, including the violence and inequity that accompany it, and they do not radically change the status or representation of women in Spanish society. *Amores prohibidos* also depathologizes lesbianism for the reader at the same time that it represents the violent consequences of the ways in which society continues to pathologize it, and so it is a text that argues for emancipation through pedagogy that addresses the perils of hate speech. In contrast to these two novels, the popular lesbian fiction currently favored by the young reading public responds to Cohler and Hammack's second model, in which lesbian and gay youth see themselves as normal and are thus able to narrate their lives without reference to models of pathology. The mainstream aspirations of *A por todas* thus reflect the revolutionary changes in the social acceptance of nonheteronormative sexual and emotional relations in Spain, which have impacted the market for lesbian-themed literature. Taken together, then, these narratives, with their disparate political goals and aesthetic models, could be seen as the voices of the different generations of activists that coexisted in queer Madrid in the years leading up to the landmark legislation regarding lesbian and gay marriage and adoption rights.

· CONCLUSION ·

Toward Lesbian Visibility

THIS BOOK has explored the various constitutions of lesbian literary identities within the construction of the geographic and symbolic space of Chueca from the end of the *movida* in the late 1980s until the Pride celebration of gay/lesbian marriage in 2005. I have argued that the changes in the barrio have responded to political and economic processes that have dramatically impacted the degree and the forms of lesbian visibility. To the extent that lesbianism was visible at all during the *movida*, it was either as sexual entertainment, *morbo*, or as an image refracted through the gay transvestite, and never quite as sexy. The transformation of Chueca from one of the *movida*'s stomping grounds to a gay village in the 1990s, however, created a safe space that allowed lesbians to become more visible with fewer risks. At the same time, the process of globalization that took hold in that decade brought with it a greater consumerism that favored gay men with money over other sexual minorities, a trend signaled by the predominance of businesses catering to men. The gender prejudices of that globalized market—which included the market for books, in an increasingly commercial business—also limited the literary choices for lesbians, who were perceived as less wealthy, and perhaps less cultured, than their gay counterparts.

The identity politics of the lesbian book business responded to this prejudice in several ways. The most surprising of these were the decisions to publish fewer books with lesbian themes in comparison to gay-themed books and to design the gay/lesbian bookstore to appeal more directly to gay male consumers, leaving women in a spatial ghetto, and their sexuality hidden in the basement. The literary representations of lesbians in lesbian literature also remained tied to the identity narrative of the activists who founded Berkana and Egales—what Bertram J. Cohler and Phillip L. Hammack call the *"narrative of struggle and success"* (49)—which found expression particularly in the latter's "Salir del armario" series.

By the end of the 1990s, however, we could note a monumental shift in all of these factors, which responded not only to economic changes throughout the country, but also to a greater social acceptance of homosexuality and a rejection of the violent forms of heterosexism. In literature this meant that lesbians could appear in literature without being pathologized and without necessarily meeting a tragic end. Nonetheless, they still risked reification and domestication through the media image of *lesbian chic,* particularly in advertising directed at straight men and in literature by straight women. Significantly, in this decade traditional identity politics became a target of ironic texts by lesbians, led by Isabel Franc, who also unshackled lesbian sexuality from conventional concepts of female passivity and love. The texts that continued her postmodern style offered not a narrative of struggle and success, but a *narrative of emancipation* (Cohler and Hammack, 49) that reflected the sensibility of writers and readers in the age of the Internet, gender construction, AIDS, massive immigration, and postcolonial sensibilities.[1]

My study ends in 2005, a year that marks a constitutional watershed in Spain. In the remaining pages, I would like to consider the impact that recent legislation on marriage, adoption, domestic violence, and the corporal punishment of children is likely to have on the pedagogy regarding lesbians and gays in two spaces that are often ignored in studies of Spanish literature: the school and the family.

The 2005 legalization of gay marriage and adoption rights in Spain and the pro-traditional family protest rally organized by the Catholic church and the conservative political party, the PP (Partido Popular [Popular Party]), highlighted a number of contradictions, ironies, and omissions regarding childhood, parenthood, gender, and sexuality. The debate between these groups, in effect, represented a battle over the separation of church and state in the definition of the family and the private realm that had profound implications for the rights of women and children in general, as well as LGBTQ adults and children.

The focus of both groups rested primarily on gay men, who were depicted in the sympathetic press as "normal" partners eager to be joined in marriage and begin a family by adopting children, and, in the opposition, as sexually frenetic deviants (usually through selective press photos of gay pride celebrations), or, at best, as unnatural marital partners who would soil the sanctity of marriage, as defined by the church, and, conservatives later argued, by the Constitution, which was represented as a text as immutable as the Bible.

The years leading up to 2005, of course, were difficult ones for the church itself, faced with multitudinous accusations of sexual abuse of young boys and, what is often forgotten, girls.[2] The idealized public image of "traditional" families based on Catholic principles was also tarnished in 2005, when the Spanish state established a special branch of the judiciary dedicated solely to cases of domestic violence, now known as "violencia machista," in response to a law passed in December 2004 that defined such violence as a continued expression of gender inequality.[3] Furthermore, a UN and EU commission published a report shortly after Pride 2005 condemning Spain as one of the few European nations that still practiced the corporal punishment of children in homes and schools ("El Consejo de Ministros"), which had long been defended as a necessary recourse for maintaining authority and preserving the structure of the family and the state.[4]

Gay marriage and domestic violence legislation, it has been argued, are responses to the violent hegemony of straight males in Spanish society, which both reflects the inequalities inherent in the family structure itself and represents a physical expression of the unequal power status of the masculine and the feminine, men and women, adults and children. It is significant, then, that in the conservative Spanish press, particularly the daily *ABC*, the gay marriage issue invoked worries about the welfare of both children and a society based on the moral Christian principles that govern the traditional family, at the same time that it overshadowed concerns about sexual abuse in the church, child abuse, and domestic violence. Unfortunately, gay marriage and pride celebrations also largely reinforced male hegemony in this instance;[5] the most visible legal issue for women during summer 2005 was domestic violence, not lesbian marriage, given that most coverage of gay marriage featured male couples. Nonetheless, it is clear that these matters are linked, and that the legislation benefited not only gay men and lesbians, but also women and children in general, at the same time that it reinforced moves by the PSOE (Partido Socialista Obrero Español [Spanish Socialist Workers' Party]) government to separate matters of church and state, which the conservative PP has strongly and consistently opposed.

The PP concepts of family, church, and state echo the beliefs fomented by Francisco Franco's dictatorship. The prejudice against homosexual parents, for example, remits to biological and religious explanations for the gendered division of labor in the traditional family, according to which women should be responsible for child rearing and other domestic work because they are biologically inclined to it and thus more suited for it, whereas men are more equipped to work in the public sphere. The idea that a normal family must have parents of the opposite sex likewise confirms the concept that the genders complement one another, which has obvious implications for gender equality in other spheres of public and private life, including employment and sexuality. According to this biological/religious interpretation of gender, male promiscuity corresponds to the procreative mandate of sexual reproduction, as does female passivity: the man sows his seed broadly, and the woman stays put to nurture the offspring.[6] This view also explains why gay men might be permitted to fit into a certain model of "discreetly promiscuous" Mediterranean masculinity, but lesbians cannot fit into any model of acceptable femininity: their sexual activity, even with a single partner, is not essentially procreative and passive, but, in common parlance, "una guarrada" (sluttiness). These were the same notions invoked during the Franco regime to justify laws forbidding women to work outside the home after they were married and to prolong their minority to the age of twenty-five, or until they married.

The discussion of "family values" also focused on the well-being of children, whose physical and emotional health, it was claimed, is at risk in families with homosexual parents. Again, conservatives invoked religious/biological concepts of sexual normality versus perversity, as well as biological definitions of parental roles, in order to promote their definition of family. They argued, for example, that gay adults are mentally ill, and thus unsuited to child rearing, that the supposed sexual promiscuity of (all) gay men puts children at risk for neglect or abuse, that homosexual relations are unnatural and thus a poor model for children, or that gay families will necessarily produce gay children.[7] Of course, domestic violence legislation and lawsuits against priests have corroborated the idea that openly gay men are not responsible for most sexual and physical abuses of children because those acts are perpetrated largely by men in traditional homes and by priests in the Catholic church, the primary defenders of "family values." The gay adults who now wish to marry and raise children, likewise, were brought up in traditional heterosexual families, not gay ones. What is more, it is likely that lesbian couples, who do not necessarily need to adopt children, have raised families without the knowledge of the state, meaning that the state does not have absolute control over this issue.

The allegations made by the PP's expert witness during the Senate debates over gay adoption that gay men and lesbians are mentally instable were thoroughly vilified at the moment they appeared and require no further comment.

The most effective path of resistance to the parental rights of gay men and lesbians combined rhetorical ploys with biological/religious arguments. For example, in denying a 2004 petition by lesbian couples for equal recognition as mothers of the biological child of one of them, the "Resolución de la Dirección General de Registros y del Notariado" (RDGRN, Resolution of the General Directorship of Registry and Notaries), specified that:

> Even accepting the unquestionable principle that homosexual couples should not be the objects of discrimination, the qualities attributed to them cannot reach the extreme that maternity should be doubly given to the woman who gave birth and her steady companion, as a result of the mere declaration of such on the part of the interested female parties. Maternity is unique in our Law and is determined by nature.... The principle of biological veracity that inspires our Order in questions of parenthood categorically denies that once maternity, which is determined by childbirth, has been established, another claim of maternity on the part of another woman can be recognized. (quoted in Rodríguez Chacón, 34)[8]

The decree clung to a biological definition of *maternity* that does not correspond to the broad affective relationship and responsibilities of *motherhood*, which heterosexual adoptive mothers, for example, are allowed to assume to the same degree as biological ones, a fact recognized by laws regarding adoption.

This ideological control of mothering by the Right exemplifies the importance of the changes in the marriage code for all Spanish women, to the degree that they eliminated gender role distinctions within the marriage institution itself. The new amendment of article 66 of the Civil Marriage Code, for example, specified that "both members of the couple are equal in rights and responsibilities" (quoted in ibid., 224),[9] and article 68 now reads: "Both partners are obliged to live together, be faithful to one another and support one another. They should also share responsibility for the home and for the care and attention of parents, children, and other people for whom they have assumed responsiblity" (ibid., 229).[10] This increased gender parity is reflected in the workplace as well, where Spanish women now have access to many of the same career opportunities as men, even in the realm of politics. As Marta Fagés pointed out in *Amores prohibidos*, language is an important tool.

Heterosexual couples, unfortunately, strongly opposed the elimination of gendered terms describing the family ("marido y mujer" [man and wife]; "padre y madre" [father and mother]) from the Constitution. This rhetorical parsing of parenthood had the sole purpose of reinforcing the biological basis of male hegemony in the family structure.[11] The linguistic solution that was finally reached reaffirmed inequality by allowing heterosexual parents to use the terms "man" and "wife," "mother" and "father," while gay and lesbian parents would use words entirely lacking that emotional charge: *cónyuges* (conjugal partners), and *progenitor/a* (male or female progenitor) (M. J. P-B.). I should point out that not all LGBTQ Spaniards approve of the marriage legislation, to the extent that it upholds the primacy of the family unit comprised of parents and children over other forms of family and sexual relations.[12]

The continued physical, psychological, and verbal violence that women face remains problematic, however, as does the threat that the parity they have achieved, particularly during the PSOE government of José Luis Rodríguez Zapatero, could be rescinded if the PP returned to power.[13] It is for this reason that I turn now to the legislation regarding gender violence, which also impacts the definition of the family in terms of the relationship between parents and children. The law penalizing gender violence, "Ley Orgánica 1/2004: Medidas de Protección Integral contra la Violencia de Género" (Organic law 1/2004: Measures for integral protection from gender violence), which was approved on December 28, 2004, and implemented in 2005, asserted explicitly that gender violence was not an issue limited to the private realm dominated by the man's discretion, but rather an extension of a society-wide discrimination against women:

> Gender violence is not a problem that affects the private sphere. On the contrary, it is the most brutal symbol of the inequality that exists in our society. It is a type of violence directed at women for the mere reason that they are women, and thus considered by the aggressors to be lacking in the same minimum rights of liberty, respect, and decision-making ability. ("Ley Orgánica," 42166)[14]

The law goes on to recognize that gender violence also affects children: "Situations of violence toward women also affect the minors in the family setting, who are direct or indirect victims of that violence" ("Ley Orgánica" 42167).[15] The recognition that violence against children violated their rights and negatively impacted their emotional development also led to legislation in 2006 to protect children from corporal punishment in the home and the school.[16] It is worth noting that conservatives also resisted this measure, claiming that it would negatively impact the family and the state by eroding parental authority (specifically, the father's authority) and social order.[17] Given that one of the behaviors that parents and schools have traditionally sought to correct was homosexuality, the measure provides significant protection for queer children.

It is still too early to determine what will be the impact of these measures, which significantly restructure the legal distinctions regarding the rights of people of different genders and ages within the family, even as they move the jurisdiction for defining marriage and parenthood from the church to the state. To the degree that the state determines pedagogical imperatives in public schools, we can expect those institutions to comply with these new definitions in designing the curriculum. Indeed, a textbook addressing questions of adolescent sexuality has appeared (*Herramientas para combatir el "bullying" homofóbico* [Tools for fighting homophobic bullying]) by Raquel Platero Méndez and Emilio Gómez Ceto, and the theme of the 2009 pride march was "Schools without Closets." Given the importance of the home in identity formation, however, real change will also require modifications to children's literature, a process that has already begun with the publication of several texts, for example: *Las bodas reales* (The real royal weddings) by Ana Rossetti, illustrated by Jorge Artajo; *El secreto de las familias* (Family secret) by Carlos de la Cruz and Antonio Acebal; *Una más en la familia* (One more in the family) by Josep Carles Laínez, illustrated by Juan Arocas; *¿De quién me enamoraré?* (Who will I fall in love with?) by Wieland Pena, illustrated by Roberto Maján; and *¡Nos gustamos!* (We like each other!) by Juanolo.

How these changes will manifest themselves in literature for adults remains to be seen. Odisea and Egales have continued to publish gay and lesbian literature, along the lines I have described in this book. Already in 2003, however, a sophisticated lesbian book, Irene Jiménez's *El placer de la Y: Diez historias en torno a Marguerite Yourcenar* (The pleasure of the Y: Ten stories based on Marguerite Yourcenar), appeared in a press not dedicated solely to gay and lesbian literature, ElCobre, which specializes in literature from "other cultures."[18] Some poets have also declared themselves openly bisexual (Ruth Toledano) or lesbian (Andrea Luca). Perhaps the social and political changes I have described will continue to impact the realm of high culture, making it unnecessary for women to remain in the land that Ana Rossetti and Jorge Artajo portray as the "armarios oscuros" (dark closets) *(Las bodas reales)*, and to become at last and truly "visibles," in tune with the theme of the 2008 gay pride celebration, which played on the phonetic similarity between the "v" and the "b" in Spanish: "Lesbianas: Con V de Visibles" (Lesbians: Spelled with a V for Visible). I close with the hope that "visibility" will also begin to include people of other races, a significant absence in lesbian literature, but one that appeared explicitly in the 2009 pride festivities, in the form of a march protesting Spanish immigration laws, with the slogan, "Con fronteras no hay orgullo" (Where there are borders, there is no pride).

Acknowledgments

THIS BOOK is the product of years of dialogue not only with a variety of written texts, but also, and most importantly, with colleagues, friends, family, activists, and artists.

First, and above all, I thank Arturo Arias, my *muso*, my critic, my ally, my love, and my infallible encyclopedia. With Arturo, all is possible.

I completed much of this research during my years at the University of California, Irvine, and I am thankful for the research support I received there from the School of Humanities. Also, for the colloquiums and bag-lunch research talks organized by the faculty of Women's Studies, I thank Inderpal Grewal, Jenny Terry, Kavita Philip, and Laura Kang. This book was shaped by conversations with my most valued interlocutors at UCI: Ana Paula Ferreira, Susan Jarratt, Carrie Noland, and Gabriele Schwab. Thanks also to my UCI graduate students, particularly Gary Atwood, Paul Cahill, Debra Faszer-McMahon, and Michael Harrison.

The Southern California Peninsularists were an invaluable sounding board, particularly (and memorably) for chapter 5. I am most grateful for the generous suggestions and support from my cherished colleagues from that group, Robert Ellis, Roberta Johnson, Mary Coffey, and Silvia Bermúdez. Maite Zubiaurre invited me to present some of this material at the University of Southern California, where I met many wonderful colleagues, among them Gabriel Giorgi and Sofía Ruiz Alfaro. To Sofía, special thanks for her complicity and marvelous sense of humor.

This book builds on the work of many other distinguished scholars (many of them dear friends), including but not limited to Debra Castillo, Elena Castro, Jackie Collins, Brad Epps, Tina Escaja, Amy Kaminsky, Jo Labanyi, Cristina Moreiras Menor, Gema Pérez-Sánchez, Inma Pertusa, Ileana Rodríguez, Dereka Rushbrook, Joana Sabadell, Doris Sommer, Noël Valis, and Nancy Vosburg.

It is safe to say that UCI helped me begin this research but the University of Texas at Austin helped me finish it. Thank you to Nicolas Shumway for bringing me to the University of Texas, where I have been privileged to work with such inspiring young colleagues as Niyi Afolabi, Jossianna Arroyo-Martínez, Héctor Domínguez Ruvalcaba, Gabriela Polit-Dueñas, and Sonia Roncador. My heartfelt gratitude to the members of the Modern European Studies Reading Group (Katie Arens, Mia Carter, Sabine Hake, and Tracie Matysik) for their generously critical reading of the first two chapters of the original manuscript. Thanks also to participants in the UT Lozano Long Conference "Contested Modernities," particularly Boaventura de Sousa Santos, Michael Hansard, Agustín Lao, and Catherine Walsh, for intellectual inspiration.

The readers and editors of the University of Minnesota Press provided invaluable feedback and suggestions. Special thanks to Richard Morrison for sending me inspiring reading and waiting patiently for the manuscript while I was associate dean at UCI, and to Adam Brunner for his unflagging support and constructive advice.

This book would not have been possible without my interlocutors in Spain. Ana Rossetti has been unstintingly generous with her time and conversations during the fifteen years we have known each other. Through her, I met some of the authors who appear in this text, including Leopoldo Alas, Noni Benegas, and Mario Merlino. Thanks to Mili Hernández for agreeing to speak with me and for putting me in contact with Julia Cela. I am grateful to Raquel Platero for her critical eye, insightful mind, and prolific pen, and to Isabel Franc for her brilliant humor. And to my many friends in the *ambiente* who assisted with fieldwork (Ana, Jennifer, Laura, María, Belén, Cristina, Churri, Maribel, Carolina, Esther, Frankie, Myriam, Reggie, and Charo): un beso. Gracias, chicas.

Finally, to my loving, feminist sons, Ben and Matt: love you beyond the moon and the stars and all the planets.

Notes

Preface

Unless otherwise noted, all translations of Spanish-language material in this volume are my own.

1. The organizers estimated attendance at two million people; the police claimed there were 95,000; and the daily newspaper *El País* settled on "more than 250,000" ("Una multitudinaria," 1).
2. These slogans would be characterized in the conservative newspaper *ABC*, in the headline, as "Vítores a Zapatero y ataques al PP y a la iglesia en la marcha de Orgullo Gay" (Hurrahs for Zapatero and attacks on the Popular Party and the church in the Gay Pride march).
3. "No estamos legislando para gentes remotas. Estamos ampliando las oportunidades de felicidad para nuestros vecinos, compañeros de trabajo, amigos y familiares. Y a la vez estamos construyendo un país más decente. Porque una sociedad decente es aquella que no humilla a sus miembros" (We are not legislating for remote peoples. We are expanding the opportunities for happiness among our neighbors, workmates, friends, and family. And at the same time, we are constructing a more decent state. Because a decent society is one that does not humiliate its members) ("Las parejas," 1).
4. The park is now infamous for prostitution, including trans prostitution, but one of the public swimming pools has been a cruising spot for decades.
5. The second Visible festival in 2006 would celebrate "GLT" culture. The omissions in the acronym and the order of the letters are, I believe, significant, especially at this late date, since they imply the continued hegemony of men, a tacit rejection of bisexuality, and a resistance to queer politics and identities. In effect, although the major collectives housed in Madrid (COGAM and FELGTB) have progressively added transsexuals and bisexuals to their names, if not their acronyms, neither includes queers. I discuss these organizations further in chapter 6.
6. For reasons of consistency, I will use the acronym "LGBTQ" as my own ideal throughout this book, except with the publishers and bookstores that emphasize gay and lesbian identities, in that order.

1. A Brief History of Chueca and Madrid's Queer Space

1. Founded in 1938, but inactive during the Franco dictatorship (1939–75), ONCE was revitalized in the 1980s, under the PSOE, the socialist government, which granted it the right to conduct a national lottery to raise funds. The blind ceased to be invisible but were initially seen largely in connection with the sale of lottery tickets. The success of this operation allowed ONCE to diversify its economic holdings, so that, even though it continues to operate the lottery, it is financially independent. The organization was originally dedicated only to the blind, but, through the ONCE foundation, it expanded its activities to promote solidarity between the blind and other disabled people in Spain in 1988, and it continues to exert political influence in an effort to improve accessibility for disabled people in Spain.

2. It was not always clear that Madrid would remain the capital, but, as Julius Ruiz explains, "It seems that the eventual decision to keep Madrid as Spain's capital was based on its imperial past. However, this decision only meant that increased importance was attached to the ideological priority of purging Madrid of the 'decadence' that made the 'Red revolution' and the murder of 'tens of thousands' possible. As Franco—in his first visit to Madrid since the end of the civil war—warned in his Victory Day Parade speech on May 19: 'People of Madrid, examine your conscience. Do you believe that without your past decadence you would have suffered Red rule? . . . I assure you that . . . the triumph of the Anti-Spanish revolution was possible due to the passivity of many Spaniards'" (49).

3. As Borja Casani put it: "Between 1975 and 1985, everyone came to Spain, just as, until recently, they used to go to Hungary or Poland. People were following the Spanish case as a very special example, perhaps because it was at the time a worldwide experiment. How do you go from a totalitarian regime to a happy and contented democracy? Journalists came to see how it had been accomplished. And it was stupendous for the government, for politics, and for the country, that we not only had a fabulous, charming, superpolite and democratic king, and a government run by young people between thirty-five and forty years of age, but also an extraordinary cultural movement" (quoted in Gallero, 14–15).

4. The critiques of these activists echo the work of David Bell and Jon Binnie on sexual citizenship in the globalized neoliberal city. Binnie defines gay villages as "sites of resistance against the oppressive structures of heterosexual society" ("Quartering Sexualities," 164), but he notes that they "have not uniformly [been] used by all sexual dissidents. Many—not only Marxists and lesbian feminists—have long disidentified with the commercialism of such venues and their celebration of artifice, conspicuous consumption and superficiality" (ibid.). For that reason, Bell and Binnie explain, the international trend toward the creation and promotion of gay spaces "can be read as an instance of 'the new homonormativ-

ity', producing a global repertoire of themed gay villages, as cities throughout the world weave commodified gay space into their promotional campaigns" (1808). Dissenters to the excessive consumerism and homogeneity of the gay village constitute the queer counterpublic (Binnie, "Quartering Sexualities," 167). Still, even these spaces perform a kind of exclusion that troubles their designation as queer utopias: "While they are not bounded, these spaces exclude on the basis of gender, so how truly queer are they? How can they be seen as 'more queer' given that they are so clearly gendered?" (ibid.).

5. I do not mean to imply that the majority of immigrants in Spain are dedicated to these activities or that only immigrants perform these roles, but simply that these are the most visible immigrant men in Chueca establishments.

6. This resignification of the street recalls the *movida*, which was taken to task for "betraying" the traditional political objectives (and hierarchies) typical of the political opposition to Franco and eventually selling out, becoming the image that the PSOE government exported as the new Spain. In much the same tone, queer lesbians have been criticized for rejecting second-generation lesbian feminism, and, as noted in the preceding paragraph, for selling out to consumerist interests.

2. Lesbian Literary Identities in the Madrid Book Business

1. This type of transformation in gay literary culture is not exclusive to Spain, of course. Suzanna Danuta Walters also comments on the phenomenon in her book *All the Rage: The Story of Gay Visibility in America*: "When I came out in Philadelphia in the late '70's, the gay bookstore, along with the gay bar, were my places of reference and often my places of reverence as well. Going to the bookstore seemed less like an act of financial support than a search for a place of affirmation and information. . . . Now, as it becomes increasingly hard to discern the difference between buying gay and being gay, the gay entrepreneur emerges as a figure to be reckoned with and gay bookstores face an increasingly uncertain future" (273). Walters describes the loss of these noncommercial functions of the bookstores and, indeed, of the bookstores themselves, with a melancholy similar to that I noted in an article regarding the disappearance of small Spanish bookstores that were sites of resistance under Franco ("Globalization").

2. It is ironic that Mili Hernández has criticized the Librería Mujeres for a similar move toward merchandising feminist T-shirts, mugs, music, and so on, and for having received subsidies from the state (personal interview, July 2000).

In a 1998 interview published in *El País*, Begoña Aguirre interviews Alonso Ramírez, a thirty-nine-year-old Madrid lawyer and director of Servi G, the first multiservice network of "pink businesses." According to Ramírez, Servi G was established because "We want to show that gays don't only know about businesses dedicated to leisure. It's a way to affirm the homosexual twenty-four hours a day and not only during the time dedicated to love and sex." Although the enterprise could be seen to reinforce the closet, Ramírez believes the opposite to be true: "There are a lot of people who live a double life, at night they're gay but at work they hide their preferences. We express them openly and this can eliminate stigmas." He goes on to insist that the network will change the image that the public at large has of the gay community from a purely sexual one into a positive image of the model citizen.

3. The bookstore El Cobertizo in Valencia, for example, closed its doors in April 2004, after seven years in business.

4. Alberto Mira also comments on this phenomenon in *Para entendernos* (Let's understand each other [or Let's come out], 155 and 509–10).

5. The Sonrisa Vertical series at Tusquets Editores published and gave prize money to the winner in the annual contest of El Premio Sonrisa Vertical. Although that series is not dedicated to gay and lesbian fiction, it has included such texts as Luis Antonio de Villena's *El mal mundo* (The Bad World, 1999) and Isabel Franc's *Entre todas las mujeres* (1992), the first openly lesbian novel by a Spanish author. The annual prize was suspended in 2004, however, per the decision of its director Luis Carlos Berlanga. A spokesperson for Tusquets, Antonio López Lamadrid, explained in an *El País* article that the prize had not been awarded for the past two years owing to the poor quality of recent entrants and the lack of serious critical review accorded to previous winners. What is more, it was the view of Tusquets that erotic literature had become mainstream. The series will continue without the prize and with the addition of erotic works in translation ("Tusquets suspende el Premio La Sonrisa Vertical").

6. The FNAC itself was bought by in 1993 by Altus Finances, a subsidiary of government-owned Crédit Lyonnais, and Phenix, a property group owned by a French waterworks company, Générale des Eaux. It was resold in 1994 to the conglomerate PPR (Pinault-Printemps-Redoute). See "FNAC" in the Bibliography.

7. See also the article on this topic by Alejandro Herrero-Olaizola.

8. Personal interview, July 1999. The book does include the following Spanish men, however: Luis Cernuda, Federico García Lorca, Salvador Dalí, Luis Antonio de Villena, Eduardo Mendicutti, Jaime Gil de Biedma, and Terenci Moix.

9. Pérez reportedly noted that "lesbian-themed books are hard to sell and they tend to maintain the same level of sales—usually very low—from the moment they appear on the market, without the increases in sales that we find with gay-themed books" ("La editorial Odisea").

10. One of the numerous events scheduled throughout Madrid to celebrate the gay marriage legislation at Pride 2005, "Visible" was advertised as a "dialogue of differences" aimed at creating a "common space for everyone." Almost all of these events, however, focused on the cultural production of gay men, with particular

attention to "queer" sexuality, male nudes, and transvestism, leaving lesbians and bisexual women as "invisible" as ever. This is not surprising, given the composition of the organizing committee, in which the only women were the political activists Mili Hernández and Beatriz Gimeno. This means that there was not a single woman from "high-culture" circles involved in organizing the First International Festival of LGTB Culture of Madrid. In contrast, the men on the organizing committee included such important artists, directors, and critics as Luis Antonio de Villena, Álvaro Pombo, Eduardo Mendicutti, Leopoldo Alas, Ventura Pons, and Guillermo Pérez Villalta.

11. Villena even commented on the absence of a bisexual roundtable and indicated his willingness to be included in that one as well, a comment that would not have been possible in the lesbian panel because, as Olga Viñuales has pointed out, bisexuality is explicitly rejected by the lesbian community: "bisexuality, despite its frequency, is perceived as a type of behavior that compromises authentic lesbian identity" (86). What is more, she argues, "bisexuality is classified simply as a sexual practice, and, as a result, it is considered promiscuous and associated with a contaminating life" (87). See also the discussion of bisexuality in Margaret Frohlich's *Framing the Margin: Nationality and Sexuality across Borders*.

12. *"Plumas"* has a specifically queer meaning in Spanish as well, as I will explain fully in the following chapter. Literally, it can mean "pens" or "feathers," but "tener pluma" means to be identifiably queer.

13. Because Franc's novels portray Barcelona, and not Madrid, I will not discuss them in depth here. For an analysis of those texts, see the articles by Jackie Collins, Silvia Rolle-Rissetto, and Nancy Vosburg in the bibliography.

14. See the following articles: "No todos los gays y lesbianas aplaudimos lo mismo," and "Mili Hernández y la morfina del poder." COGAM is the Gay, Lesbian, Bisexual, and Transexual Collective of Madrid.

3. The New Safita

1. Indeed, David Halperin states clearly in *Saint Foucault: Toward a Gay Hagiography* that "much of the impetus for Foucault's late work on *pratiques de soi* came from insights into the transformative potential of sex which he gained from his experiences in the bathhouses and S/M clubs of New York and San Francisco" (160). See also James Miller's *The Passion of Michel Foucault* (1993) and David Macey's *The Lives of Michel Foucault* (1993).

2. Ironically, Villena's own writing performs discursive critiques of identities.

3. See my article "Globalization, Publishing, and the Marketing of 'Hispanic' Identities."

4. Cristina Moreiras Menor defines this change as a shift "from the lettered national tradition to the visual international one" (*Cultura herida*, 199).

5. Fernando Villaamil also argues that heterosexist men maintain control, even while appearing to be tolerant, by dictating the terms of the discourse regarding homosexuality (22). Beatriz Gimeno makes a similar point regarding lesbianism and feminism (*Historia*, 203–24).

6. Garlinger notes that Monserrat Roig made a similar observation when discussing Bibi Andersen's performance as a transsexual: "Roig's image of Bibi focuses on how the transvestite body, only female in appearance, is completed by the unveiling of the penis. Creating a mirror in which men can view themselves and their own desires, Bibi's body offers up a Lacanian fantasy of having and being the phallus in one complete package. For Roig, who reiterates that Bibi was not born a woman, the penis continues to operate as the true object of desire, in spite of (or perhaps because of) the fact that her feminine appearance makes Bibi an object of desire for the mostly heterosexual male audience. Roig perceptively notes that transgenderism in this context functions as a masculine attempt to usurp a feminine space for other men. Her remarks are not so much directed at Andersen as at the audience, which only focuses on the penis, thus eliminating any identification with femininity: the masquerade falls by the wayside, and the intellectuals in the audience, implicitly all men in Roig's passage, can identify with Andersen now that she is once again a man" ("Sex Changes," 38).

7. Umbral apparently did not experience a similar desire for phallic women, or lesbians. As Aurelio Martín wrote in an article for *El País*, "Rosa Chacel critica con dureza a Umbral: La nonagenaria escritora le califica de 'cretino y verdadero imbécil'" (Rosa Chacel harshly criticizes Umbral: The ninety-year-old writer calls him a "cretin and a true imbecile"): "Francisco Umbral writes about Rosa Chacel in his latest book that she 'is a cross between a witch and Mary Poppins,'" and continues: "In the latest novels in Madrid by Rosa Chacel she shows a lot of love, too much, for the daughters of the portresses." He warns a friend of his, a journalist from San Sebastián, to "be careful of charming old women." The journalist, according to Umbral, confirmed to him after her interview with Chacel: "How right you were, Paco. The old woman hit on me." In other places, he says things like "Rosa Chacel is a dapper old woman, and she runs around with vague, evanescent poetesses like Clara Janés."

8. *Destape* literally means "nakedness," but historically it refers to the sexual permissiveness and full nudity in Spanish culture in the immediate post-Franco period.

9. José Enrique Monterde describes these films as follows: "But the ultimate expression of the *españolada* and possibly the most authentic example of the genre films can be found in the 'folkloric cinema,' situated pointedly in Andalusian settings, structured generally around the more or less flamenco-ish songs and dances inserted at the service of—or benefiting from the commercial pull of—the

great crooners of the moment, like Concha Piquer, Lola Flores, or Estrellita Castro" (238).

10. In an article on Jane Gallop's use of feminine costume in a gender performance for an academic conference, Debra Silverman explores the question of whether or not women can perform drag: "if all womanliness is worn as a disguise, how can we read Gallop's performance, as she herself identifies it, as drag? One way would be to discuss her reappropriation of the term 'drag' to counter the more problematic, heavily encoded notion of 'masquerade.' But what, then, does it mean to perform a masquerade and, through this performance, turn it into drag—the kind of free-play with gender identity that Butler's analysis connotes? The move from masquerade to drag makes a vital difference. Noting how Joan Crawford [in *Johnny Guitar*] camps up her anxiety, if we can call such an exhibition drag, we can begin to make sense of the ways this performance of gender mocks the fixed expectations of the male/female binary" (79).

11. Barbara Johnson makes this point in "Gender and Poetry: Charles Baudelaire and Marceline Desbordes-Valmore": "When men employ the rhetoric of self-torture, it is *read* as rhetoric. When women employ it, it is confession. Men are read rhetorically; women, literally. Yet within the poetic tradition, it is the rhetorical, not the literal, that is taken seriously.... When men have described love as an experience of fragmentation, wounding, or loss of psychic intactness and control, it has been read as an expression of 'The Nature of Desire.' When women have described something analogous, it has been read as an expression of 'What a Woman Wants.' Rhetoric, in other words, is a way of shifting the domain of a poem's meaning to a higher, less referential, more abstract and theoretical level. And this is done by universalizing, that is, by denying the presence of the sexual difference out of which the poem springs" (176).

12. This is the type of female drag Silverman describes: "For Gallop, a hyperbolic 'femme' constitutes a disunity between her inside and her outside which 'unconsciously' inflects her presentation. The audience must be clued to this disunity because it is not fully visible on the surface. In other words, in her femme suit, Gallop is another woman. Yet because its style hearkens to an outdated mode of femininity, the suit is clearly part of a costume, something that points to, even as it masks, a 'real' Gallop underneath it. Gallop must dress herself as the forties melodrama heroine in order to put on her show. She needs the suit to make the statement; her drag depends on it" (72).

13. "For while Patela's sex will not be disguised, or while it still imposes itself in disguise and makes the narrator at times almost giddy with exasperation and desire, Miguel/Milady's sex is another matter. It is Miguel/Milady who comes closest to resisting, blurring, or cutting the gender divide, though here too, as we shall see, the divide reasserts itself. Miguel/Milady fails to stay on the slash

and is all too successfully identified as, at bottom, a man" (Epps, "The Queer Case," 161).

14. "una serie de artículos con todo rigor y sin ninguna concesión a la curiosidad morbosa."

15. Valis agrees that Rossetti is penning camp: "What Rossetti, who is closely identified with the Movida of the late 1970s and early 1980s, 'camps up' in her novel is largely Francoist culture or its remnants, as parodied in the much diminished images and cultural objects of provincial, middle-class Spanish society" (59). What Valis omits is the gender component of this game. I will argue that Rossetti also evokes the gender implications of Spaniards' fascination with transvestites and transsexuals at the time of the transition.

16. "¿Le has visto tú por si acaso algún santo en su casa? ¿Una estampilla siquiera?"

"Bueno... tiene... ¡una Virgen!"

"¿Una Virgen? Me gustaría verla. ¿Y por qué sabes tú que es una Virgen? Será a lo mejor una de esas artistas, indecentes todas, vestidas de los tiempos antiguos."

"No es una foto... es una estatua así."

"Bien chica es. ¿Y por qué sabes tú que es una Virgen?"

"Porque tiene las manos así puestas, con un rosario, y es toda blanca, la cara y todo."

"Estará muerta."

"No, sino que cuando la mete en la alacena..."

"¿Mete a la Virgen en la alacena? ¿Con las habichuelas y el pimiento molido? ¡Qué falta de irreverencia [sic], por Dios!"

"No. Es que la mete en la alacena, porque como está oscuro... se pone verde ¡y brilla!"

"¡Ay! ¡Ay! ¡Que te quiere hipnotizar con el achaque de la Virgen!"

"¡Que no, abuela!... ¡Que es una Virgen de las que llevan ahora! ¡Que la ha traído ella... de Gibraltar, me parece!"

"¡¡¡De Gibraltar!!! ¡Cuidado como yo te vea entrar más en la casa esa!— (¡Zas!)—¡Menuda Virgen! ¡Menuda Virgen esa!—(¡Zas!)—¡Ni mirarla! ¿Te enteras? ¡Ni mirarla!—(¡Zas!) (¡Zas!)—Una Virgen que debe de ser ¡¡¡hasta protestante!!!"

17. "Venía el nieto y la vestía de azul. Venía la abuela y la vestía de rojo. El nieto le traía rosas. La abuela las quitaba y le ponía nardos. El nieto, blanco. La abuela, negro.

"Harto el nieto, se compró un candado, pero la abuela desenroscó los cáncamos e impuso su voluntad en los altares.

"No le quedó otro remedio que ponerle a la puerta cerradura.

"Dignamente la anciana soportó la afrenta pero cuidadosamente rumió la venganza y cautelosa acechó la oportunidad.

"Una noche, mientras eran evacuados al pasillo los innumerables floreros, tomó la fortaleza por sorpresa.

"En efecto: el nieto, inmóvil, con dos frágiles violeteros en sendas manos presenció cómo, rauda, su abuela se abalanzaba a la imagen, y que de un tirón le arrebataba el pañuelo, que se lo llevaba a la cara y que con gran estruendo vaciaba en él sus fosas nasales.

"'¡Ay!'—exclamó estupefacto. '¡Que me recuerdas los tiempos de la República!'"

18. "Sobrevino mi fin de carrera a causa de un cuaderno de ejercicios que olvidé abierto y la curiosidad de tía Teresa que lo leyó. . . . Montó en cólera hasta un extremo inconcebible y supurando santa ira por todos los poros de su piel, se abalanzó al teléfono y censuró agriamente, a la secretaria de la academia, semejante programa que incluía lenguas fuera de la jurisdicción de Roma. Y canceló mi matrícula con un: ¡¡¡Sinvergüenzas!!! Acto seguido se dirigió a la cocina, abrió el fogón, metió todo el material británico que encontró su mirada rapaz y le prendió fuego."

19. "los desnudos, enjabonados y, desde luego, en mejor forma que los de Signorelli."

20. "No te decepciones, que ahora viene lo mejor: la muchacha, pero apúntalo, era un castrado."

"¿Quée?"

"No te sobresaltes, querida: el número de castrados en el mundo es infinito."

"Me asombra tanta ligereza."

"¿Tú no? ¿No has echado alguna vez de menos cierto adminículo?"

"¿Yo?"

21. "O sea, que cualquiera puede estar castrado sin que se note."

22. Epps makes a similar point: "Though personages associated with the españolada may predominate, women, both real and fictional, from a variety of times, places, and positions, swirl together as so many models of womanliness and, by no small coincidence, of creativity. They are most clearly models for the transvestitic (male to female) characters who are central to the (female) narrator's endeavors as author, but they are also models for the narrator herself. Tellingly, the transvestites mediate the female models for the narrator in a way that complicates authority, authorship, authenticity, and nature. For all of these names, and others, conjure up an image of womanliness as spectacle, a flashy making up or making over, a masquerade, which in Joan Riviere's now classic essay involves anxiety over public (male) recognition. Said anxiety is coupled to the woman's supposed fear of retribution for having dared to claim a position of public equality and authority that, in Riviere's reading, entails the symbolic castration of men and the symbolic assumption, on the woman's part, of phallicism" ("The Queer Case," 159–60).

23. "Quisiera rogar a los lectores de *Plumas de España* que sean benevolentes

e intenten disculpar mi impericia, pues jamás abordé un proyecto tan ambicioso como éste que me ocupa.

"No es capricho ni frivolidad decidirme a presentar en forma novelada un asunto, no por cotidiano menos profundo y en cierto modo desconocido. Si yo fuese avezada en la materia e instruida, sin duda lograría con algún acertado e inspirado ensayo, acercaros a la íntima esencia que en toda acción se esconde, a la verdadera razón que palpita detrás de la más fútil conducta. Mas, pobre de mí, qué otra cosa puedo hacer, si sólo soy un testigo de la realidad que apenas consigue transcribirla.

"Así pues, ya que no me es dado penetrar en lo que la mente piensa y comprende, o el corazón siente, o la voluntad desea, me limitaré a enunciar lo que veo hacer y a repetir lo que escucho, sin adentrarme en juicios ni detenerme en emitir opiniones que puedan empañar la objetividad que pretendo....

"Deseo fervientemente que el relato que hoy inicio más que recrearos os haga reflexionar, porque debo advertir que en él no he consentido la menor intrusión a la fantasía, no he omitido, por otra parte, detalle, y no he tenido indulgencia con nada que pudiera deformar los hechos.

"Por tanto, todo los personajes que irán apareciendo no sólo son verídicos, son reales y no me importan las consecuencias que de esta afirmación se puedan derivar."

24. "Por qué se mete usted en esas vulgaridades que no le pegan nada. Usted sabe escribir como los ángeles, no sé por qué se ha empeñado en hacerlo como una perdida."

Él piensa en su necedad, que una tiene que llevarse toda la vida escribiéndole sonetos a los santos patrones, al puente, a la alameda, y "al niño que falta en mi cintura."

4. Lesbian-Themed Best Sellers and the Politics of Acceptance

1. Etxebarría's first novel, *Amor, curiosidad, prozac y dudas* (Love, curiosity, Prozac, and doubts, 1997) was successful, but it sold many more copies after *Beatriz* became a hit, and it has now been made into a motion picture, despite some controversy regarding possible plagiarism ("Me han hecho mucho daño, pero tengo la conciencia muy limpia" [They have done me a lot of harm, but I have a clear conscience], interview with Leandro Pérez Miguel, *El Mundo* [Internet edition] October 2, 2001).

2. Beatriz, the protagonist, does experiment with drugs (cocaine and Ecstasy), but it is her childhood friend, Mónica, who is the drug addict.

3. Walters also notes that, with this visibility comes a high incidence of antihomosexual violence and condemnation of homosexuality by religious groups.

The same dichotomy may be seen in Spain, where, despite greatly increased tolerance, many still believe that homosexuality is perverse.

4. "La mayoría llevaba el pelo corto y vestía pantalones, aunque también había alguna que otra disfrazada de *femme*, con falda de tubo y melena de leona. Si una se fijaba, acababa por comprender que existía una sutil demarcación de territorios. Las radicales resistentes ocupaban el flanco izquierdo, uniformadas en sus supuestos disfraces de hombres, fumando cigarrillos con gesto de estibador y ceño de mal genio, las piernas cruzadas una sobre la otra, tobillos sobre rodilla, en un gesto pretendidamente masculino. En la pista bailaban jovencitas más despreocupadas, que podían haber estado en una discoteca hetero sin llamar en absoluto la atención. Una rubia bastante llamativa se había permitido incluso ponerse un traje largo y coqueteaba con una pelirroja que se la comía con los ojos, mientras correspondía a la conversación de su amiga con una sucesión de carcajadas nerviosas y forzadas."

5. "Un dato gracioso que leí en un libro de texto: En la antigua Roma las bailarinas de Lesbos eran las preferidas para animar los banquetes. . . . Pero la fama erótica de las muchachas de Lesbos no se debía a sus habilidades acrobáticas, sino a otra especialidad: el sexo oral, que según los griegos había sido inventado en la isla. Una habilidad que las lesbianas se enseñaban las unas a las otras."

6. "Paseábamos cogidas de la mano y todos los peatones nos dirigían miradas de soslayo. En parte, porque les resultaba chocante la imagen de dos chicas paseando enlazadas. En parte, porque las dos éramos jóvenes y guapas y daba gusto mirarnos. Yo lo sabía y me sentía orgullosa."

7. "¡Fuera de aquí! ¡Guarras! ¡Basura! ¡Éste no es un sitio para vosotras!"

8. In 2008, however, Parrondo's homophobia was publicly punished by a radical lesbian happening, a lesbian *besada* (public kissing) in front of the *sidrería* (cider shop), an event that was covered in the daily *El País* on July 18.

9. The *"okupa"* movement, which began in Spain in the mid-1980s, proposes that abandoned buildings be occupied by squatters.

10. "Al incorporarse para apagar el cigarrillo de maría en el cenicero de la mesilla, la breve tela de la camiseta dejó al descubierto el tribal negro y redondo que Rosalía tenía tatuado en la zona lumbar. Irene no pudo resistirse a acariciarlo y lo fue recorriendo lentamente con la yema de sus dedos sin que Rosalía se moviera. Inclinada hacia ella, lo iba dibujando con su dedo corazón, deteniéndose voluptuosamente en cada punta angulosa del grabado como si ella misma lo estuviera tatuando en aquel momento.

—Es muy atrayente—dijo, reafirmando su gusto por aquella figura que la tenía como embrujada—. ¿Por qué te lo has tatuado?—inquirió—. Siempre hay una razón de peso para estos arrebatos que duran toda la vida. . . ."

—Pues verás—dijo Rosalía—. Me lo hice, precisamente, para conseguir que alguien lo acariciara del mismo modo que tú lo estás haciendo ahora....
—Los tatuajes suelen hacerse por amor—continúa hablándole Rosalía ya en un susurro mientras la besa reiteradamente en la boca—. Por amor o por despecho."

11. "Aquella noche aprendió Irene que el tacto metálico y frío de los piercings revitaliza en su contacto muchas zonas erógenas del cuerpo, que impacta cuando contacta con la piel y te sorprende su frialdad cuando te roza involuntariamente el metal; que absolutamente todo el vello que cubre tu cuerpo se rebela, voluptuoso, y se erotiza, alzándose en pie como un soldado en guardia pendiente del ataque."

12. "promesa de quedar otro día en casa parar contarle más detalles de la novela y ver juntas en dvd la película *Frida*, que no hace mucho acaban de estrenar. No le digo a Ana que ya la he visto un par de veces."

13. "En el semisótano que ocupa un pequeño restaurante sirio asentado en una transitada calle de Lavapiés, una mujer árabe de cabello anaranjado por la henna baila la danza del vientre para un reducido número de personas. Rosalía, entregada a sus movimientos y a la música, se deja llevar libremente por el ritmo sensual de la danza que mece las caderas de la egipcia de un modo inigualable....

La egipcia danza meciendo rítmicamente sus caderas y Rosalía no puede sacarse de la cabeza una escena de aquella noche en la que Irene, en un gesto invisible para los presentes, le pasaba sus uñas delicadamente por la base del cuello, mientras una preciosa muchacha libanesa de no más de diecisiete años bailaba al ritmo sensual de la música norteafricana. Sus ojos eran tan verdes y su piel tan morena, que resaltaban de su rostro tanto como los pañuelos multicolores que a modo de falda rodeaban sus caderas y de los que más tarde se despojaría de uno en uno, jaleada por los habituales en la sala.... No era un lugar de ambiente como los anteriores que habían visitado aquella noche, estaba lleno de extranjeros, árabes en su mayoría, pero la mujer danzó para ellas especialmente, dedicándoles el baile, deteniendo el tiempo delante de su mesa, como si deseara que su danza bautizara sensualmente la relación que acababa de comenzar."

14. "En apenas unos minutos surge en el fondo del café un coqueto escenario y en medio del local una pista de baile abre a la noche. Las luces cambian, el local se oscurece, la música se recicla al paso de una drag vampiresca, con grandes senos siliconados y un aparatoso vestuario cargado de espumillón plateado y lentejuelas brillantes, que cruza caminando a grandes zancadas el local, manteniendo difícilmente el equilibrio sobre unas inexpugnables botas de charol naranja, hasta situarse en el coqueto escenario que ha surgido en el fondo del café como por arte de magia. Junto a ella un policía bien parecido, fornido y correctamente uniformado, con un paquete excepcional en cuanto a proporciones se refiere, y una porra exageradamente grande que subraya más aún el contenido fálico de la es-

cena, intenta cachear a la drag queen mientras ésta grita y protesta desaforadamente, dejándose meter mano, escenificando una resistencia falsa ante los atentos espectadores. El policía insiste en solicitar su documentación y ante la negativa de la drag a entregársela, comienza a registrarla, toqueteándola por todas partes hasta que acaba cobrándose allí mismo la multa en carne. La escena concluye en un gran polvo simulado entre el poli y la drag, que gozan como posesos con un ruido de fondo de sirena policial que ridiculiza aún más la escena y acentúa, para los más críticos, la hipocresía y el abuso de autoridad al que siempre ha estado sometido este colectivo.

"La breve representación se repite todos los últimos sábados del mes, a eso de las doce, no sólo para rememorar con orgullo la clandestinidad de los lugares de ambiente de entonces—no hay nada que una más a la gente que la clandestinidad compartida—sino también como excusa para cambiar el entorno y dejar paso a un local diferente en el que la música y el baile cobran ahora total protagonismo."

15. Carmen Díez "believes we have a long way to go to break the binarism regarding being a man or a woman, which prevents a variety of models from becoming visible or possible. Finally, she points out that the appearance of new forms of masculine behavior and attitudes influences the emblematic models (for good or ill) as well as the relational contexts for friendships and love, as well as work" (Esteban, 48).

16. "No me gusta ni mi cara ni mi nombre."

17. "Era en los últimos tiempos de mi madre, imagina, su afición al armario, tener que atarla, lo que se hacía, o aquella tarde en que untó la pared con sus propios excrementos."

18. "Yo estoy marcada, marcada. Rosario, ésa es mi marca. La marca del niño que es raro. Y Milagros reconoció mi marca desde el principio. Desde ese curso, quinto o sexto, en el patio de la escuela. La rara, que era ella, la rara recién llegada del pueblo, reconoció a la rara que era yo. Los raros nos olemos. La diferencia es que yo me he esforzado durante toda mi vida en ser normal y apartarme de mi tribu. Pero no me han dejado. Máxima aspiración en mi vida: ser normal."

19. "A Milagros le gustaba llamar la atención, aunque fuera haciendo el monstruo. La monstrua, la llamaban. La Monstrua se sentó a mi lado en el pupitre, o me la sentaron, ya no me acuerdo, y me contagió su condición. Nos señalaron como monstruas a las dos."

20. "Esas cosas formaban parte ya de mi experiencia cuando Milagros se asomó para verme manipular la compresa, doblarla, enrollarla hasta hacerla mínima y envolverla en una tira de papel higiénico, dos años en que no preguntó a nadie ni nadie le preguntó a ella, sólo escuchó conversaciones de las otras niñas, las espió, supo en qué consistía ese ritual mensual y decidió apuntarse a él aunque ella nunca tuvo sangre, nunca fue mujer, como decíamos las niñas."

21. "como decíamos las niñas."

22. "¿Milagros bollera? Yo no lo sé. Yo sé que no lo soy. Así mismo se lo dije a Morsa."

23. "la cerveza me ayuda y el furioso deseo de que todos sepan que no, que no soy lesbiana, y las piernas se me abren y parece que todo es húmedo, que yo también soy húmeda como cualquier mujer."

24. "Milagros se acostaba con tías."

25. "Lo que creo es que Milagros necesitaba cariño, así de simple, y se arrimaba a quien se lo daba, pero que no era sexo puro y duro lo que ella buscaba."

26. "hubiera necesitado que alguien, ese ángel de la guarda que nunca tienen los niños desgraciados, le hubiera ido desenredando la gran confusión mental que le produjo esa pérdida que ya estaba cantada."

27. "haciendo que su voz se convirtiera en todas las voces necesarias para un niño, jugando muchas noches alrededor de la madre dormida o perdida en la bruma, actuando con una madurez que luego perdió, estancada como se quedó en una infancia rara."

28. "Ella siempre decía que veía más para mí y para cualquier mujer femenina (mi madre siempre añadía lo de femenina, cosa que me dolía) el trabajo en la agencia de viajes que el de capataza de basureros."

29. "Yo no hice de Pocahontas, eso está claro, a mí siempre me encasquetaban en todas las funciones escolares el papel del chico, imagino por mi gesto serio, un tanto grave, lo cual por un lado me facilitaba salir en todas las obras, porque parece que no había otra niña que tuviera tanta cara de tío como yo, pero por otro, me acomplejaba."

30. "esos pequeños encasillamientos a los que te someten los adultos casi desde que naces y que determinan tu vida." At the same time that Rosario rejects the masculine image of herself, she recognizes that masculinity confers a freedom from domestic relationships, exemplified in her father's abandonment of the family, which would eventually force Rosario to abandon plans for her own career, because she, as a woman, could not claim the same right to focus exclusively on her own needs and desires: "huele a padre ausente, traidor, a padre que se fue hace tantos años que ya casi ni puedes acordarte y al que ahora comprendes, por muy hijo de puta que sea, él siguió su deseo, él hizo lo que tú querrías hacer todos los días, dar un portazo y hacer otra vida, ser otro, dejarla . . . pero tú no puedes, Rosario, tú no tienes esa suerte, y toda la rebeldía se pudre en tu interior, como un niño que no llegara a nacer" (62) (It smells of absent father, traitor, of the father who left so many years ago and who you can barely remember and who you now understand, no matter what a son of a bitch he was, he followed his desire, he did what you would have wanted to do every day, slam the door and have another life, be different, let it go . . . but you can't do it, Rosario, you don't have that kind of luck, and all your rebelliousness rots inside you, like a child that could never be born).

31. "Yo siempre he tenido ideas negras, desde niña, desde cuando me dio por pensar, por ejemplo, que cualquier mañana me levantaría, iría al baño a hacer pis y al limpiarme con el papel higiénico me daría cuenta de que me estaba creciendo pene."

32. "No sé si su lesbianismo era lesbianismo en estado puro, quiero decir que Milagros se acostaba con tías, de eso sí que tenía alguna noticia, pero lo hacía como yo cuando tenía ocho años y me acostaba desnuda con la hija de mi vecina y nos poníamos la una encima de la otra y la hija de mi vecina decía, hay que besarse el chichi, como los matrimonios, y ella me lo besaba un rato y luego decía, ahora es tu turno, pero yo nunca llegué a hacerlo porque a mi vecina le olía demasiado y me daba repugnancia y entonces ella se enfadaba y me echaba de su casa."

33. "Yo ya me siento ajena mientras está sucediendo, en pleno acto. Ajena, ajena al cuerpo de ese hombre que tengo al lado y que jadea encima de mí. De pronto lo veo como un animal babeante y me muevo, y jadeo y me muevo, para que todo acabe cuanto antes mejor."

34. "Yo no era bollo, que no era su novia, ni su amiga íntima, como ella quería que yo dijera al menos ('no lo soy, Milagros, ni lo seré nunca'), y que aquello que había sucedido aquella noche cuando se quedó a cuidarnos a mi madre y a mí sólo había sido una necesidad casi enfermiza de cariño.

"Pero tú te dejaste, me decía, te dejaste."

"Milagros, tú sabes en qué situación física y psicológica me encontraba, estaba derrotada, Milagros, y sucedió mientras yo estaba medio dormida, le dije, y por la mañana pensé que era un sueño provocado por la fiebre."

"Eso es lo que hacen todos los maricones y todas las bolleras del mundo que se avergüenzan de serlo, hacerse los dormidos para que al día siguiente parezca que no ha pasado nada. Ah, pero sí que pasó, Rosario, aunque tú estés ahora por negarlo, pasó y pasó, a mí no se me olvidan los detalles. Para mí no cuenta lo que tú opines ahora, para mí cuenta lo que tú decías aquella noche."

"¿Qué dices, le decía yo, de qué estás hablando?"

"Que si uno se corre, si uno se corre, y dice, ay, Milagros, Milagros, es porque a uno le gusta."

35. "Me acerqué lentamente a su lado, recuperando todavía el equilibrio que sus palabras me habían hecho perder, y ella debió entender que me había convencido, que ya no avisaría a nadie, y dejó de presionar la caja contra su pecho para acercármela, como si quisiera compartir a la criatura conmigo."

36. "Pienso que a Milagros le hubiera dado una gran alegría verme allí entre todas aquellas mujeres en las que se apreciaba un parecido físico con ella, verme como una más de la familia."

37. "Noto el olor de madre, el olor de madre con la cabeza perdida, el olor de todo aquello que no quiero ser."

38. "Sanchís dice que eres virgen porque las lesbianas son vírgenes y dice que tú eres lesbiana."

39. "las piernas se me abren y parece que todo es húmedo, que yo también soy húmeda como cualquier mujer."

40. "Y tuve claro que esa noche y la siguiente y la siguiente [Morsa] se quedaría en casa, tuve claro todos y cada uno de los pasos siguientes. Casi sentí en ese momento su cuerpo sobre mí, el abandono, el polvo que me dejaría embarazada, que me daría un hijo. No se puede cambiar el pasado, ni podemos evitar lo que ya somos, así que hagamos que empiece otra vida, pensé, una vida nueva que crezca de esta Rosario de la que ya no puedo librarme, esa Rosario a la que no le gusta ni su cara ni su nombre, hagamos una criatura inocente y hermosa que salga de ese yo que siempre he odiado. Tal vez sea la única oportunidad de borrar de mi alma la tara con la que nací, pensé, de buscar una redención, de hacerme perdonar el pecado original."

41. Wracked with guilt for having to tie her mother up and leave her in the closet while she is at work and when she has sex with Morsa, Rosario seeks advice, not only from a psychologist, but also from a priest. She comments on their similarity and on the uselessness of their suggestions.

5. Dislocations

1. In his subsequent discussion of MUDs (Multi-User Domains) and MOOs (MUD Object-Oriented), William Mitchell explains that the online participants in fantasy games like Dungeons and Dragons jointly create and modify an elaborate fiction: "These participants enter textual descriptions of imaginary places that others can visit, and of objects and robotic characters that populate those places, awaiting scripted interaction with future visitors. The underlying software ties all the descriptions and scripts together to create a single, continually evolving environment and provides an opportunity for you to meet and interact with other participants within that environment" (114).

2. "la mitad de las contertulias eran hombres sin escrúpulos que se hacían pasar por lesbianas, y el resto, mujeres acomplejadas, inseguras u obsesionadas con el sexo, que mentían más que callaban."

3. Although some of my comments apply to various forms of cybersexuality, my focus in this article is limited to linguistic intercourse because I am comparing the verbal re-creations of sexuality in the chat and the collection of short stories.

4. "By the late twentieth century, our time, a mythic time, we are all chimeras, theorized and fabricated hybrids of machine and organism; in short, we are cyborgs. The cyborg is our ontology; it gives us our politics. The cyborg is a condensed image of both imagination and material reality, the two joined centres structuring any possibility of historical transformation. In the traditions of

'Western' science and politics—the tradition of racist, male-dominant capitalism; the tradition of progress; the tradition of the appropriation of nature as resource for the productions of culture; the tradition of reproduction of the self from the reflections of the other—the relation between organism and machine has been a border war. The stakes in the border war have been the territories of production, reproduction, and imagination. This chapter is an argument for *pleasure* in the confusion of boundaries and for *responsibility* in their construction" (Haraway, 150).

5. For more on this topic, see my essay "Globalization, Publishing, and the Marketing of 'Hispanic' Identities" and Mario Santana's *Foreigners in the Homeland*.

6. Juan Manuel Cendoya writes: "In Iberian America the Spanish banks have the advantage of language and a tremendous cultural and social proximity" (78).

7. "¿qué puede tener de infiel chatear con algunas chicas?"

8. "el rol de las lesbianas en las familias alternativas."

9. "Quizá lo mejor del sexo virtual es que te alienta para el real, que si tu pareja te tiene un poco harta a fuerza de rutina, primero te follas a una por Internet y luego llegas a su cama a hacer el amor; que, como dijo la uruguaya, no es lo mismo pero está requetebién. Mañana a la misma hora ... con otra, y mi pareja deberá volver a hacer el amor todos los días, costumbre que la rutina nos ha robado. Hasta mañana, amor."

10. "una carta manuscrita, con sello, desde sitios lejanos; una carta que intuíamos antes de abrirla lentamente, reservando el olfato para percibir el aroma de la tinta, del papel."

11. It is interesting to note that letters figure prominently in several other stories, including "Cartas" and "Otras cartas." They are, however, only one form of discourse highlighted in the collection as a whole.

12. "Me corro, uruguayita ... Ahhh ... No puedo más ..."

13. "Yo leía lo que escribía la uruguaya y me estaba haciendo una paja brutal ... con mi novia a un paso.... Me metía dos o tres dedos en el coño, los sacaba, los remetía con fuerza, me mojaba las tetas con lo que juntaba abajo, me pasaba los dedos húmedos por los labios, me aplastaba una teta mientras la otra mano se frotaba contra la seda del pijama a la altura de mis labios."

14. "es que cuando una comienza con esto, pareciera tener personalidad adictiva: cada día estás más enganchada."

15. "—¿Nunca lo hiciste?
—No, la verdad es que soy nueva en esto ... y no me parece que se pueda hacer el amor por *chat*.
—Yo te propongo follar, no hacer el amor."

16. "—Esto me parece una locura, el sexo virtual no tiene ninguna gracia.
—Y ¿cómo lo sabes si nunca lo has hecho? Prueba.
—¿Estás muy desesperada?

—Estoy caliente y sola y me gustaría que hubiera alguien a mi lado para deshacerme de este calentamiento.
—Yo, justamente, tengo a mi pareja a unos metros, muy metida en su libro.
—¿Entonces?...
—Y... es que soy muy tímida y no sé cómo hacerlo."
17. "había un océano entre nosotras."
18. "'¿Estás ahí, españolita? ¿Te estás tocando?' Y mi mano bajó sin mi autorización a mi entrepierna, la seda del pijama estaba húmeda y el contacto de mis dedos fue espectacular."
19. "—¿Cómo son tus pelos?
—Rojos, abundantes, enrulados y se mojan tanto como mi cosita.... ¿Cómo llaman en España a la cosita?"
20. "Me estoy hamacando en la silla, tengo la concha al aire y me refriego contra el tapizado."
21. "Chau, españolita.... Como decimos nosotras: que cojas bien y a fondo." *Ciao* is used primarily in those Latin American countries—Argentina and Uruguay—with the greatest influx of Italian immigrants, but it is not used in Spain. Likewise, *coger* is the Latin American equivalent of *follar*, but it does not have that meaning in Spain.
22. "¿Sabes cómo se llama esto en el sur de América? La cosita."
23. I am grateful to Robert Richmond Ellis for pointing this out to me at the MLA Convention in December 2004.
24. "Paula es atractiva, seductora, inquieta, inteligente, elegante y, además guapa. Es directora de grandes cuentas en el banco más importante de este país. Vive colgada del teléfono, trepada a aviones, con una agenda que le resta tiempo hasta para ver a su madre, a la que tiene ingresada en la residencia más cara de Madrid y a la que le paga una acompañante permanente para que la sustituya. Cualquier cosa menos sumar problemas. No tiene tiempo y el que tiene lo quiere sólo para ella.

"Responde sólo ante el dueño y director general del banco, se tutea con él, deciden la política institucional en Latinoamérica, la caída en la bolsa, hasta cuánto se puede perder.... Sabe que parte de su éxito es ella misma, su forma de vestir, su forma de moverse, las faldas en el límite que distrae a los hombres y causa envidia a las mujeres, los trajes en tonos pastel, pañuelos de seda auténtica, gafas innecesarias para ver pero imprescindibles para su ultrasimpática sinceridad."

25. "Pese a sus crisis, pese a su decadencia, pese a las librerías nocturnas que ya no funcionaban, Buenos Aires era para ella como una segunda casa: allí estaba cómoda, suelta, doce mil kilómetros lograban relajarla, hacerle olvidar que era una ejecutiva."
26. "háblame en argentino que me fascina vuestro idioma."
27. "cada vez que se quitaba la ropa de alta ejecutiva iba perdiendo poco a poco

sus modales femeninos, comenzaba a sentirse un seductor: le gustaba el juego de seducción entre mujeres pero sentía que ocupaba una posición dominante, que su atractivo les gustaba pero las inhibía; y para contrarrestar el efecto, se ponía un poco masculina, campechana."

28. "—Te gusta morder... Mordé..., me gusta que me muerdan. —Mordé... Mordé..., me gusta tanto este dialecto..., me gusta tanto tu ciudad, tu país. Los argentinos no sabéis lo que tenéis. —Vos mordé, que yo te cuento. Tenemos unos gobiernos de mierda que se roban todo y un pueblo de mierda que los deja."

29. "Y ella obedeció mansamente, la besó a boca abierta, con lengua llegando hasta la garganta."

30. "Quedaron para verse unos meses después in Río de Janeiro, sin agenda y sin ejecutiva."

31. "Pero la crisis se agudizó: las despidieron de la tienda, ya no podrían mantener el apartamento, no había trabajo, la violencia era diaria, cotidiana. Lima era un infierno, el Perú y toda Latinoamérica, un polvorín que empujaba a todos al exilio."

32. "¡España, la madre patria, sentía una cierta fobia contra los peruanos! ¡No tenían la suerte de ser europeos y blancos, sí occidentales y católicos pero del tercer mundo!"

33. "éstas que sólo quieren dinero pero trabajar nada de nada."

34. "La tomó de la cintura y se la llevó a la pista de baile. La besó apenas se hubieran entrelazado.... Salieron, subieron al coche de Charo y se fueron a casa. Por fin dejó de follar y comenzó a hacer el amor. Se sentía [que]... todo era posible, hasta triunfar en esta ciudad. Charo la obligó a dejar la casa de su abuela, alquiló un pequeño apartamento a dos calles del de Charo, consiguió un trabajo semilegal en una clínica, esperó pacientemente la homologación del título y, colorín, colorado, este cuento se ha acabado."

6. Popular Lesbian Fiction

1. "'La noción sociológica del matrimonio describe como elemento sustancial del mismo la unión doble y estable de un hombre y una mujer, generalmente ordenada a la procreación', explicó [the PP representative, Leocadio] Bueso fijando la postura del PP. Esta exigencia de heterosexualidad, según el PP, se da por supuesta en el Código Civil y en la Constitución, aunque no las recojan" (Pastor, "El PP impide") ("The sociological notion of matrimony describes the stable union of a man and a woman, generally aimed at procreation, as a substantial element," Bueso explained in defining the PP's position. This requirement that the union be heterosexual, according to the PP, is implicit in the Civil Code and in the Constitution, although they don't state it directly).

2. Villaamil also makes this point in his analysis of gay marriage.

3. Valerie Lehr explains: "Although the contractually agreed-to marriages of today may seem like a significant advance over the pre-arranged, clearly economic arrangements made for many men and women in the past, this understanding presupposes that monogamous, dyadic sexual relationships should have higher status and receive greater benefits than other forms of relationships. This superiority is asserted often through a variety of disciplinary mechanisms, including mental health experts, the media, schools, religious institutions, and the law. In this sense, marriage itself can—and should—be seen as a disciplinary system, one that promotes social goals, such as creating households of consumers and promoting a dual-wage structure, rather than as a natural institution that enhances individual freedom" (23).

4. *Su cuerpo era su gozo* is a realistic novel that attempts to reconstruct the challenges that a lesbian couple, originally from a small town, would have faced during the Franco dictatorship. Their relationship and their lives are systematically undermined by the mechanisms of various social institutions—the university, mental health institutions, inheritance laws—permeated by Francoist values and activated by members of their own families. The novel, in this sense, performs the important task of filling in the history of Spanish lesbians at the same time that it provides a rationale for the political agenda of women of Gimeno's generation.

5. "Me había usado a mí, también lo había hecho con sus hijos; los cuatro habíamos sido su gran tapadera."

6. "¿No se les pasó nunca por la imaginación que aquello pudiese ser lo que era, su verdadera identidad, y estar viviendo a mi lado una farsa y, por lo tanto, ser incapaces de ser felices?"

7. "que más me atrajo y al que yo también atraje."

8. "En sus brazos me sentí como una barca varada sobre una cala solitaria, de fina arena y olas suaves que me mecían acompasadamente, lamiendo mi madera algo resquebrajada por el sol, penetrando en todas mis hendiduras, refrescándolas, salpicándolas con pequeñas gotas juguetonas y saltarinas, entrando por todos los poros, por todos los nudos, y dilatando toda aquella madera estructurada en barca."

9. "no dejé de maquillarme, de curvar mis cejas, de sombrear mis ojos y de perfilar mis labios, cosas que sigo haciendo, y que sin duda haré hasta que no pueda sostener ni las tenacillas ni el perfilador de labios en mis manos."

10. This same Jaime, however, who brags about having a lesbian friend and verbally defends "alternative lifestyles," reacts with violence and homophobia when Julia breaks off her relationship with him to pursue another with Lucía, claiming to be disgusted by her sexual acts: "'¡Me das asco! . . . ¿Dónde lo hicisteis? ¡Como haya sido en esta cama te mato, zorra!'" (You disgust me! Where did you do it? If it was in this bed, I'll kill you, you slut!") (78).

11. "Lucía estaba convencida de que el activismo era la única vía posible para la mujer, fuera lesbiana o no, mientras que Julia creía firmemente en que la igualdad estaba ya lograda y que tampoco había por qué dar la vuelta a la tortilla. "El tema que provocó el enfrentamiento había sido sacado a la palestra por Jaime. . . . Él quería que ésta se diera cuenta de que su punto de vista era totalmente erróneo, fruto del discurso tendencioso elaborado por el Poder para controlar el avance femenino. Argumentaba que lo que habían logrado las mujeres se podía borrar de un plumazo. El día a día demostraba que la más ferviente defensa de los valores patriarcales se hallaba precisamente entre las propias mujeres; y esas mujeres, continuadoras voluntarias de las prácticas discriminatorias, serían el primer vehículo de transmisión de la ideología machista y sexista."

12. "Desde mi adolescencia he apostado por una diversidad de géneros y orientaciones y donde más cómoda me puedo sentir es en un garito en donde haya hombres y mujeres, heteros, gays y bisexuales, blancos, negros y cualquier otra etnia."

13. "Luego está el tema de la llamada literatura lésbica. Si hay algo que me jode de esas historias de lesbianas es su gravedad. Me refiero a que tú coges cualquiera de esos libritos de imitadoras sáficas de Corín Tellado y ¿qué es lo que encuentras? Relatos de amores sufridos, correspondidos o no correspondidos, con final feliz o sin él, protagonizado por niñas monísimas de la muerte que tienen unos trabajos de la hostia y una cuenta corriente que les permite hacer continuas escapaditas a bucólicos parajes donde van con la novia de turno, otra niña monísima de la muerte y profesión liberal, a hacer el amor durante horas y horas, lánguidas horas, tiernas horas, placenteras horas repletas de orgasmos sublimes, cósmicos, que eleven su percepción espiritual y las unen hasta el infinito y más allá... Porque ésa es otra, las lesbianas no follan. No, señorita, está usted muy equivocada. Las lesbianas hacen el amor. Siempre. Los gays follan. Los heteros practican el coito. Los animales copulan. ¿Y las lesbianas? Las lesbianas hacen el amor. Claaaro."

14. "Dejo caer el bolso sobre el sofá y entro en la cocina en busca de una coca-cola. Le doy un sorbo y la pongo sobre la mesita del salón mientras me voy desnudando y entro en mi dormitorio. Me quedo solamente con una vieja camiseta y salgo al salón donde enciendo un cigarrillo y continúo bebiendo de la lata de coca-cola." Most descriptions in the novel are done in this style, or through analogies to popular U.S. films.

15. The GYLA and GYLIS of the novel allude to two major collectives associated with Madrid, FELGTB (Federación Española de Lesbianas, Gays, Transexuales y Bisexuales [Spanish Federation of Lesbians, Gays, Transsexuals, and Bisexuals]) and COGAM (Colectivo de Gays, Lesbianas y Transexuales de Madrid [Collective of Gays, Lesbians and Transsexuals of Madrid]), which has never changed its acronym since its foundation in 1985. COGAM sponsored the creation in 1992 of what was then called the FEGL, which put gays before lesbians.

In 2002, the name changed to FELGT, and in 2007, to FELGTB (FELGTB Quiénes) (http://www.felgtb.org/es/quienes-somos/historia). *A por todas* also alludes indirectly (pp. 244–45) to the president of the FEGL from 1997 to 2002, Pedro Zerolo, whose presidency of the organization launched his career in state and city politics. He was succeeded by Beatriz Gimeno, president from 2003 to 2007, and the spouse of Boti García Rodrigo, president of COGAM from 2000 to 2004. COGAM has received criticism from queer organizations for its dedication to "pink business" as a political tool.

Conclusion

1. "The emerging narrative of emancipation, though, is tied not only to a dissatisfaction with the science of normal gay adolescence previously undertaken. Rather, it is linked to shifts in the larger culture, particularly for youth growing up in more affluent and sophisticated urban and suburban communities who, emboldened by positive internet accounts and the media, assume leadership in establishing gay-straight alliances in schools and feel empowered to live a diverse sexual lifeway outside the boundaries of a conventional taxonomy" (Cohler and Hammack, 54).

2. The John Jay College of Criminal Justice report titled "The Nature and Scope of the Problem of Sexual Abuse of Minors by Catholic Priests and Deacons in the United States" was filed in 2004, and the Ferns Report in Ireland was published in 2005. The John Jay report states: "The survey responses make it clear that the problem was indeed widespread and affected more than 95% of dioceses and approximately 60% of religious communities" (26).

3. The Royal Decree regarding the creation of new courts dedicated exclusively to domestic violence cases (Real Decreto 233/2005) was issued on March 4, 2005. An article published in the daily *El País* on April 30, 2005, explains the creation of twenty-six new courts and twenty-seven magistrate positions, in compliance with the mandates of the decree, to begin functioning on June 29, 2005 ("El Consejo de Ministros").

4. The countries cited in the report were France, Hungary, Malta, Poland, Romania, the Slovak Republic, Slovenia, Spain, and Turkey. Spain amended Article 154 of the Civil Code to ban the corporal punishment of children in 2007. The amendment was opposed by the defenders of the traditional family, in particular the conservative party, the PP, which claimed that it weakened the authority of parents (Pérez de Pablos).

5. See my discussion of the "Visible" festival in the preface and chapter 2.

6. The sexual promiscuity of *heterosexual* males is not only widely recognized in Spanish culture but has even been institutionalized in the form of the "casas chicas" that men have traditionally maintained for their mistresses, so the argu-

ment that gay men are exceptionally promiscuous seems absurd. The crucial issue for all Spanish men has always been discretion, rather than sexual practices, so that, as Fernando Villaamil has explained, gay marriage could be justified as a respect for "privacy," preferable to public displays of undomesticated sexuality (22). The tactic of deflecting a critique of male sexual behavior onto gay ("perverse") males clearly marks the continued domination of heterosexual men in relation to homosexual men, but the tacit public acceptance of male homosexuality, discreetly practiced, also signals the recognition, even encouragement, of a common male proclivity for illicit sex that is not considered "natural" in women.

7. Famously, or perhaps infamously, during the debates on gay marriage the conservative PP called as an expert witness to the Senate Aquilino Polaino Lorente, professor of psychopathology from the Universidad Complutense de Madrid, who explained homosexuality as a pathological condition caused by inadequate parenting.

8. "Aún partiendo del principio incuestionable que las parejas de homosexuales no deban ser objeto de discriminación, los efectos atribuidos a las mismas no pueden llegar al extremo de que se establezca doblemente, por la sola declaración de las interesadas, la maternidad tanto respecto a la mujer que ha dado a luz como respecto de la compañera estable de ésta. La maternidad es única en nuestro Derecho y queda determinada por naturaleza. . . . El principio de veracidad biológica que inspira nuestro Ordenamiento en materia de filiación se opone frontalmente a que determinada la maternidad por el hecho del parto, puede sobrevenir otro reconocimiento de la maternidad por otra mujer."

9. "Los cónyuges son iguales en derechos y deberes."

10. "Los cónyuges están obligados a vivir juntos, guardarse fidelidad y socorrerse mutuamente. Deberán, además, compartir las responsabilidades domésticas y el cuidado y atención de ascendientes y descendientes y otras personas dependientes a su cargo."

11. It is pertinent to recall Gayatri Spivak's words on this matter: "The institution of phallocentric law is congruent with the need to prove paternity and authority, to secure property by transforming the child into an alienated object named and possessed by the father, and to secure property by transforming the woman into a mediating instrument of the production and passage of property" (184).

12. The idea that gay marriage marginalizes queers and upholds the economic rationale of the marriage institution is not new. Valerie Lehr writes that "the family-household system exists and works to reinforce a sex/gender system embedded in the family and the economic realm" (21). She goes on to note that "Although the contractually agreed-to marriages of today may seem like a significant advance over the pre-arranged, clearly economic arrangements made for many men and women in the past, this understanding presupposes that monogamous,

dyadic sexual relationships should have higher status and receive greater benefits than other forms of relationships. This superiority is asserted often through a variety of disciplinary mechanisms, including mental health experts, the media, schools, religious institutions, and the law. In this sense, marriage itself can—and should—be seen as a disciplinary system, one that promotes social goals, such as creating households of consumers and promoting a dual-wage structure, rather than as a natural institution that enhances individual freedom" (23).

13. The PP candidate for prime minister in 2008, Mariano Rajoy, pledged to overturn gay marriage and adoption if he was elected: "Rajoy 'quitaría el derecho' a los homosexuales a adoptar" (Rajoy "would take away the right" of homosexuals to adopt). In a later article, a spokesperson for the party clarified that Rajoy did not like the legislation but would not necessarily overturn it.

14. "La violencia de género no es un problema que afecte al ámbito privado. Al contrario, se manifiesta como el símbolo más brutal de la desigualdad existente en nuestra sociedad. Se trata de una violencia que se dirige sobre las mujeres por el hecho mismo de serlo, por ser consideradas, por sus agresores, carentes de los derechos mínimos de libertad, respeto y capacidad de decisión."

15. "Las situaciones de violencia sobre la mujer afectan también a los menores que se encuentran dentro de su entorno familiar, víctimas directas o indirectas de esta violencia."

16. Gill Valentine, Tracey Skelton, and Ruth Butler point out the importance of the household for gay/lesbian identity formation in a 2003 article, "Coming Out and Outcomes: Negotiating Lesbian and Gay Identities with, and in, the Family": "Little attention has been paid to how young people's transitions from childhood to adulthood are embedded in day-to-day family life, and to the emotional functioning of the space of the home. Although we recognise that young people grow up in a variety of family forms, and may have experiences of living in more than one household, home(s) is still the site where young people spend lengthy periods of time with a parent or parents and siblings. It is in the home that understandings about young people's maturity and morality are often constructed by parents through rules about spatial and temporal boundaries. Even when young people leave home, the family home is still the site through which many of their individual biographies and expectations are routed and consequently where the emotional functioning of the family is often played out. As such, it is important to recognise the transitional processes that take place within the family home(s), rather than just those that occur at the wider macroscale of society, and to understand how what goes on within family homes can have consequences for young people's identities and social relations in the spaces that stretch beyond them" (481).

17. Here are a few examples of their thinking: "Gracias papá, por aquel zapatillazo que un día me propinaste, cuando te falté al respeto y me hiciste ver cla-

ramente que iba por mal camino. Puede que tu 'agresión,' me hiciera reflexionar y encontrar la senda correcta" (Lozano Herrera) (Thank you, Father, for hitting me with a shoe that day when I was disrespectful and you made me see clearly that I was going down the wrong path. It could be that your "aggression" made me reflect and find the right path); "La autoridad ha perdido fuerza y los padres prefieren tener buenas relaciones con los hijos, quienes cada vez más ponen en entredicho las normas de convivencia" (Derqui) (Authority has lost its force and parents prefer to get along with their children, who have more and more say about the rules of the home); "Los hijos necesitan ver a un padre con autoridad y cariño, que les sirva de ejemplo con su vida y su trabajo, un padre siempre dispuesto a escuchar y comprender sus confidencias, y junto a él la figura de la madre" (Toranzo) (Children need to see a father with authority and affection, who can serve as an example through his life and his work, a father who is always willing to listen to and understand their confidences, and next to him, the figure of the mother). The most extreme condemnation of gay marriage and families can be found in the article by Ignacio Sagarra Renedo, which ends with a quote about the father from the Bible and another about the mother from the Fascist poet José María Pemán.

18. The Web site (http://elcobre.es/portada1024X768.htm) explains that these cultures, "más que no occidentales, están más allá de las occidentales, que más que 'étnicas,' son reflejo del mestizaje y la diversidad que identifica los comienzos del siglo XXI" (more than non-Occidental, are beyond Occidental; not just "ethnic," they are a reflection of cross-breeding and the diversity that defines the beginning of the twenty-first century).

Bibliography

Aguirre, Begoña. "Chueca ha sacado la imagen del homosexual del cuarto oscuro." *El País* (Internet edition), September 11, 1998.

Alas, Leopoldo. *Ojo de loca no se equivoca: Una irónica y lúcida reflexión sobre el ambiente*. Barcelona: Planeta, 2002.

Aliaga, Juan Vicente. *Identidad y diferencia: Sobre la cultura gay en España*. Barcelona: Egales, 1997.

Aliern Pons, Francesca, et al. *Otras voces*. Madrid/Barcelona: Egales, 2002.

Apter, Emily. *Feminizing the Fetish: Psychoanalysis and Narrative Obsession in Turn-of-the-Century France*. Ithaca, N.Y.: Cornell University Press, 1991.

Arguedas, José María. *Los ríos profundos*. Buenos Aires: Losada, 1958.

Asturias, Miguel Ángel. *Mulata de tal*. Buenos Aires: Losada, 1963.

Baudrillard, Jean. *Seduction*. Trans. Brian Singer. New York: St. Martin's Press, 1990.

Bauman, Richard, and Charles L. Briggs. *Voices of Modernity: Language Ideologies and the Politics of Inequality*. Cambridge: Cambridge University Press, 2003.

Bell, David, and Jon Binnie. "Authenticating Queer Space: Citizenship, Urbanism and Governance." *Urban Studies* 41.9 (2004): 1807–20.

Bell, David, and Mark Jayne, eds. *City of Quarters: Urban Villages in the Contemporary City*. Hants, England: Ashgate, 2004.

Benegas, Noni, and Jesús Munárriz. *Ellas tienen la palabra: Dos décadas de poesía española*. Madrid: Hiperión, 1997.

Bermúdez, Silvia. "Sexing the Bildungsroman: *Las edades de Lulú*, Pornography, and the Pleasure Principle." In *Bodies and Biases: Sexualities in Hispanic Cultures and Literatures*, ed. David William Foster and Roberto Reis. Minneapolis: University of Minnesota Press, 1996. 165–83.

Bieder, Maryellen. "Gender and Language: The Womanly Woman and Manly Writing." In *Culture and Gender in Nineteenth-Century Spain*, ed. Lou Charnon-Deutsch and Jo Labanyi. Oxford: Clarendon, 1995. 98–119.

Binnie, Jon. "Quartering Sexualities: Gay Villages and Sexual Citizenship." In *City of Quarters: Urban Villages in the Contemporary City*, ed. David Bell and Mark Jayne. Hants, England: Ashgate, 2004. 163–72.

Bourdieu, Pierre. *The Rules of Art: Genesis and Structure of the Literary Field.* Trans. Susan Emanuel. Stanford, Calif.: Stanford University Press, 1996.

Boyd, Carolyn P. *Historia Patria: Politics, History, and National Identity in Spain, 1875–1975.* Princeton, N.J.: Princeton University Press, 1997.

Braudel, Fernand. "Divisions of Space and Time in Europe." In *The Global Cities Reader,* ed. Neil Brenner and Roger Kell. London: Routledge, 2006. 25–31. (From *The Perspective of the World,* 1984.)

Brenner, Neil. "Global Cities, 'Glocal' States: Global City Formation and State Territorial Restructuring in Contemporary Europe." In *The Global Cities Reader,* ed. Neil Brenner and Roger Kell. London: Routledge, 2006. 259–66. (From *Review of International Political Economy,* 1998.)

Brenner, Neil, and Roger Kell, eds. *The Global Cities Reader.* London: Routledge, 2006.

Bruquetas de Castro, Fernando. *Outing en España: Los españoles salen del armario.* Majadahonda (Madrid): HMR (Hijos de Muley-Rubio), 2000.

Buero Vallejo, Antonio. *Historia de una escalera.* Barcelona: Josep Janés, 1950.

Bush, Andrew. "Ana Maria Moix's Silent Calling." In *Women Writers of Contemporary Spain: Exiles in the Homeland,* ed. Joan L. Brown. Newark: University of Delaware Press, 1991. 136–58.

Butler, Judith. *Bodies That Matter: On the Discursive Limits of "Sex."* New York: Routledge, 1993.

———. "Is Kinship Always Already Heterosexual?" In *Left Legalism/Left Critique,* ed. Wendy Brown and Janet Halley. Durham, N.C.: Duke University Press, 2002. 229–58.

———. *The Psychic Life of Power.* Stanford, Calif.: Stanford University Press, 1997.

———. *Undoing Gender.* New York: Routledge, 2004.

Buxán, Xosé M., ed. *conCiencia de un singular deseo: Estudios lesbianos y gays en el estado español.* Barcelona: Laertes, 1997.

Califia, Pat. *El don de Safo: El libro de la sexualidad lesbiana.* Trans. Carlos Benito González and María Elena Casado Aparicio. Madrid: Talasa, 1997.

Carranco, Rebeca. "'Este bar no es para vosotras': Una pareja denuncia que las expulsaron de una sidrería por lesbianas." *El País,* July 6, 2008, 3.

Casani, Borja, and José Tono Martínez. "Madrid 1984: ¿La posmodernidad?" *La luna de Madrid* 1 (1983): 6–7.

Casani, Borja, Nanye Blázquez, José María Parreño, Gonzalo García Pino, and José Luis Gallero. "Sale la luna." In *Sólo se vive una vez: Esplendor y ruina de la movida madrileña,* ed. José Luis Gallero. Madrid: Ardora, 1991. 8–21.

Castle, Terry. *The Apparitional Lesbian: Female Homosexuality and Modern Culture.* New York: Columbia University Press, 1993.

Cela, Julia. *Galería de retratos: Personajes homosexuales de la cultura contemporánea.* Barcelona: Egales, 1998.

Cendoya, Juan Manuel. "La expansión de Santander Central Hispano en Iberoamérica." *Quórum* 5–6 (2003): 76–82.
Cervera, Rafa. *Alaska y otras historias de la movida*. Barcelona: Plaza y Janés, 2002.
Chisholm, Dianne. *Queer Constellations: Subcultural Space in the Wake of the City*. Minneapolis: University of Minnesota Press, 2005.
Chuecatown. Dir. Juan C. Flahn. Canónigo Films, 2007.
Clarke, Eric O. *Virtuous Vice: Homoeroticism and the Public Sphere*. Durham, N.C.: Duke University Press, 2000.
Cohler, Bertram J., and Phillip L. Hammack. "The Psychological World of the Gay Teenager: Social Change, Narrative, and 'Normality.'" *J Youth Adolescence* 36 (2007): 47–59.
Collins, Jacky. "(Un)natural Exposure: Lola Van Guardia's *Plumas de doble filo*. Creating a Real and Imagined Lesbian Space." In *Mujeres Malas: Women's Detective Fiction from Spain*, ed. Jacky Collins and Shelley Godsland. Manchester: Manchester Metropolitan University Press, 2005. 78–90.

———. "'A World Beyond': The Lola van Guardia Trilogy." In *Hispanic and Luso-Brazilian Detective Fiction: Essays on the Género Negro Tradition*, ed. Renée W. Craig-Odders, Jacky Collins, and Glen S. Close. Jefferson, N.C.: McFarland & Company, 2006. 79–90.
Colmeiro, José. "*Canciones con historia*: Cultural Identity, Historical Memory, and Popular Songs." *Journal of Spanish Cultural Studies* 4.1 (March 2003): 31–46.
Corbin, J. R. *The Anarchist Passion: Class Conflict in Southern Spain, 1810–1965*. Brookfield, Vt.: Avebury, 1993.
Cruz-Malavé, Arnaldo, and Martin F. Manalansan IV. *Queer Globalizations: Citizenship and the Afterlife of Colonialism*. New York: New York University Press, 2002.
de Certeau, Michel. *The Practice of Everyday Life*. Trans. Steven Rendall. Berkeley: University of California Press, 1984.
de la Cruz, Carlos, and Antonio Acebal. *El secreto de las familias*. Oviedo: Coleutivu Milenta Muyeres, 2005.
de Prada, Juan Manuel. *Las esquinas del aire: En busca de Ana María Martínez Sagi*. Barcelona: Planeta, 2000.
Deleuze, Gilles. *Masochism: Coldness and Cruelty and Venus in Furs*. Trans. Jean McNeil. New York: Zone Books, 1991. 9–138.
Delicado, Francisco. *La lozana andaluza*. Madrid: Espasa-Calpe, 1988.
Derqui, L. "La familia tradicional deja paso al modelo de 'familianegociadora' en la que son los hijos quienes deciden." *ABC* (Internet edition), June 20, 2006.
"El Consejo de Ministros aprueba la creación de 26 nuevos juzgados y de 27 plazas de magistrados." *El País* (Internet edition), April 30, 2005.
El derecho a la propia identidad: La acción en favor de los derechos humanos de gays y lesbianas. Madrid: Amnistía Internacional, 1999.

BIBLIOGRAPHY

"El mercado de Fuencarral echa el cierre en enero." *El País* (Internet edition), October 6, 2008.

Ellis, Robert Richmond. *The Hispanic Homograph: Gay Self-Representation in Contemporary Spanish Autobiography.* Urbana: University of Illinois Press, 1997.

Enguix Grau, Begoña. *Poder y deseo: La homosexualidad masculina en Valencia.* Valencia: Edicions Alfons El Magnànim, 1996.

Epps, Brad. "The Queer Case of *Plumas de España.*" In *P/Herversions: Critical Studies of Ana Rossetti,* ed. Jill Robbins. Lewisburg, Pa.: Bucknell University Press, 2004. 146–82.

———. "Virtual Sexuality: Lesbianism, Loss, and Deliverance in Carme Riera's 'Te deis, amor, la mar com a penyora.'" In *¿Entiendes? Queer Readings, Hispanic Writings,* ed. Emilie Bergmann and Paul Julian Smith. Durham, N.C.: Duke University Press, 1995. 317–45.

Esteban, Mari Luz. "Estrategias corporales masculinas y transformaciones de género." In *Sexualidades: Diversidad y control,* ed. Óscar Guasch and Olga Viñuales. Barcelona: Bellaterra, 2003. 45–67.

Etxebarría, Lucía. *Amor, curiosidad, prozac y dudas.* Barcelona: Plaza y Janés, 1997.

———. *Beatriz y los cuerpos celestes.* Barcelona: Destino, 1998.

Evans, Peter. "Cifesa: Cinema and Authoritarian Aesthetics." In *Spanish Cultural Studies: An Introduction,* ed. Helen Graham and Jo Labanyi. Oxford: Oxford University Press, 1995. 215–22.

Fagés, Marta. *Amores prohibidos.* Madrid: Odisea, 2002.

FELGTB. "Quiénes somos." http://www.felgtb.org/es/quienes-somos/historia.

Fernández Cubas, Cristina. "Mundo." In *Con Agatha en Istambul.* Barcelona: Tusquets, 1994.

Ferrán, Ofelia, and Kathleen M. Glenn, eds. *Women's Narrative and Film in Twentieth-Century Spain: A World of Difference(s).* New York: Routledge, 2002.

Fielding, Helen. *Bridget Jones's Diary.* London: Picador, 1996.

"FNAC." http://www.fundinguniverse.com/company-histories/FNAC-Company-History.html.

Foucault, Michel. *Discipline and Punish: The Birth of the Prison.* Trans. Alan Sheridan. New York: Vintage, 1979.

———. *The History of Sexuality. Volume I: An Introduction.* Trans. Robert Hurley. New York: Vintage, 1980.

———. *Language, Counter-Memory, Practice: Selected Essays and Interviews.* Trans. Donald F. Bouchard and Sherry Simon. Ithaca, N.Y.: Cornell University Press, 1977.

———. *Power/Knowledge: Selected Interviews and Other Writings, 1972–1977.* Ed. Colin Gordon. New York: Pantheon, 1980.

Franc, Isabel. *Entre todas las mujeres.* Barcelona: Tusquets, 1992.

Freixas, Laura. *Literatura y mujeres: Escritoras, público y crítica en la España actual.* Barcelona: Destino, 2000.

Frohlich, Margaret G. *Framing the Margin: Nationality and Sexuality across Borders.* Tempe: Asociación International de Literatura y Cultura Femenina Hispánica, 2008.

Galán, Mabel. *Donde comienza tu nombre.* Madrid: Odisea, 2004.

Gallero, José Luis. *Sólo se vive una vez: Esplendor y ruina de la movida madrileña.* Madrid: Ardora, 1991.

García-Calvo, Carlos. "Mujeres, mujeres, pero ¡qué mujeres!" *La luna de Madrid* 15 (1985): 64–65.

García Canclini, Néstor. *La globalización imaginada.* Mexico City: Paidós, 1999.

García Lorca, Federico. *La casa de Bernarda Alba.* Buenos Aires: Losada, 1945.

García Martín, Antonio, and Andrés López Fernández. *Imagen social de la homosexualidad en España.* Madrid: Asociación Pro Derechos Humanos, 1985.

Garlinger, Patrick Paul. "Dragging Spain into the 'Post-Franco' Era: Transvestism and National Identity in *Una Mala Noche La Tiene Cualquiera.*" *Revista Canadiense de Estudios Hispánicos* 24.2 (2000): 363–82.

———. "Sex Changes and Political Transitions; or, What Bibi Andersen Can Tell Us about Democracy in Spain." In *Traces of Contamination: Unearthing the Francoist Legacy in Contemporary Spanish Discourse,* ed. Eloy E. Merino and H. Rosi Song. Lewisburg, Pa.: Bucknell University Press, 2005. 27–52.

———. "Transgender Nation: Bibi Andersen, Postmodernity, and the Spanish Transition to Democracy." *Revista de Estudios Hispánicos* 37.1 (2003): 3–30.

Garlinger, Patrick Paul, and H. Rosi Song. "Camp: What's Spain to Do with It?" *Journal of Spanish Cultural Studies* 5.1 (2004): 3–8.

Gilmore, David D. "The Democratization of Ritual: Andalusian Carnival after Franco." *Anthropological Quarterly* 66.1 (1993): 37–47.

Gimeno, Beatriz. *Historia y análisis del lesbianismo: La liberación de una generación.* Barcelona: Gedisa, 2005.

———. *Su cuerpo era su gozo.* Madrid: Akal, 2005.

Giorgi, Gabriel. "Madrid en Tránsito: Travelers, Visibility, and Gay Identity." *GLQ* 8.1–2 (2002): 57–79.

Gómez Pereira, Marosa. *Un amor bajo sospecha.* Madrid, Barcelona: Egales, 2001.

Graham, Helen, and Jo Labanyi. *Spanish Cultural Studies: An Introduction.* Oxford: Oxford University Press, 1995.

Grandes, Almudena. *Las edades de Lulú.* Barcelona: Tusquets, 1989.

Guasch, Óscar. *La sociedad rosa.* Barcelona: Anagrama, 1991.

Halperin, David. *Saint Foucault: Toward a Gay Hagiography.* Oxford: Oxford University Press, 1995.

Haraway, Donna J. *Simians, Cyborgs, and Women: The Reinvention of Nature.* New York: Routledge, 1991.

Herdt, Gilbert H., and Andrew Boxer. *Children of Horizons: How Gay and Lesbian Teenagers Are Leading a New Way Out of the Closet.* Boston: Beacon Press, 1996.

Hernández, Mili. "Cuando una librería se cierra..." *B: Revista Cultural de la Librería Berkana* 30 (no date). http://www.libreriaberkana.com/revista/numero30/index.htm.

Hernández, Wilfredo. "From the Margins to the Mainstream: Lesbian Characters in Spanish Fiction (1964–1979)." In *Tortilleras: Hispanic and U.S. Latina Lesbian Expression,* ed. Lourdes Torres and Inmaculada Pertusa. Philadelphia: Temple University Press, 2003. 19–34.

Herrero Brasas, Juan A. *La sociedad gay: Una invisible minoría.* Tres Cantos (Madrid): Foca, 2001.

Herrero-Olaizola, Alejandro. "Consuming Aesthetics: Seix Barral and José Donoso in the Field of Latin American Literary Production." *MLN* 115.2 (2000): 323–39.

Huhtamo, Erkki. "From Cybernation to Interaction: A Contribution to an Archaeology of Interactivity." In *The Digital Dialectic: New Essays on New Media,* ed. Peter Lunenfeld. Boston: MIT Press, 2000. 96–110.

Irigaray, Luce. *Speculum of the Other Woman.* Trans. Gillian C. Gill. Ithaca, N.Y.: Cornell University Press, 1985.

Jaime, María Felicitas. *Cenicienta en Chueca.* Madrid: Odisea, 2003.

Jiménez, Irene. *El placer de la Y: Diez historias en torno a Marguerite Yourcenar.* Barcelona: ElCobre, 2003.

John Jay College of Criminal Justice. "The Nature and Scope of the Problem of Sexual Abuse of Minors by Catholic Priests and Deacons in the United States." 2004. http://www.usccb.org/nrb/johnjaystudy/.

Johnson, Barbara. "Gender and Poetry: Charles Baudelaire and Marceline Desbordes-Valmore." In *Displacements: Women, Tradition, Literatures in French,* ed. Joan DeJean and Nancy K. Miller. Baltimore: Johns Hopkins University Press, 1991. 163–81.

Jordan, Barry, and Mark Allison. *Spanish Cinema: A Student's Guide.* London: Hodder Arnold, 2005.

Juanolo. *¡Nos gustamos!* Valencia: Tándem, 2006.

Krauel, Ricardo. "Funambulismo sobre una frontera de un género: 'Una novela' de Ana María Moix." *Anales de la Literatura Española Contemporánea* 23.1–2 (1998): 641–53.

Kristeva, Julia. *Powers of Horror: An Essay on Abjection.* Trans. Leon S. Roudiez. New York: Columbia University Press, 1982.

"La editorial Odisea entregó sus premios de literatura gay y lésbica." *Yahoo! Noticias,* February 7, 2003.

Labanyi, Jo, ed. *Constructing Identity in Contemporary Spain: Theoretical Debates and Cultural Practice.* Oxford: Oxford University Press, 2002.

Laínez, Josep Carles. Illustrated by Juan Arocas. *Una más en la familia.* Valencia: Llambert Palmart, 2004.

"Las parejas homosexuales ya pueden contraer matrimonio y adoptar niños." *El País,* July 1, 2005, 1, 31–38.

Lefebvre, Henri. *The Production of Space* (1974). Trans. Donald Nicholson-Smith. Oxford: Blackwell, 1991.

Lehr, Valerie. *Queer Family Values: Debunking the Myth of the Nuclear Family.* Philadelphia: Temple University Press, 1999.

Ley Orgánica 1/2004, de 28 de diciembre, de Medidas de Protección Integral contra la Violencia de Género. *Boletín Oficial de Estado* 313. December 29, 2004. 42166–97.

Lindo, Elvira. *Una palabra tuya.* Barcelona: Seix Barral, 2005.

Llamas, Ricardo. *Miss Media: Una lectura perversa de la comunicación de masas.* Barcelona: Ediciones de la Tempestad, 1997.

———. *Teoría torcida: Prejuicios y discursos en torno a "la homosexualidad."* Madrid: Siglo XXI de España, 1998.

Llamas, Ricardo, and Fefa Vila. "Spain: Passion for Life: Una historia del movimiento de lesbianas y gays en el estado español." In *conCiencia de un singular deseo: estudios lesbianos y gays en el estado español,* ed. Xosé M. Buxán. Barcelona: Laertes, 1997. 189–224.

Llamas, Ricardo, and Francisco Javier Vidarte. *Homografías.* Madrid: Espasa, 1999.

Lozano Herrera, Antonio. "Polémica decisión judicial." *ABC* (Internet edition), April 9, 2007.

Macey, David. *The Lives of Michel Foucault.* London: Hutchinson, 1993.

Manalansan, Martin F. "'Out There': The Topography of Race and Desire in the Global City." In *Global Divas: Filipino Gay Men in the Diaspora.* Durham, N.C.: Duke University Press, 2003. 62–88.

Manuel, Peter. "Andalusian, Gypsy, and Class Identity in the Contemporary Flamenco Complex." In *Gypsies: An Interdisciplinary Reader.* New York: Garland, 1998. 175–97. Also in *Ethnomusicology* 33.1 (1989): 47–65.

Martín, Aurelio. "Rosa Chacel critica con dureza a Umbral: La nonagenaria escritora le califica de 'cretino y verdadero imbécil.'" *El País* (Internet edition), March 12, 1994.

Martín Gaite, Carmen. *Usos amorosos de la posguerra española.* Barcelona: Anagrama, 1987.

Martínez Castellanos, Rafael. *Chuecatown.* Madrid: Odisea, 2002.

Martos Montiel, Juan Francisco. *Desde Lesbos con amor: Homosexualidad femenina en la antigüedad.* Madrid: Clásicas, 1996.

Massey, Doreen. *For Space*. London and Thousand Oaks, Calif.: Sage, 2005.
Maurell, Pilar. "El Nadal premia el erotismo y la 'carga poética' de Lucía Etxebarría." *El Mundo* (Internet edition), January 7, 1998.
McDowell, Linda. *Gender, Identity and Place: Understanding Feminist Geographies*. Minneapolis: University of Minnesota Press, 1999.
Medina Domínguez, Alberto. *Exorcismos de la memoria: Políticas y poéticas de la melancolía en la España de la transición*. Madrid: Libertarias, 2001.
Mendicutti, Eduardo. *El palomo cojo*. Barcelona: Tusquets, 1991.
———. *Una mala noche la tiene cualquiera*. Barcelona: Tusquets, 1988.
Mérida, Rafael M., ed. *Sexualidades transgresoras: Una antología de estudios queer*. Barcelona: Icaria, 2002.
"Mili Hernández y la morfina del poder." *Esdificil.com*, www.esdificil.com/editorial/mili_hernandez.htm.
Miller, James. *The Passion of Michel Foucault*. New York: Simon and Schuster, 1993.
Mira, Alberto. *De Sodoma a Chueca: Una historia cultural de la homosexualidad en España en el siglo XX*. Madrid: Egales, 2004.
———. *Para entendernos: Diccionario de cultura homosexual, gay y lésbica*. 2d ed. Barcelona: Ediciones de la Tempestad, 2002.
Mirizio, Annalisa. "Del carnaval al drag: La extraña relación entre masculinidad y travestismo." In *Nuevas Masculinidades*, ed. Marta Segarra and Angels Carabí. La Coruña, Spain: Icaria, 2000. 133–50.
Mitchell, Timothy. *Passionate Culture: Emotion, Religion and Society in Southern Spain*. Philadelphia: University of Pennsylvania Press, 1990.
Mitchell, William J. "Replacing Place." In *The Digital Dialectic: New Essays on New Media*, ed. Peter Lunenfeld. Boston: MIT Press, 2000. 112–28.
M. J. P-B. "Justicia rectifica y dicta una orden para aclarar que 'padre' y 'madre' siguen en los registros." *ABC* (Internet edition), March 9, 2006.
Moix, Ana María. *A imagen y semejanza*. Barcelona: Lumen, 1983.
———. *Julia*. Barcelona: Seix Barral, 1970.
———. "Las virtudes peligrosas." In *Las virtudes peligrosas*. Madrid: Alfaguara, 1998. 11–51.
Monterde, José Enrique. "El cine de la autarquía (1939–1950)." In *Historia del cine español*, by Román Gubern, José Enrique Monterde, Julio Pérez Perucha, Esteve Riambau, and Casimiro Torreiro. Madrid: Cátedra, 1995. 181–238.
Montoliú Camps, Pedro. *Enciclopedia de Madrid*. Barcelona: Planeta, 2002.
Morán, Libertad. *A por todas*. Madrid: Odisea, 2005.
———. *Llévame a casa*. Madrid: Odisea, 2003.
Moreiras Menor, Cristina. *Cultura herida: Literatura y cine en la España democrática*. Madrid: Libertarias, 2002.
Moret, Xavier. "La joven Lucía Etxebarría recibe el Nadal con una novela que trata de la iniciación sexual." *El País* (Internet edition), January 7, 1998.

Myrata, Ramón. "El financial times de la mendicidad." *La luna de Madrid* 1 (1983): 4-5.

Nash, Mary. *Defying Male Civilization: Women in the Spanish Civil War*. Denver: Arden, 1995.

Nieto, José Antonio. "La intersexualidad y los límites del modelo 'dos sexos/dos géneros.'" In *Sexualidades: Diversidad y control*, ed. Óscar Guasch and Olga Viñuales. Barcelona: Bellaterra, 2003. 69-104.

"No todos los gays y lesbianas aplaudimos lo mismo." Opinion section, naciongay.com, September 10, 2001.

Noel, Eugenio. *Semana santa en Sevilla*. Ed. Jorge Jiménez Barrientos and Manuel J. Gómez Lara. Seville: University of Seville, 1991.

Ocaña: Retrato intermitente. Dir. Ventura Pons. Prozesa Teide, 1978.

Olmeda, Fernando. *El látigo y la pluma: Homosexuales en la España de Franco*. Madrid: Oberon, 2004.

Palma Borrego, María José. "Un recorrido por la novela lesbiana española." In *Ars homoerótica: Escribir la homosexualidad en las letras hispanicas*, ed. Nicolas Balutet. Paris: Publibook, 2006. 15-19.

Parsons, Deborah L. *Streetwalking the Metropolis: Women, the City and Modernity*. Oxford: Oxford University Press, 2000.

Pastor, Enric. "El PP impide que se legalicen los matrimonios homosexuales." *El Mundo* (Internet edition), September 26, 2001.

Pavlović, Tatjana. *Despotic Bodies and Transgressive Bodies: Spanish Culture from Francisco Franco to Jesús Franco*. Albany: State University of New York Press, 2003.

Pena, Wieland. Illustrated by Roberto Maján. *¿De quién me enamoraré?* Madrid: Fundación Triángulo, 2007.

Pérez Cánovas, Nicolás. *Homosexualidad, homosexuales y uniones homosexuales en el derecho español*. Granada: Comares, 1996.

Pérez de Pablos, Susana. "El bofetón queda fuera de la ley: El Congreso aprueba eliminar el último resquicio legal del castigo físico infantil." *El País* (Internet edition), December 21, 2007.

Pérez Miguel, Leandro. "Me han hecho daño, pero tengo la conciencia limpia." *El Mundo* (Internet edition), October 2, 2001.

Pérez Sánchez, Gema. *Queer Transitions in Contemporary Spanish Culture: From Franco to La Movida*. Albany: State University of New York Press, 2007.

Pertusa, Inmaculada. *La salida del armario: Lecturas desde la otra acera (Sylvia Molloy, Cristina Peri Rossi, Carme Riera, Esther Tusquets)*. Gijón: Llibros del Pexe, 2005.

Petit, Jordi. *25 años más: Una perspectiva sobre el pasado, presente, y futuro del movimiento de gays, lesbianas, bisexuales y transexuales*. Barcelona: Icaria, 2003.

Platero Méndez, Raquel. "Derechos civiles o matrimonio heterosexista." *Diagonal* (June 23–July 6, 2005): 14.

———. "The Limits of Equality: The Intersectionality of Gender and Sexuality in Spanish Policy Making." *Kvinder, Køn og Forskning* 1 (2007): 33–47.

———. "Overcoming Brides and Grooms: The Representation of Lesbian and Gay Rights in Spain." In *Multiple Meanings of Gender Equality: A Critical Frame Analysis of Gender Policies in Europe*, ed. Mieke Verloo. Budapest: Central European University Press, 2007. 207–31.

Platero Méndez, Raquel, and Emilio Gómez Ceto. *Herramientos para combatir el "bullying" homofóbico.* Madrid: TALASA, 2007.

Preciado, Beatriz. *Manifiesto contra-sexual: Prácticas subversivas de identidad sexual.* Madrid: Opera Prima, 2002.

"Rajoy 'quitaría el derecho' a los homosexuales a adoptar: El líder del PP afirma además que no habría 'dinero público' para recuperar el pasado." *El País* (Internet edition), February 9, 2008.

Reina, Manuel Francisco, ed. *Mujeres de carne y verso.* Madrid: La Esfera de los Libros, 2001.

Resina, Joan Ramon, and Dieter Ingenschay, eds. *After-Images of the City.* Ithaca, N.Y.: Cornell University Press, 2005.

Ribeiro, Margardia Calafate, and Ana Paula Ferreira. *Fantasmas e fantasias imperiais no imaginário português contemporâneo.* Porto: Campo das Letras, 2003.

Robbins, Jill. "An Introduction: Postmodern by Design." In *P/Herversions: Critical Studies of Ana Rossetti*, ed. Jill Robbins. Lewisburg, Pa.: Bucknell University Press, 2004. 31–62.

———. "Globalization, Publishing, and the Marketing of 'Hispanic' Identities." *Iberoamericana* 3.9 (2003): 89–101.

———. "The (In)visible Lesbian: The Contradictory Representations of Female Homoeroticism in Contemporary Spain." *Journal of Lesbian Studies* 7.3 (2003): 107–31.

Rodríguez Chacón, Rafael. *Matrimonio, separación y divorcio en España: Nueva regulación. Estudio sistemático de las leyes 13/2005, de 1 de julio, y 15/2005, de 8 de julio.* Barcelona: Ediciones Experiencia, 2005.

Rodríguez Fisher, Ana, ed. *De mar a mar: Epistolario Rosa Chacel-Ana María Moix.* Barcelona: Península, 1998.

Rolle-Rissetto, Silvia. "La escritura de Isabel Franc: Una pluma de doble filo (Entrevista 2004)." *Letras peninsulares* 18.1 (2005): 151–155.

———. "La reconceptualización de la identidad lésbica en *Plumas de doble filo*: Una vocación lúdico-amorosa." *Letras peninsulares* 18.1 (2005): 143–50.

Rossetti, Ana. *Plumas de España.* Barcelona: Seix Barral, 1988.

———. Illustrated by Jorge Artajo. *Las bodas reales: Cuento para colorear.* Barcelona: Bellaterra, 2005.

Ruiz, Julius. *Franco's Justice: Repression in Madrid after the Spanish Civil War.* Oxford: Clarendon; New York: Oxford University Press, 2005.

Ruiz, Sofía. *Sexutopías.* Madrid: Egales, 2006.

Rushbrook, Dereka. "Cities, Queer Space, and the Cosmopolitan Tourist." *GLQ* 8.1/2 (2002): 183–205.

———. "Sexuality and Space: Queering Geographies of Globalization." *Environment and Planning D: Society and Space* 21 (2003): 383–87.

Sagarra Renedo, Ignacio. "Matrimonio homosexual: El altar de Moloc." *ABC* (Internet edition), October 29, 2004.

Salinero Cascante, María Jesús. "El cuerpo femenino y su representación en la ficción literaria." In *Piel que habla: Viaje a través de los cuerpos femeninas,* ed. M. Azpeitia. Barcelona: Icaria, 2001. 39–76.

Sánchez, Carlos. "Contra el placer light: Pornódromos madrileños." *La luna de Madrid* 15 (1985): 44–45.

Santana, Mario. *Foreigners in the Homeland: The Spanish American New Novel in Spain, 1962–1974.* Lewisburg, Pa.: Bucknell University Press, 2000.

Sedgwick, Eve Kosofsky. *Between Men: English Literature and Male Homosocial Desire.* New York: Columbia University Press, 1985.

Silverman, Debra. "Making a Spectacle, or Is There a Female Drag?" *Critical Matrix* 7.2 (1993): 69–89.

Smith, Michael Peter. "The Global Cities Discourse: A Return to the Master Narrative?" In *The Global Cities Reader,* ed. Neil Brenner and Roger Kell. London: Routledge, 2006. 377–83.

———. *Transnational Urbanism. Locating Globalization.* Malden, Mass., and Oxford: Blackwell, 2001.

Smith, Paul Julian. "Los estudios lesbianos y gays en el mundo anglosajón y en el estado español." In *(Trans)formaciones de las sexualidades y el género,* ed. Mercedes Bengoechea and Marisol Morales. Alcalá: University of Alcalá Press, 2001. 43–54.

———. "Pedro Almódovar's Cinema of Desire. 1: Homosexuality, Postmodernism, and Self-Publicity. 2: Pepi, Luci, Bom: Lesbian Comedy." In Paul Julian Smith, *Laws of Desire: Questions of Homosexuality in Spanish Writing and Film, 1960–1990.* Oxford: Clarendon, 1992. 163–203.

Smith, Richard G. "World City Topologies." In *The Global Cities Reader,* ed. Neil Brenner and Roger Kell. London: Routledge, 2006. 400–406. (From *Progress in Human Geography,* 2003.)

Soriano Rubio, Sonia. *Cómo se vive la homosexualidad y el lesbianismo.* Salamanca: Amarú, 1999.

Spivak, Gayatri. "Displacement and the Discourse of Woman." In *Displacement: Derrida and After,* ed. Mark Krupnick. Bloomington: Indiana University Press, 1983. 169–95.

Stavrides, Stavros. "Heterotopias and the Experience of Porous Urban Space." In *Loose Space: Possibility and Diversity in Urban Life*, ed. Karen Franck and Quentin Stevens. London: Routledge, 2007. 174–92.

Suárez Briones, Beatriz. "De cómo la teoría lesbiana modificó a la teoría feminista (y viceversa)." In *(Trans)formaciones de las sexualidades y el género*, ed. Mercedes Bengoechea and Marisol Morales. Alcalá: University of Alcalá Press, 2001. 55–68.

Sullivan, Nikki. *A Critical Introduction to Queer Theory*. New York: New York University Press, 2003.

Toral, Pablo. "Las motivaciones político-económicas de las inversiones españolas." *Quórum* 5–6 (2003): 130–56.

Toranzo, Carmen. "La figura del padre." *ABC* (Internet edition), March 5, 2002.

Torres, Rafael. *La vida amorosa en tiempos de Franco*. Madrid: Temas de Hoy, 1996.

Trujillo, Gracia. "Sujetos y miradas inapropiables/adas: El discurso de las lesbianas queer." In *Lesbianas: Discursos y representaciones*, ed. Raquel Platero. Madrid: Melusina, 2008.

Tubert, Silvia, ed. *Del sexo al género: Los equívocos de un concepto*. Madrid: Cátedra, 2003.

Tusquets, Esther. *Siete miradas en un mismo paisaje*. Barcelona: Lumen, 1981.

"Tusquets suspende el Premio La Sonrisa Vertical." *El País* (Internet edition), May 25, 2004.

Ugarte, Michael. "Madrid: From 'Años de Hambre' to Years of Desire." In *Iberian Cities*, ed. Joan Ramon Resina. New York: Routledge, 2001. 93–121.

"Umbral dice que Rosa Chacel tiene derecho a defenderse." *El País* (Internet edition), March 12, 1994.

"Una multitudinaria marcha celebra en Madrid el matrimonio gay." *El País*, July 3, 2005, 1, 32–36.

Valentine, Gill, and Tracey Skelton. "Finding Oneself, Losing Oneself: The Lesbian and Gay 'Scene' as a Paradoxical Space." *International Journal of Urban and Regional Research* 27.4 (2003): 849–66.

Valentine, Gill, Tracey Skelton, and Ruth Butler. "Coming Out and Outcomes: Negotiating Lesbian and Gay Identities with, and in, the Family." *Environment and Planning D: Society and Space* 21.4 (2003): 479–99.

Valis, Noël. "The 'Cursilería' of Camp in Ana Rossetti's *Plumas de España*." *Journal of Spanish Cultural Studies* 5.1 (2004): 57–68.

Valle-Inclán, Ramón del. *Tirano Banderas: Novela de tierra caliente*. Madrid: Espasa-Calpe, 1993. 1st ed., 1926.

Van Guardia, Lola. *Con pedigree (Culebrón lésbico por entregas)*. Madrid: Egales, 1997.

———. *La mansión de las tríbadas*. Madrid: Egales, 2002.

———. *No me llames cariño*. Madrid: Egales, 2004.

———. *Plumas de doble filo*. Madrid: Egales, 1999.
Veksler, Bernardo. *Del Barquillo a Chueca: Transformaciones y glamour de un barrio madrileño*. Madrid: Vision Net, 2005.
Vigara Tauste, Ana María, and Rosa María Jiménez, eds. *"Género," Sexo, Discurso*. Madrid: Ediciones del Laberinto, 2002.
Vilarós, Teresa. *El mono del desencanto: Una crítica cultural de la transición española, 1973–1993*. Mexico City and Madrid: Siglo Veintiuno, 1998.
Villaamil, Fernando. *La transformación de la identidad gay en España*. Madrid: Los Libros de la Catarata, 2004.
Villena, Luis Antonio de, ed. *Amores iguales: Antología de la poesía gay y lésbica*. Madrid: La Esfera de los Libros, 2002.
Viñuales, Olga. *Identidades lésbicas*. Barcelona: Bellaterra, 2000.
"Vítores a Zapatero y ataques al PP y a la iglesia en la marcha de Orgullo Gay." *ABC*, July 3, 2005, 1, 52.
Vosburg, Nancy. "Barcelona in Spanish Women's Detective Fiction: Feminist, Postfeminist, and Lesbian Perspectives." In *Mujeres Malas: Women's Detective Fiction from Spain*, ed. Jacky Collins and Shelley Godsland. Manchester: Manchester Metropolitan University Press, 2005. 22–30.
Walters, Suzanna Danuta. *All the Rage: The Story of Gay Visibility in America*. Chicago: University of Chicago Press, 2001.
Williams, Bruce. "Camping at the Margins: Naked Myth and Its Intertext in the Films of Pedro Almodóvar." In *Mitos, III: Actas del VII Congreso Internacional de la Asociación Española de Semiótica*, ed. Túa Blesa et al. Saragossa, Spain: Asociación Española de Semiótica, with Universidad de Zaragoza, 1998. 807–11.
Yarza, Alejandro. "Estudios cinematográficos: 'La herida al aire: Travestismo y ansiedad cultural en el cine de Pedro Almodóvar.'" In *El hispanismo en los Estados Unidos: Discursos críticos/prácticas textuales*, ed. and introd. José del Pino and Francisco La Rubia Prado. Madrid: Visor, 1999. 191–209.
———. "Iconografía Religiosa y Estética Camp en ¡Atame!, de Pedro Almodóvar." *Revista Canadiense de Estudios Hispánicos* 22.1 (1997): 109–24.

Index

abjection: causes of, 71; of the self, 77
activism: lesbian, 103; in *A por todas*, 113; lesbian versus queer, 30; LGBTQ, 101–2
adolescence, gay, 148n1
adoption rights for gays, 115, 118, 120; resistance to, 121
Aguirre, Begoña, 129n2
AIDS activism, 13
Alas, Leopoldo, 9–10; on cybersex, 89, 90; on homogenizing identity, 34; *Ojo de loca no se equivoca*, 33, 82–83
Alaska (Olvido Garo), 5
Alianza (publisher), 23–24
Almodóvar, Pedro, 4
ambiente (gay space): Alas on, 33; of Chueca, 112; of Madrid, 7, 8. *See also* queer spaces, Spanish
Andalusia: anarchism in, 48; in cine folclórico, 42; Falange in, 40–41, 50; in lesbian fiction, 107; Semana Santa processions of, 39, 43, 44; during Spanish civil war, 50; Virgin cult in, 48. *See also* culture, Anadalusian
Andersen, Bibi, 39, 132n6
A por todas (Morán), xiv, 29, 103, 111–14; activist groups in, 113; gender identities in, 114; LGBTQ politics in, 111; mainstream aspirations in, 115; queer space in, 111, 112
Apter, Emily, 42
Arabs, expulsion from Spain, 67, 69

Argentina: dialects of, 97
Argentina, Imperio, 40
Arias, Arturo, ix, x
authors, women: humility imposed on, 53. *See also* lesbian authors, Spanish

Baker, Josephine, 67
Barcelona: Andalusian imagery in, 43; lesbians of, 29, 79; LGBTQ culture of, 1
Barral, Carlos, 23
Baudrillard, Jean: on fetishism, 42; on transvestism, 36, 37
Beatriz y los cuerpos celestes (Etxebarría), xiii, 57–58; commercial success of, 80; Francoism in, 59; gay culture in, 59; lesbian content of, 58, 60–61; middle-class readers of, 61; responses to, 58
Bell, David, 128n4
Benegas, Noni, ix–x
Berkana (bookstore), xii, 16; economic viability of, 23; Latin American authors of, 20; lesbian-oriented stock of, 19–20; marketing to men, 19; niche marketing by, 18; nonprint stock of, 18, 19; relocations of, 18
Biblioteca Breve Prize, 70
Binnie, Jon, 128n4
biological determinism: conservative invocation of, 121; in gender identity, 104; male hegemony in, 122
bisexuality, lesbian rejection of, 131n11
bookstores, anti-Franco, 129n1

bookstores, LGBTQ: Etxebarría's works in, 58; future of, 129n1; of Madrid, 16–23; role in gay communities, 129n1; variety among customers, 30
Bourdieu, Pierre, xii, 30
Brun, Helle, 25
Buero Vallejo, Antonio: *Historia de una escalera*, 108
Bueso, Leocadio, 145n1
bullying, homophobic, 123
Burgos, Carmen de, 25
Butler, Judith, 53, 84; on gay marriage, 102; on gender identity, 133n10; *The Psychic Life of Power*, 71, 74
Butler, Ruth, 150n16

camp: *coplas* in, 42; gay associations of, 37; in *Plumas de España*, 134n15; in post-Franco Spain, 37–38
Canut, Nacho, 5
capitalism: global versus local, 15
carnival: aggression in, 44; homosocial aspects of, 43. See also Semana Santa processions
Casa de Campo park (Madrid), xi, 127n4
Casa del Libro (bookstore), 21–22, 62, 63
Casani, Borja, 5, 37, 128n3
Castile, cultural hegemony of, 86
castration: fear of, 53; in *Plumas de España*, 52–53, 55; symbolic, 135n22
Catholicism, national, 41, 69; commercialism of, 51; and Francoism, 51; gay evocation of, 43–44; in *Plumas de España*, 49–50, 51, 52; and popular culture, 51; satirization of, 43–44
Cela, Julia: *Galería de retratos*, 25, 130n8
Cendoya, Juan Manuel, 95
Chacel, Rosa, 132n7
chat rooms: cybersex in, 82–83, 86, 87–90; linguistic freedom in, 87; multiple possibilities of, 88. See also communications technology
chicas raras, 71, 72, 106

children: corporal punishment of, 119, 123, 148n4, 150n17; violence against, 120
Chisholm, Dianne, 7, 8, 9
Chueca (barrio, Madrid): bookstores of, 16–23; boundaries of, 1–2; creation of, 3–4; economic relations of, xii; exclusions in, 9–10; in Franco era, 3–4; Fuencarral Market, 2; gay males of, 11, 12; history of, 2–4; homogenization of, 14; identity negotiation in, xii, xiv; immigrant population of, 11; lesbian tourists in, 11; literary practices of, xii; pickup spots of, 112; political space of, xii; Pride party in, xi; as product of interrelations, xii; queer consciousness of, 13; queer space of, xii, xiii, 9, 117; San Antón Market, 2; self-satisfaction in, 9–10; sociocultural milieu of, 2; during Spanish civil war, 3; symbolic space of, 117
Chueca, Federico, 1
Chueca Plaza, 1–2; bookstores of, 17, 18; pink businesses of, 1
Chuecatown (film), 19
church and state, Spanish: separation of, 119
cine folclórico, 39, 42, 132n9
Civil Marriage Code (Spain), 121–22, 145n1
civil war, Spanish: Andalusia during, 50; Chueca during, 3
Clarke, Eric O., 106
ClubCultura.com, 58
COGAM (Colectivo de Gays, Lesbianas y Transexuales de Madrid), 13, 65, 68, 127n5, 147n15
Cohler, Bertram J., 117; "The Psychological World of the Gay Teenager," 114–15
Colmeiro, José, 41
commerce, Spanish: and Latin American commerce, 95–96, 97
communications technology: codes underlying, 85, 86; control through, 85–86; effect on social structures, 89;

language as, 99; lesbians' use of, 82; liminal practices in, 86; sociopolitical implications of, xiv. *See also* chat rooms
consumption: of gay males, 12; in gay spaces, 15, 117, 128n4; in Spanish queer culture, xii
coplas, flamenco, 40, 41–42
corporal punishment: of children, 119, 123, 148n4, 150n17. *See also* violence
counterpublics, queer, 129n4
courts, Spanish: domestic violence cases in, 119, 148n3
Crawford, Joan, 133n10
cultural authority: creation of, 30
culture, Anadalusian, xiii; gender in, 51; in Madrid, 43; in *Plumas de España*, 48; resistance through music in, 40, 41–42, 43; in Spanish drag, 44; transgressive, 39–44
culture, gay, 1; colonized subject in, 93; consumption in, 12, 15, 117; egocentrism of, 10; Francoist repression of, 43; homogenization of, 14, 30, 34; identity development in, 114; marginalization of, 111; production of, 130n10; trendiness in, 59
culture, lesbian: colonized subject in, 93–94, 96–98; ghettoization of, 111
culture, Spanish: Arabic influence in, 68, 69, 70; Castilian, 86; Francoist, 35; gender in, 25, 120; kitsch in, 49–50, 51, 52; male heterosexual promiscuity in, 148n6; masculinism of, 15; women in, 30, 34; women intellectuals in, 29
cuplé shows, 49
cybersex, 142n3; in chat rooms, 82–83, 86, 87–90; international, 82; masturbation during, 82, 83. *See also* communications technology
cyborgs, 85, 97, 98–99, 142n4

Dagas, Connie, xii, 24, 25
De Lauretis, Teresa, 74

Deleuze, Gilles, 93
Delicado, Francisco: *La lozana andaluza*, 48
destape (sexual permissiveness), 39, 132n8
Diéz, Carmen, 139n15
Different Life, A (bookstore), xii, 16; economic viability of, 23; gay male clients of, 18; Latin American authors of, 20; nonprint stock of, 19
discourse, feminist: lesbianism and, 132n5
discourse, role in sex, 83, 89
divas, Spanish: transvestite imitation of, 39
domesticity, bourgeois ideals of, 8–9
drag shows: Andalusia in, 44; bourgeois spectators of, 47; in *Donde comienza tu nombre*, 69–70; effect on spectator, 37; full frontal nudity in, 38, 39; literary texts associated with, 37–38; in Madrid, 44–45; music in, 39; in post-Francoist Spain, 35–39; women's performance of, 133n10, 133n12

Egales (publishing house), xii, 123; association with Berkana, 24–25; coming-out stories of, 27; gay male publications of, 25; gender of buyers, 26; identity politics of, 29; lesbian textual politics of, 15; Salir del armario series, 25, 28, 29, 33, 59, 102, 115
El Cobertizo (bookstore), 130n3
ElCobre (press), 124
emancipation: narratives of, 114, 118
English language: proliferation of, 91
Epps, Brad, 45, 47, 135n22
eroticism: resistance to power in, 70
Espasa-Calpe (publisher), 21
Etxebarría, Lucía: *Amor, curiosidad, prozac y dudas*, 136n1; *Beatriz y los cuerpos celestes*, xiii, 57–58; celebrity of, 57–58, 62; Nadal Prize of, 5. *See also Beatriz y los cuerpos celestes*

European Union: role of language in, 97; Spain in, 57
Evans, Peter, 42

Fagés, Marta: *Amores prohibidos*, xiv, 29, 102–3, 107–11, 122; gossip in, 108, 109, 110; homophobia in, 109, 110–11; patriarchy in, 108, 110; violence in, 115
Falange, in Andalusia, 40–41, 50
families: alternative, 76–77, 88; Catholic principles of, 119; heteronormative, 102, 113; in LGBTQ parlance, 113–14; role in identity formation, 150n16
FELGTB (Federación Española de Lesbianas, Gays, Transexuales y Bisexuales), 127n5, 147n15
femininity: conventional constraints on, 55; imitation of, 35, 36–37; Spanish models of, 39
feminism: discourse of, 132n5; lesbian, 12
Ferreira, Ana Paula, 67
fiction, Spanish: sentimental, 59–60, 107. *See also* lesbian fiction, Spanish
Fielding, Helen: *Bridget Jones's Diary*, 112
flamenco, Andalusian, 40, 41–42
FNAC (Fédération nationale d'achats pour cadres, bookstore), 21, 22; international ownership of, 130n6
Fombella, Enrique, 5
Fontanus, Nicolaus, 84
Foucault, Michel, 83; experience of gay culture, 131n1
Franc, Isabel, 118; *Entre todas las mujeres*, 29; fiction of, 29, 131n13
Franco, Francisco: anticommunism of, 128n2
Francoism: in *Beatriz y los cuerpos celestes*, 59; cultural practices of, 35; national Catholicism and, 51; Popular Party's reflection of, 119; repression of gay culture, 43. *See also* Spain, Franco era
free expression: marketing choices and, 20, 130n4

Freixas, Laura: *Literatura y mujeres*, 25–26
Freud, Sigmund: on female sexuality, 71; on maturation, 74
Frida (film), 67, 70
Fuenmayor (Andalusia): carnival in, 43
Fundación Triángulo (LGBT group), 13

Galán, Mabel: chat rooms in, 64, 82; cover art of, 63; crossover audience of, 63; diegetic narrative of, 64; *Donde comienza tu nombre*, xiii, 22, 29, 57, 62–70; drag shows in, 69–70; genres of, 64; globalization in, 67; lesbian characters of, 64–66, 67, 70, 80; Lisbon in, 68; metaliterary narrative of, 63–64; *okupas* in, 65, 66
Gallop, Jane, 133n10, 133n12
García-Calvo, Carlos, 7
García Canclini, Néstor, 15
García Lorca, Federico: *La casa de Bernarda Alba*, 108
García Rodrigo, Boti, 30, 147n15
Garlinger, Patrick Paul, 36, 37, 39, 132n6
gay identity, Spanish: homogenization of, 34; politics of, 23, 103, 118; role of family in, 150n16. *See also* lesbian identity
gay literature, Spanish, 27, 28; high and low culture in, 33–34. *See also* lesbian literature
gay marriage: economic aspects of, 149n12; heteronormative aspects of, 102
gay marriage, Spanish: activism for, 101–2; government approval of, ix, xi; legislation for, 115, 130n10; in lesbian fiction, 103; Popular Party on, 101, 145n1, 149n7, 150n13; privacy issues in, 149n6
gay pride parades: Semana Santa processions and, 40. *See also* Spanish Pride parades
gays, Spanish: closeted, 33; cultural production of, 130n10; cultured, 33; feminized image of, 102; during Franco

era, x–xi; hierarchies among, 35; promiscuous image of, 120; in public sphere, 34–35; purchasing power of, 10; resistance to queer politics, 127n5; visibility of, 38. *See also* culture, gay; homosexuality; lesbians, Spanish
gay villages, 128n4; Chueca as, 11
gender equality, 120; legislation protecting, 122, 123; in workplace, 122
gender identity: acquisition of, 74; in *A por todas*, 114; binarism in, 139n15; biological determinism in, 104; in drag shows, 133n10; Freud on, 74; in Spanish culture, 120
Gilmore, David D., 43, 44
Gimeno, Beatriz, 28, 115, 131n10, 132n5; feminism of, 12; on lesbian chic, 12–13, 58–59; on lesbian depoliticization, 10–11; on lesbophobia, 62; presidency of FELGT, 148n15; *Su cuerpo era su gozo*, 9, 103, 146n4
globalization: in *Donde comienza tu nombre*, 67; effect on LGBTQ literature, 15–16, 30, 117; literary representations of, 81; of post-Franco Spain, 63, 80, 97–98; of queer aesthetic, 67; sexual citizenship in, 128n4; of Spanish economy, xii, 1; of Spanish publishing, 15, 24, 30, 57, 87
Gómez Ceto, Emilio: *Herramientas para combatir el "bullying" homofóbico*, 123
Gómez Pereira, Marosa: biological determinism in, 104; maritime imagery of, 105–6; *Un amor bajo sospecha*, xiv, 102, 103–7
González, Felipe, 36
Guasch, Óscar: *La sociedad rosa*, 26
gypsies, in cine folclórico, 42

Halperin, David, 131n11
Hammack, Phillip L., 117; "The Psychological World of the Gay Teenager," 114–15

Haraway, Donna, 97, 98–99, 142n4; *Simians, Cyborgs, and Women*, 85–86
Hayek, Salma, 67
Hernández, Mili, 30, 131n10; bookstore of, xii, 17; on bookstores, 22; on lesbian literature, 25, 26, 27–28, 115; on Librería Mujeres, 129n2
Herralde, Jorge, 23
heterosexism, violent, 118
heterosexuality: promiscuous, 148n6; and Spanish transvestism, 36; technologies of, 83–84
Hiperión (publishing house), 21
Homografías (Llamas and Vidarte), 7, 9–10
homophobia: aggressive, 102; in *Amores prohibidos*, 109, 110–11; bullying in, 123
homosexual discourse, heterosexual control of, 132n5
homosexuality: abject, 53; acceptance of, 118; in children's literature, 123; during Franco era, 16; heteronormative, 65, 67, 69, 106, 115; legitimization of, 102; in post-Franco era, xi, 1
homosexuality, male: in *La luna de Madrid*, 6; in Spanish public sphere, 34–35; visibility of, 105
Huhtamo, Erkki, 86
hysteria: lesbianism and, 84–85

Iberia: Arab occupation of, 67
identity politics: gay/lesbian, 23; in lesbian literature, 103, 118
immigrants, 68, 124, 129n5; of Chueca, 11; lesbian, xiv
intellectuals, Spanish gay, 33–34
International Festival of LGTB Culture (First, Madrid), 131n10
Internet: lesbian literature on, 20–21; military-industrial origins of, 86; modernity of, 89. *See also* communications technology

Jaime, María Felicitas: "Cartas," 81, 143n11; *Cenicienta en Chueca*, xiv, 29, 81, 99; "Cenicienta en Chueca," 81, 97–98; "Chateo," 82, 87–90, 92–93; "Ejecutivas," 81, 93–97; "Otras cartas," 81–82, 143n11; "Soledades," 81, 97
James, Zondra (pseudonym), 6
Jews: expulsion from Spain, 67
Jiménez, Irene: *El placer de la Y*, 123–24
John Jay College of Criminal Justice: sexual abuse report of, 148n2
Johnson, Barbara, 46, 133n11

Kristeva, Julia: *The Powers of Horror*, 71

labor: gendered division of, 119
La Celestina (bookstore), 21
La Juguetería (sex shop), 13
language, sexed positions within, 53
Las Costus (Enrique Naya Igueravide and Juan Carrero Galofré), 5
Latin America: commerce in, 95–96, 97; dialects of, 92, 93, 97; exoticism of, 94; neo-imperial relations with Spain, 93–98
law, phallocentric, 149n11
Lazarillo de Tormes, 48
Lefebvre, Henri, xii
Lehr, Valerie, 146n3, 149n12
Lele, Ouka (pseudonym), 7
lesbian authors, Spanish: critiques of sexual identity, 31; high-culture, 59; output of, 27–28
lesbian chic, 12–13, 58–59; media image of, 118
lesbian fiction, Spanish, xii, xiii, 16, 102; Andalusia in, 107; best-sellers, 57–80; bourgeoisie readers of, xiv; gay marriage in, 103; heterosexual readers of, 106; popular, 101–15; romance, 103, 104, 115; set in Franco era, 146n4; women's spaces in, 9
lesbian identity: components of, 13;

development of, 114, 150n16; role of family in, 150n16; Spanish publishers on, 28
lesbianism: and feminist discourse, 132n5; heteronormative, 106; and hysteria, 84–85; as immaturity, 74, 78; as original sin, 79; technological regulation of, 84. *See also* sexuality, lesbian
lesbian literature, Spanish: arbiters of, 15; availability of, 16–28; in global market, 117; identity politics in, 103, 118; Internet access to, 20–21; literary style of, 111; marketing of, 30; narrative of struggle in, 115; nonheteronormative, 115; racial diversity in, 124; romantic, 103, 104, 111–12, 115; sales of, 130n9
lesbian marriage, xiv. *See also* gay marriage
lesbian readers, Spanish: buying habits of, 25, 26–27, 28; numbers of, 30; sophistication of, 27
lesbians, Spanish: of Barcelona, 29, 79; Catalan, 79; closeted, xi, 8; cybersex among, 82–83; depoliticization of, 11; differences among, 34; equal rights for, 62; feminine norms of, 79; feminist, 13; during Franco era, x–xi, 8–9, 102, 105; heterosexist moral values of, 88; immigrant, xiv; invisibility of, xi, 13, 25, 55, 101, 105, 117, 124, 131n10; during *movida madrileña*, 117; postfeminist, 12–13; rejection of bisexuality, 131n11; transnational relationships of, xiv, 93–94, 96–99; violence against, 107, 115; working-class, 71. *See also* sexuality, lesbian
lesbophobia, 61–62
LGBTQ community, Spanish, 1; activism in, 101–2; of Barcelona, 1; bookstores of, 16–23, 30, 58; equality for, 102; parlance of family, 113–14
LGBTQ literature, Spanish: bookstores carrying, 16–23; effect of globalization

on, 15–16, 30, 117. *See also* gay literature, Spanish; lesbian literature, Spanish
LGBTQ politics: of Madrid, xii; role of literature in, 31
LGBTQ publishing, Spanish: globalization of, 30; pedagogical mission of, 15
Librería Mujeres (bookstore), 20, 21, 129n2
Lichtenstein, Roy: *Girl with Hair Ribbon*, 63
Lindo, Elvira: the abject in, 71, 73, 74, 77; alternative family in, 76–77; chicas raras in, 71, 72; gender ambiguity in, 72–73, 74, 75, 78; queer space in, 70–71; *Una palabra tuya*, xiii, 57, 70–79
Lisbon: Arab culture of, 70
literary space: politics of, 14
literature, Spanish: heterogeneity in, 87; transition in, 35, 131n4. *See also* gay literature, Spanish; lesbian literature, Spanish; LGBTQ literature, Spanish
Llamas, Ricardo, 1
LSD (Lesbianas Sin Duda), 13–14
Luca, Andrea, 124
Lumen (publisher), 23, 24
Luna de Madrid, La (journal), 5–6; male homosexuality in, 6; women contributors to, 7

machismo: of Franco era, xi; and misogyny, 39
Madrid: Andalusian imagery in, 43; Arab culture of, 70; Barquillo neighborhood, 2–3, 6; drag shows in, 44–45; during Franco era, xi, 3–4; Fuencarral street, 17; gay space of, 7, 8; Guardia Civil, 4; Hortaleza street, 17–18; Justicia district, 3; Lavapiés neighborhood, 14, 68; LGBTQ bookstores of, 16–23; LGBTQ culture of, 1; Malasaña neighborhood, 17; okupations of, 68; pornodromes of, 6–7; queer space of,

xii; The Rastro, 5; sexual tourism in, 6; during Spanish civil war, 3; status as capital, 128n2
marriage: contractual, 146n3, 149n12; disciplinary mechanisms in, 146n3, 150n12; in Spanish civil law, 121–23. *See also* gay marriage
Martín, Aurelio, 132n7
Martínez Castellanos, Rafael, 19
Mary, Virgin: Andalusian cult of, 48; luminous statues of, 49–50
masculinismo, Spanish, 36, 37
masculinity: Mediterranean, 120; subordinated forms of, 39
maternity: biological definition of, 121
McDowell, Linda, 9
Mendicutti, Eduardo: *Una mala noche la tiene cualquiera*, xiii, 26, 45
Merlino, Mario, ix–x
Mira, Alberto, 130n5; on Catholicism, 43; *De Sodoma a Chueca*, 25; on transvestism, 36, 38, 47
Mitchell, Timothy, 43
Mitchell, William J., 82–83
Monterde, José Enrique, 132n9
Montliú Camps, Pedro, 3
MOOs (MUD Object Oriented), 142n1
Morán, Libertad, 22; *A por todas*, xiv, 29, 103, 111–14. *See also A por todas*
Moreiras Menor, Cristina, 35, 45, 131n4
motherhood: ideological control of, 121
Moura, Beatriz de, 23, 24
movida madrileña (1980s), xii; aesthetics of, 91; intellectuals of, 5; lesbians during, 117; nightlife of, 4, 5; roots of, 91–92; sexual pleasure in, 37; transvestism during, 46; urban space of, 4–6
MUDs (Multi-User Domains), 142n1
music, resistance through, 40, 41–42, 43
Myrata, Ramón, 5

Nadal Prize, 57, 58
novelas rosas, 59–60, 107

nudity, full frontal: in transsexual shows, 38, 39

Odisea (publishing house), xii, 15, 102, 123; association with A Different Life, 24, 25; circulars of, 12; gender of buyers, 26; Safo collection, 18, 62–63
Odisea Prize, 25, 29, 102, 107
okupas (drug dens), 65, 66, 68, 137n9
Olmeda, Fernando, 43
ONCE (National Organization for Blind Spaniards), 2, 128n1
orgasm, female, 84–85

parental authority: conservative view of, 123, 150n17
parents, homosexual: rights of, 120–21
Parrondo, Nicolás, 62; homophobia of, 137n8
Pérez, Óscar, 25, 26, 27, 130n9
Pérez Galdós bookstore, 18, 21
Pérez Sánchez, Gema, x–xi
phallicization, feminine, 53
phallus: absent, 38, 44, 54; cyber-, 83; *pluma* as, 55
pink business, 10, 18, 129n2; of Chueca Plaza, 1; as political tool, 148n15
Planeta literary prize, 55
Plantadit-Bageot, Karine, 67
Platero Méndez, Raquel: *Herramientas para combatir el "bullying" homofóbico*, 123
Plaza y Janés (publisher), 24
Plumas de España (Rossetti), xiii, 35, 44–56; Andalusian culture in, 48; camp in, 134n15; castration in, 52–53, 55; Catholicism in, 49–50, 51, 52; critical assessments of, 46; gender issues in, 46, 47; global culture in, 56; inauthenticity charges against, 45; kitsch culture in, 49–50, 51, 52; misreadings of, 56; provincial literary climate in, 55; *señorita cursi* figure of, 45–46, 53; *travestís* of, 47

Polaino Lorente, Aquilino, 149n7
Pons, Ventura: *Ocaña*, 45
Popular Party (PP): conservatism of, ix, 149n7; family policies of, 118, 119–20; in gay marriage debate, 101, 145n1, 149n7, 150n13; reflection of Francoism, 119
pornodromes of Madrid, 6–7
pornography, lesbian, 6–7
Preciado, Beatriz: *Manifiesto contrasexual*, 83–85
promiscuity, male: in Spanish culture, 148n6
PSOE (Partido Socialista Obrero España), 9, 119, 122; ONCE and, 128n1
public sphere, Spanish: gay men in, 34–35
publishing, global: lesbian characters in, 80; Spain in, 15, 24, 30, 57, 87
publishing, lesbian: identity politics of, 29, 30; textual politics of, 15
publishing, Spanish, 23–30; commercial aspects of, 35; globalization of, 15, 24, 30, 57, 87; LGBTQ, 15, 30; of mid-twentieth century, 15; women in, 23

queer aesthetic, globalized, 67
queer culture, Spanish: consumption in, xii
queer lesbian movement, 13–14
queer spaces, Spanish, 15; of Chueca, xii, xiii, 9; in *A por todas*, 111, 112; in *Una palabra tuya*, 70–71. See also *ambiente* (gay space)

Rajoy, Mariano, 150n12
Ramírez, Alonso, 129n2
Resolución de la Dirección General de Registros y del Notariado (RDGRN), 121
Riviere, Joan, 135n22
Rodrigo (artist), 6
Rodríguez Zapatero, José Luis, x, 122
Roig, Monserrat, 132n6
Rose, John, 86
Rossetti, Ana: association with *movida*

madrileña, 134n15; *La luna de Madrid* contributions, 7; *Plumas de España*, xiii, 35, 44–56. *See also Plumas de España*
Ruiz, Julius, 3, 128n2
Ruiz, Sofía, x, 29; *Sexutopías*, ix

Sagarra Renedo, Ignacio, 151n17
Said, Edward, 93
same-sex unions, Spanish, 101–2. *See also* gay marriage, Spanish
Sánchez, Carlos, 6
Santana, Mario, 23
Seix Barral (publisher): Latin American Boom novels of, 23
self-torture: rhetoric of, 133n11
Semana Santa processions, 39; gay pride parades and, 40; homosocial aspects of, 43; social norms of, 44; women in, 44
Servi G (pink business network), 129n2
sex: as function of discourse, 83, 89; linking with love, 92
sexual identity: narratives of, 114–15, 118
sexual identity, women's: visibility of, xiv
sexuality: cultural construction of, 89, 91; technological control of, 84, 85; verbal re-creations of, 142n3; virtual, 82–83
sexuality, female: Catholic concepts of, 8; Freud on, 71; hysteria in, 84; masculine paradigm of, xiii; regulation of, 84; working-class, xiii, 57
sexuality, lesbian: in *Beatriz y los cuerpos celestes*, 61; bourgeoisie acceptance of, xiv; homonormative, 28; marketing of, 12; and models of femininity, 120; in Spanish society, 19; visibility in cyberspace, 89
sexuality, male: globalized image of, 12
sexual politics: of Franco era, 21–22; gendered nature of, 33
Shangay (circular), 12
Silverman, Debra, 133n12
Skelton, Tracy, 150n16

Soja, Edward, xii
Song, H. Rosi, 37
Sonrisa Vertical (literary prize), 130n5
Spain: expulsion of Arabs from, 67, 69; imperial past of, 67–68
Spain, Franco era: Andalusia during, 40–41; Chueca during, 3–4; concept of family in, 119; gays/lesbians during, x–xi, 8–9, 102, 105; gay space during, 8; homosexuality during, 16; lesbian spaces of, 8–9; machismo in, xi; Madrid during, xi, 3–4; *masculinismo* of, 37; national Catholicism of, 51, 69; sexual politics of, 21–22; women's fiction of, 59–60; working class of, 108. *See also* Francoism
Spain, post-Franco: camp during, 37–38; Civil Marriage Code, 121–22, 145n1; Constitution (1978), 4, 122, 145n1; drag shows in, 35–39; drug use in, 91; economic imperialism of, 95–98; in European Economic Community, 57; gay tourists in, xii; globalization of, xii, 1, 63, 80, 97–98; homosexuality in, xi, 1; immigrants to, xiv, 11, 68, 124, 129n5; lesbian activism in, 103; linguistic hegemony of, 86–87, 91; *masculinismo* in, 36; neo-imperialism of, 93–98; neoliberalism of, 24, 80; relations with Latin America, 93–98; surface change in, 36; transitions to democracy, xiii, 3–4, 24, 35, 38; transsexuality in, 38, 39
Spanglish, 86
Spanish language: Argentine, 97; foreign words in, 86, 91; hegemony of, 86–87, 91, 97; Latin American, 92, 93, 97; regional sexual vocabularies of, 93
Spanish Pride parades: of 1990s, xi; participants in, x; of 2005, ix–xi, 127nn1–2; of 2008, 62; of 2009, 124
Spanish Royal Academy, 86, 91
Spivak, Gayatri, 55; on phallocentric law, 149n11; on virginity, 78

stereotypes, gay/lesbian, 62
struggle: narratives of, 114, 115, 117
success: narratives of, 117

Tierno Galván, Enrique, 4
Toledano, Ruth, 124
Tono Martínez, José, 5, 37
Toral, Pablo, 95
tourism, Spanish, 128n3; gay/lesbian, xii, 11; sexual, 6
transsexuality: authenticity issues for, 36; of post-Franco era, 38, 39; rhetorical use of, 36; usurpation of feminine space, 132n6
transvestism: global understanding of, 56
transvestism, Spanish: heterosexist use of, 36; during *movida madrileña*, 46; of post-Franco era, 38
transvestites, Spanish: authenticity issues for, 36–37; performance of *coplas*, 42
Trujillo, Gracia, 66; "Sujetos y miradas inapropiables/adas," 13
Tusquets, Esther, 23; *Siete miradas en un mismo paisaje*, 9
Tusquets, Óscar, 23
Tusquets Editores: Sonrisa Vertical series of, 22, 130n5

Ugarte, Michael, 4
UGT (Unión General de Trabajadores), 2
Umbral, Francisco, 36, 39, 132n7
urban space: of *movida madrileña*, 4–6. *See also* queer spaces, Spanish

Valentine, Gill, 150n16
Valis, Noël, 45, 46, 134n15
Van Guardia, Lola: *Con pedigree*, 112
Vásquez, Dolores: murder trial of, 62
Veksler, Bernardo, 1–2

Vidarte, Francisco Javier, 1
Villaamil, Fernando, 9, 132n5; on gay marriage, 146n2, 149n6; on masculinity, 38–39
Villena, Luis Antonio de, 33–34, 131n11; critique of identities, 131n1
Viñuales, Olga, 131n11; *Identidades lésbicas*, 79
violence: antihomosexual, 136n3; against children, 120; domestic, 119, 120, 122–23, 148n3; heterosexist, 118; against lesbians, 107, 115
virginity: patriarchal concept of, 78
Visible 2005 festival (Madrid): gay men in, xi, 130n10; lesbian roundtable of, 27, 29, 103, 115
Visible 2006 festival (Madrid), 127n5

Walters, Suzanna Danuta: *All the Rage*, 59, 129n1; on antihomosexual violence, 136n3; on gay consumers, 12; on homoerotic imagery, 63
womanliness as spectacle, 134n22
women: phallic, 39, 132n7; rhetoric of self-torture, 133n11
women, Andalusian: disciplinary limits on, 48, 52–53; Falangist attacks on, 50; in Semana Santa processions, 44; *señoritas cursis*, 46, 47
women, Spanish: absence from literary politics, 35; high-culture, 25, 59; political immaturity of, 27
women, working-class: lesbians, 71; sexuality of, xiii, 57
workplace, gender equality in, 122

Yarza, Alejandro, 39

Zerolo, Pedro, 148n15

JILL ROBBINS is professor of Spanish literature and culture, and chair of the Department of Spanish and Portuguese at the University of Texas, Austin.